Manny
A
Criminal-Addict's
Story

Manny
A
Criminal-Addict's
Story

Richard P. Rettig

Manual J. Torres

Gerald R. Garrett
University of Massachusetts at Boston

Houghton Mifflin Company Boston
Atlanta Dallas Geneva, Illinois
Hopewell, New Jersey Palo Alto London

Printed in the U.S.A.

Library of Congress Catalog Card Number: 76-14654
ISBN: 0-395-24838-8

Contents

Foreword

The tradition of firsthand accounts of experience with crime has produced such excellent works as Sutherland's *The Professional Thief* and Chambliss's *The Box Man.* The present work has features that should place it securely in the front ranks of that tradition.

Certainly it is time that a good account of contemporary criminal existence is developed. Many of the best available works in this tradition describe behavior of fifty or even seventy years ago. When Manny speaks, he speaks to conditions of the present. The senseless brutality of prison life, the life of the addict, the emergent highly mobile armed robber, these are couched in terms that are relevant to the contemporary scene of muggings, the violence of Attica, the tragedy of George Jackson, and the hopelessness, and helplessness, in prisons everywhere.

A unique and outstanding feature of *Manny: A Criminal-Addict's Story* is that it traces an elaborate career of deviance. It begins with his early experiences with gang life, then passes on through encounters with gambling, experiences in New York, with Synanon, and with the California Department of Corrections.

This work is then a rich source of data on crime for which there is no substitute. Manny's variegated career provides experiences that are not renderable by the techniques of social science as we know them today. Criminologists using the accepted and conventional tools of the research trade cannot touch the long span of time, the evolution of a career, and the varied character of that career, that we find in this account. To be sure, Manny's experiences cannot be used to test or refute formed hypotheses regarding the development of a criminal career. What the book can provide, however, are experienced descriptions that can fill out and illustrate, in a dramatic way, many of the key issues touched by the more abstract concepts of formalized theories of criminal behavior.

For the sociologist, especially, this account is revealing. Manny's life as a gang member can be used to examine the fit of such accounts of gang behavior as developed by Cohen, by Cloward and Ohlin, or by Yablonsky. Concepts such as "stigma," "degradation," or "depersonalization" as found in the works of such writers as Garfinkle or Goffman are vividly illustrated, say, in Manny's experiences on entering Sing Sing prison.

Manny's words also provide ample illustration of the brutal failure of our so-called correctional institutions. Hostility, depersonalization, and dependence were produced for Manny not only in Sing Sing, but also in such reformist settings as Chino or Synanon. As he says, "basically, the way things come down for the inmates, it is similar, one lock-up to another." Penologists and reformers would do well to read this book carefully, and ponder why what are hoped to be different settings are eventually perceived by those who experience them as the same.

It may be, in fact, that much of the writings by criminologists lack both the drama and the content of *Manny*. Manny's description of his prison experience persistently sounds a theme of interwoven sameness, routine hustling, depersonalization, hostility, and powerlessness that are connected together in a way that is yet to be captured adequately by the more formal language of social science.

For the student, the sections on the connection between Manny's experiences and more formal studies of deviant behavior are invaluable. An important question always is what are we learning? The significance of Manny's career lies in our assumption that there are many more Mannys out there in the world. It becomes important, then, that we try to draw out of the first-hand account those elements which help us to generalize to other situations and persons. These sections provide an essential bridge to other writings and other experiences necessary to widen the scope of possible generalizations.

Finally, the work is readable. Manny's words are not hindered by the shackles of dullness that we criminologists often impose upon ourselves in generating more formalized theory.

A book that has as much content as this, and yet is consistently interesting, is a rarity indeed.

Kenneth Polk

Acknowledgments

It is ironic that much of the content of this book deals with events that take place principally in New York and California—ironic because much of our work in writing it has been in locations throughout the United States, Canada, and Europe. But we have each accumulated through our mobility debts that deserve recognition.

Acknowledgments due on the part of Richard Rettig must go back to those years spent "on the bricks" and "in the joint" during his sojourn "in the life." Surely my sociological point of view is broader and deeper because of past experience. To all my old friends, wherever you are, thanks! To my wife Margaret and children, Marie, Lynn, Jay, and Terral, who put up with a lot and carried my share of family responsibilities during the long hours of composition and revision, I express my deep sense of gratitude.

Our work has profited from the contributions of our colleagues, associates, and students. For their important suggestions and criticisms of early versions of the manuscript, we acknowledge our indebtedness to: Kenneth Polk, University of Oregon; John Irwin, San Francisco State University; Ernest K. Alix, Southern Illinois University at Carbondale; Benedict S. Alper, Boston College; and Carolsue Holland, Boston University, Overseas Division. To an extraordinary group of Maryland students in Wiesbaden and Heidelberg, who were in their own way enormously helpful, goes a very special thanks. Virginia Calvert and Elizabeth Zeller, who gave us valuable input from the student perspective, and Werner H. Bruer and Michael Hoffner, who helped one of the authors in countless ways, deserve recognition for their contributions.

R. H. R
M. J. T.
G. R. G.

Introduction

Life histories have always been popular as well as an important source of information to social scientists. This is particularly true of biographies that deal with a social world that is not easily accessible to social researchers. Clifford Shaw's *The Natural History of a Delinquent Career* (1931), for example, became an important test of culture transmission theory, and Edwin Sutherland's *Professional Thief* (1937) helped to stimulate the growth of his theory of differential association. Even more recently, sociologists have incorporated the autobiographical approach in text readers in criminology and deviance.

Although this volume adds yet another biography to an already vast number, it may very well be unique. This is the life history of Manny Torres. It traces the life of a young Puerto Rican boy in New York City from his involvements in delinquent gang activities to those in the rackets and underworld. We follow Manny through his desperate years as a heroin addict, as a criminal, as a prison inmate, and as a parolee. His life is discussed in an unusually frank and straightforward way in the language of street people, dope addicts, and prison cons. In sum, we do not know of other books that present a biographic account of a criminal-addict career in quite the same way.

It may also be a unique book in that it is written expressly for an academic audience with interests in deviance, crime, correction, and criminal justice. In this respect, the book is an effort to go well beyond Manny's biography by using what is—from a sociological viewpoint—an unusually rich life to elucidate a variety of theories in deviance and criminology. Our aim is both to expose students to a social world that very few of us experience firsthand and to enrich their understanding of that world and the theories that purport to explain it.

Plan of the Book

One reason for an introductory chapter is to indicate what the book is all about; still another is to explain its organization and how it might be best utilized by an academic audience. These tasks seem especially important to a book that is divided into two parts, each of which contains very different levels of content and uses very different forms of language.

The Biography

Manny begins by contrasting his street experiences as a "bottom-level" addict in New York City with his childhood years which, until the point of his father's death, were filled with the advantages of a middle-class family. In this respect, Manny's early life is probably atypical of most Puerto Rican families. This contrast, however, provides us with an advance picture of what may very well be the high and low points in Manny's life. The death of his father reconstitutes family life for Manny, his mother, and his brother Bobby. The family moves to a poor neighborhood in the Bronx, and Manny and his brother soon find their way into a local gang, the Young Stars. Homelife and the school become relatively unimportant to Manny as the gang begins to play a critical role in defining his identity and in providing him with a source of self-esteem. But Manny's account of ganging goes well beyond charting the changes that take place in his personal life, for he provides us with a detailed picture of the group structure, values, and activities that typified delinquent gangs in the 1950s.

In Chapter 2, Manny graduates from delinquency into the fringe of a criminal career by means of a successful gambling streak. The neighborhood "boss," Leo, who controls the local numbers racket, comes to be an important figure in Manny's life, and Manny soon becomes a dedicated worker in Leo's organization. This shift in deviant activities can be seen as still another turning point in Manny's life in that his self-identity now comes to be that of a professional racketeer. As Manny comments, "In my head I thought I was a big-time gangster," and so in a very real sense he was one.

Not unlike many young people in urban neighborhoods, Manny is led into his first experimentation with marijuana. But, unlike most teenagers, Manny is later introduced to "snorting" heroin. Though the first is an unpleasant experience, Manny finds the second time around to be "something else . . . all of the colors of Times Square explode in your eyeballs . . . and the world levels out." In a matter of months, Manny's initial fears of heroin gradually ease and he moves from "snorting" to "skinpopping" and finally to "mainlining." The shift in his lifestyle is dramatic, and his increasing commitment to heroin disenfranchises him from Leo's organization. Instead, he drifts in and out of relationships that lead to "capers" and "heists" that make "scoring" heroin almost easy. We see his involvements in professional thievery and "boosting," as well as the fast action of street hustling. But what differentiates Manny from most professional criminals and hustlers is that his life is organized around an ever-increasing commitment to heroin. In the end, his career is interrupted by his first "bust." Manny is off to Sing Sing Prison in New York State.

Manny's account of prison life in Chapter 3 gives credence to the widely held claim that getting caught functions to confirm and strengthen one's commitment to criminality rather than weaken it. From his very first encounter in the admissions process to his experiences as a "well-seasoned con," we can see almost precisely step by step how Manny becomes prisonized and how his self-identity becomes solidified as both criminal and convict. His relationship with Raul, his "homeboy" from the Bronx, is especially significant. Raul provides Manny with an immediate friendship and an inside track to "doing time" the easy way. Thus, Raul helps Manny in making the transition from the naiveté of a "fish" to a con who knows and understands the ways of prison life. But in this chapter Manny goes well beyond a chronicle of personal experiences by taking a more analytical and impersonal view of life in a maximum-security penal facility. We are given an inside perspective of the prison culture of the 1960s: the inmate power structure, prison sex and homosexual roles, the social codes that govern the inmate society, and the ways in which racism is manifested in the prison experience.

Still another turning point in Manny's life comes soon after his time in prison. Almost from the day of his release, Manny is back to "fixing dope every day . . . right back to hustling . . . and shooting." In Chapter 4, Manny relates how he came to do his first "stretch" in Synanon, an involvement in addict rehabilitation that was to consume nearly three years of his life. He tells how he gradually learned to tolerate, even profit, from the Synanon "haircut," a process whereby initiates are "cut down to size." For Manny, it came to be an invasion of his façade as a street hustler and as an experienced con artist. He shares with us the often pragmatic, sometimes spiritual and emotional, commitment of people to Synanon experience. His account is especially illuminating in this respect in that we can sense the smothering comfort of total commitment to Synanon, as well as the agony of submission to absolute rule. For Manny, however, Synanon comes to be an exercise in tolerating oppression by leaders whom he sees as skillful in methods of subterfuge, manipulation, and dictatorial control. "You never use dope if you never leave," says Manny, "but who wants to stay in prison forever?"

Chapter 5 finds Manny in the years following Synanon reliving all of his past experiences—crime, hustling, and dope. And, while there are new events in his criminal career, new characters, and new locales in his travels, his personality is remarkably similar to the Manny revealed to us in earlier chapters. It is important, however, that Manny share with us what is perhaps a rerun of earlier scenes in his life. For one thing, these accounts reveal what often happens to those who are suddenly deinstitutionalized and how returning to the "old life," whether a consequence of personal failure or a result of restricted opportunities to take up a new life, becomes a matter of following a path of least resistance. In the end, Manny is once again arrested, but this time he is off to Chino, California, to serve a long-term sentence.

In the final biographical chapter, the now familiar cycle—jail, streets, and back to jail—repeats itself. Beginning with his time in the Chino Diagnostic Center, his almost miraculous salvation from a long sentence, and yet another bust, Manny shows no evidence of a commitment to personal change. However, his final "stretch" in the California Rehabilitation Center opens up new possibilities for a turnaround. And, though Manny voices in this chapter harsh criticisms of the CRC experience, it is here that his energies are rechanneled into education. His biography concludes with a narrative of his parole to Humboldt County, California, the start of his college career at Humboldt State University, and an account of what evidently has become a powerful influence in reconstituting his personal life.

A concluding chapter, entitled, "From the Horse's Mouth," is included partly because the biography ends at a point that does not offer a picture of Manny that clearly sets him apart from his past. Written at a time when his street and prison experiences are well behind him, Manny discusses in a series of interview dialogues some of the more salient happenings in his life, using these to touch upon what he sees as critical issues in understanding deviant lifestyles, criminal identities, criminal justice, and corrections. That there remains hostility and resentment over the events in his past is evident in the early part of this chapter. Yet it is also clear that Manny has given considerable thought to his life, and at points in these dialogues we can see the shift from "street observer" to "intellectual" that takes place even while the book is progressing.

Although this overview will be useful in preserving the continuity of Manny's life history, there are two notes of caution that should be entertained before reading the biography itself. First, it is important to bear in mind that the biographical narrative is essentially a self-report of Manny's life. While self-reported life histories offer the special advantage of an "inside view," this can also be seen as one of its principal disadvantages. That is, self-reports often raise the question of how much the author may have distorted the events of his or her life. Many times the concern is less that the author has deliberately or consciously misportrayed events than that there is a type of distortion that is a natural consequence of how the author presently perceives the world. Thus, one's interpretation of events and personal experiences undergoes a filtering process in which there may be a tendency to portray the facts in ways that enhance one's own image. There exists, then, a potential distortion factor in any self-reporting of events in which one has had personal involvement.

Although it is important to understand that this biography for the most part represents Manny's perceptions of his social world, and thus carries the potential risks of self-reporting, so too does much of the data utilized by sociologists and social scientists. A great deal of the information gathered through questionnaires and interviews represents the respondent's perception of reality and events, and rarely are these perceptions subject to verification by external criteria. Thus, if we ask respondents to evaluate the importance of events in their childhood, we are seldom in a position to dispute their claims or responses. This does not mean, of course, that these data are unuseful or invalid. Rather, they represent perceptions and interpretations of events that are seen as real by the respondent, even though they may appear a distortion of reality to the researcher.

Manny, who is himself a student of sociology, is well aware of the pitfalls of writing a life history. We believe that the biography presented here indicates that at times he has been able to step outside of the world of crime, prison, and heroin in which he was once an active member and to see himself and the circumstances surrounding his life with a significant degree of detachment and objectivity. Although this does not in itself add veracity to the accuracy of the events he portrays, it does function to make this biography something more than a chronicle of personal experiences and con stories. At the very least, Manny provides us with perspectives on social contexts—the prison, Synanon, street life, among others—that in an analytical way go well beyond his personal involvements. Finally, it goes almost without saying that we have given scrupulous attention to insuring an accurate portrayal of the major facts of Manny's life history. Editing of the biography itself has been confined to eliminating passages or sections that were unnecessarily repetitive of earlier events or dialogue or where his street language obscured intended meaning. With these exceptions, the language in the biography, which at times is profane and abusive, at times almost lyrical, is Manny's original prose. For the protection of Manny's family, his friends, and his private life, some of the factual matters in his early life and his underworld activities have been altered slightly, yet in our opinion, these alterations in no way distort the sociological substance or significance of those events, nor do these minor changes damage the facticity of the biographical account.

Perspectives

For students in the social sciences the task of linking theory and reality is a crucial test of scholarship. It is not always an easy test to pass, either because we misunderstand the function of a theory or because we lack experiences in the "real world" that could facilitate a deeper understanding of its phenomenology.

One of the problems in examining theory is that we frequently consider it to be nothing more than an abstract enterprise of unproven speculations, separate and distinct from the "real world." While there is a thread of truth to this, it obscures the interlocking relationship of theory and reality. For example, theory defines the kinds of data and observations that are necessary to explain phenomena. In other words, theory tells us what kinds of data are needed to explain events in reality. Second, "facts" in the "real world," that is, empirically verifiable observations, have a special kind of significance to any theoretical system because one of the functions of theory is to explain relationships between facts. Put another way, theory enables us to see relationships between two observations or facts that might otherwise remain obscure. Finally, observations in the "real world" not only test the validity of a theory but function to build and expand theoretical systems.

Sometimes our inability to appreciate theory and its intrinsic link to the "real world" derives from the distant relationship that theory has to our personal lives and to "our" empirical world. Students who have had little or no personal contact with the criminal world, for example, often find it difficult to appreciate and understand a theory that purports to explain criminality. This is not altogether surprising, since it is not always easy to comprehend an abstract explanation of phenomena that we have neither experienced nor directly observed. And while a theory that has little bearing on our personal world hardly invalidates the theoretical perspective itself, at the very least it makes difficult the task of understanding as well as appreciating its explanatory power.

It is precisely because the task of linking theory and the "real world" is difficult yet so important to undergraduate students that we include as an addendum to each chapter of the biography a section entitled "Perspectives." These are compiled in Chapter 8, "Perspectives on Manny's Life History." Our central purpose is to help students reach a deeper understanding of theories of deviance and crime by means of discussions that use the general circumstances of Manny's biography as touchstones. In sum, the Perspectives should facilitate the student's understanding of the formal literature and theories in deviance and crime. We feel that they will

stimulate fruitful and worthwhile theoretical group discussions by providing for students identifiable touchstones on common grounds.

Each Perspective introduces a number of theories, and in some we have
included citations from research literature that have a special relevance to
the subject under discussion. We have introduced a theory or concept at
a point where it offers a relevant context in which to examine the sociological circumstances of Manny's life as it was conveyed in the corresponding chapter of his biography. Taken as a whole, the Perspectives expose
readers to a wide range of theories, ranging from the structural-functionalist
approach and Durkheim's anomie theory, together with its contemporary
offshoots; to symbolic interactionism; theories of criminality, such as
Sutherland's differential association theory, Reckless' containment theory,
and the labeling perspective on crime; theories of delinquency, including
those of Miller, Cloward and Ohlin, Yablonsky, Cohen, Karaki and Toby,
Polk and Schafer, and others; to theoretical perspectives on the social organization of prison, including such works as Schrag, Sykes and Messinger,
McCorkle, Irwin, and Wheeler. (All of these references are cited in the
Perspectives.)

Although we believe that the Perspectives will be useful in introducing
and elucidating concepts and theories in deviance and crime, it should be
emphasized that they serve as summaries rather than as compendia of
sociological theory. The utility of the Perspectives for students rests partly
in their brevity, and thus our discussions focus on the more salient elements
and concepts of a theory.

Taken together the Perspectives do not give special emphasis to a particular approach or theory. While this offers the advantage of achieving
broader coverage of materials, it also carries the disadvantage of leaving
readers without a unified theoretical framework from which to examine
the issues and problems raised in the substance of Manny's biography. It is
for this reason that we include a final chapter, which integrates competing
and complementary theories of deviance and delinquency, drawing on
many of the perspectives reviewed in Chapter 8. The student will want
to give special attention to this chapter, for it provides an orientation
that gives a relatively new interpretation to the sequence of developmental
stages in a deviant career, including street-criminal careers of the Manny
Torres variety.

It should be pointed out that the organization of this book offers at
least two options with regard to how it can be read. For example, the biography can be read in its entirety, followed by the Perspectives. This approach offers the advantage of preserving the continuity of Manny's life
history. As an alternative, each biographical chapter can be read, followed
by the corresponding Perspective in Chapter 8, and then Chapter 9. For

some students this approach may be more helpful in facilitating an immediate understanding of theoretical concepts, and it offers the additional advantage of accumulating conceptual tools that can make the reading of subsequent chapters a more useful exercise in sociological analysis.

Finally, in reading the chapter Perspectives it is also important to bear in mind that sociological theories are not usually intended to explain a single case. Durkheim, for example, sought to explain deviant behavior not in terms of individual characteristics of the deviant but by stressing social conditions and the weakening of collective sentiments as causal factors in deviance. As we shall see later, labeling theory directs attention not only to the characteristics of deviants but it also amplifies the social processes whereby behaviors are assigned deviant labels and stresses the societal reaction to those who are successfully labeled. Our point here is that the student should not expect that each of the theories will explain the specific facts of Manny's life. Some theories, for example, may provide us with insights into how Manny's life came to be structured in such a way that his opportunities or options were limited and restricted or were channeled into alternative "opportunities"; yet, these can lack the explanatory power to tell us why Manny pursued the choice he made. The latter question is more within the purview of the psychologists, whereas the former is of interest to sociologists. It will become obvious, too, that some theories are better suited than others to answer the questions of causality raised in the biography. In still other instances, we will find that the circumstances surrounding Manny's experiences will raise questions with respect to the validity of a theory's premises.

Concluding Comments

Although this book has as a central feature a provocative life history, our purpose in writing it has been to provide students with an academic exercise in examining the interrelationship of theory and the "real world." The events in Manny's life and his lucid descriptions of the street existence of addicts, his experiences in crime and in prison, are especially rich in sociologic substance. No less important is the fact that Manny's life history opens up a social world that few readers will experience firsthand.

We would be derelict in our commitment to scholarship and education, however, were we to avoid pointing to the moral dimensions in the life of Manny Torres. Readers will not find it easy to remain neutral to Manny as the chapters of his biography unfold. In fact, at times one cannot help but feel a sense of disgust and moral outrage over his thievery, dishonesty, self-waste, and his episodes of violence. Simultaneously, one cannot avoid feeling a compassion for a life that has been so filled with trouble and hurt. Perhaps the experience of feeling such contradictions in emotions will in itself be an important educational exercise. And if this book leads its readers to contemplate the types of social change that might ultimately minimize recurrences of the Manny Torreses in our society, it will have accomplished a very special objective.

Selected References

Some recent examples of biographies and life-history accounts are:

Behan, Brendan
1958 *Borstal boy*. New York: Knopf.

Bone, Edith
1957 *Seven years solitary*. New York: Harcourt Brace Jovanovich.

Brown, Claude
1965 *Manchild in the promised land*. New York: Macmillan.

Burroughs, William
1953 *Junkie*. New York: Ace Books.

Chessman, Caryl
1954 *Cell 2455, Death Row*. Englewood Cliffs, N.J.: Prentice-Hall.

Cleaver, Elridge
1968 *Soul on ice*. New York: McGraw-Hill.

Jackson, George
1970 *Soledad brother*. New York: Bantam Books.

Leopold, Nathan F., Jr.
1958 *Life plus 99 years*. New York: Doubleday.

Malcolm X
1964 *The autobiography of Malcolm X*. New York: Grove Press.

Rubin, Theodore
1961 *In the life*. New York: Ballantine Books.

Sands, Bill
1964 *My shadow ran fast*. Englewood Cliffs, N.J.: Prentice-Hall.

Sutton, Willie
1953 *I, Willie Sutton*. New York: Farrar, Straus & Giroux.

Thomas, Piri
1967 *Down these mean streets.* New York: The New American Library.

Two useful anthology texts in criminology and deviance are:

Minton, Robert J.
1971 *Inside: Prison American style.* New York: Random House.

Peterson, David M., & Truzzi, Marcello (Eds.)
1972 *Criminal life: Views from the inside.* Englewood Cliffs, N.J.:
 Prentice-Hall.

A recent text that uses a considerable amount of autobiographical material obtained from interviews is:

Winslow, Robert, & Winslow, Virginia
1972 *Deviant reality: Alternative world views.* Boston: Allyn & Bacon.

For an especially interesting account of the lives and activities of delinquent boys from a novelist's perspective see:

Price, Richard
1974 *The wanderers.* Boston: Houghton Mifflin.

Chapter 1

Young Star Here!

The conflict of fighting gang subculture was found to flourish in Puerto Rican neighborhoods where there was little opportunity to succeed either in a criminal or a noncriminal fashion. (Geis, 1965)

Most people don't really know what it is to be hooked on dope. I mean, to be really sick. Like me and my brother Bobby in the Bronx back in the early sixties, after we were using for over a year. We were on a real heavy run. It was colder than the tail end of an iceberg, right in the dead of winter, and we're sleeping in the car parked out in the street because the cops were looking for me at my apartment. I remember that wind! It whistled down those concrete canyons thirty miles an hour, hanging icicles on everything that moved and freezing what little blood we had left in our veins. This night we've got fifteen dollars between us. And we have to decide should we get a hotel room for the night and get down, man, or should we wait until six o'clock in the morning? If we get a room at six we can hold on to it for twenty-four hours, till the following day at six. So we're arguing this and it's cold and we're sick. But we just got enough bread to score once and we're trying to hold off. But it gets to be too much, so we finally decide, "No, to hell with it, we have to get down."

I mean, we have to fix; we have to get down. Not for the fun of getting loaded, but just to keep from getting sicker. So finally my brother says, "Okay, we'll go to a connection and score." This is two o'clock in the morning and it is in the middle of winter, and all I have on is a long-sleeved white shirt that I must have been wearing for over two weeks. No undershirt, no sweats, no coat. Just a thin, dirty, white shirt. And we're walking all over the neighborhood. We're trying to run down four or five different connections and they're either out of dope or they're laying low out of sight. We can't score and we begin to wonder if we're into a run of bad luck.

Finally, we run into this other dope fiend who's looking to score. And he says he thinks he knows somebody who's holding the bag. So we walk all the way across town, must have been ten miles or so, walking in the damn cold in the middle of the night. We get to the connection and he has the dope so we score.

Then we gotta go upstairs. Seems like we spent half our lives getting upstairs to fix. We used to stash our outfits to fix with all over town in apartment buildings, usually up on the top landing. And, like it would be six or seven stories up. We'd go up to the top floor and on up one more landing before we'd get out on the roof. And we'd get up there and we'd have no water to fix with so we'd knock on somebody's door—

we'd just knock like hell and ask them if we could get some water. Usually they'd look at us like we were crazy. We'd stand there and shout at them, "Goddamn you, we got to have water. Just give it to us in a Coke bottle or a paper cup or something. It makes no difference, we got to have some water now!"

And we'd just stand there needing water for all our lives and they'd slam the door on us like they were trying to kill us. But we'd just knock again and shout louder.

"We got to have water. We have to fix and it makes no difference what you want! We gotta have water and you better give it to us."

And it don't make a damn that you're knocking some dude out of bed in the middle of the night. You don't even think of it that way. You're so damn sick, you know. You're feeling so bad that you know you're going to die, and you have the remedy for all your problems right in your hand. You have the cure in your hand. That little dab of white powder is gonna make you feel good. And you feel terrible, so you don't care. All you want is that fix. And you just knock, y'know. And it's like they didn't understand what was happening. So you'd just be yelling at them to get a point across.

"I'm sick, man, and I don't give a damn. I don't care, I gotta get down, so just give me some water."

And finally they would usually give me the water in something like a Coke bottle. And we'd run back up to the top landing and get ready to fix. We'd break open this three-dollar bag of dope and start heating it up. And then we'd get into an argument over who's gonna get off first, 'cause we only got one outfit, y'know, only one syringe.

Okay, we're all sick and we all want to go first. It was me and my brother and this other dope fiend, and we're just standing there arguing like hell with each other. I mean, it's unreal that all we gotta do is somebody go first and get down to the nod, and then the others can get off, but we argued for over an hour. And, I mean, we're ready to fight! It was really getting out of hand. And my brother threatened me. I mean, he pulled a knife and threatened to stick me right there, if I didn't knock off the bullshit and let him fix.

That little dab of white powder is gonna make you feel good.

Well, then I didn't have no choice so I said, "Okay, all right, you go first, man."

So, my brother went first and got down. When you're watching someone else fix and you're sick, and you're watching someone else cook the stuff and you get that sulfur smell up your nose, y'know, what a hell of a sensation! I'll always remember that rotten feeling, because you're already sicker'n shit and you get a whiff of that sulfur and you just throw up. I mean, you just puke it all up right there. I mean, you start gettin' cramps because the stuff is so close but you haven't got it in your arm yet. And finally, when my turn came, boy, I hit it! Y'know, and everything was smoother'n silk and real fine. I mean, man, I was dirty, I hadn't had a bath or a change of clothes for weeks. I was hungry and I had no place to live, no place at all. I mean, nothin! I had no friends. Y'know, I would con my own brother out of his shoes for a fix. I had nothing in the world, but I felt great. I just fixed heroin and I felt like a million dollars cash.

There is something fantastic and fatal about heroin, and no nonuser can ever dig it. Like, it's the ultimate tranquilizer. It anesthetizes the whole damn ugly world. All your troubles become forgotten memories, lost on another dimension, when you're in the nod. And you don't even consider that it will soon wear off and the gentle nod will turn into a screaming want. And the nose-dripping, crawling, wormy feeling of needing a fix always follows the mellowest nod.

When you tell people things like that, they don't believe it. But that's the way it is and it's really strange. You have no values. There's no such thing as values for a dope fiend, none at all. The only livin' thing that counts is the fix. That's all that counts, nothin' else means a shit.

Like, I would steal off anybody—anybody at all, my own mother gladly included if it meant the difference between a fix and no fix. I would do anything for money to fix. I would con, I would beg, I would cry; I would break bad and threaten. I would do anything at all to get enough money to fix. If I hadn't of been so skinny and ugly I'd of sold my ass for dope.

I had a lot of friends at one time. But I burned all my friends for dope. And that's not all, I'd of killed them too, for heroin, if that'd been necessary.

Oh yeah! If it came to the point where I had a gun in my hand and you had the dope and you didn't give it to me, I'd take it off of you. And I'd of used the gun if I had to. I would kill you! Certainly! If you had the dope and that's the only way I could get it.

Now, if you just had money . . . I'm not sure. I don't think I would've. 'Cause, you see, I still had to score. Scoring can be just as hard as raising the bread sometimes. So if you got the nose-running, crawling, ice-cold shits—like, your guts are going to blow up and your muscles are snapping like rubber bands, and someone's got dope and ain't givin' it up, you're going to kill him. No sweat. No sweat at all.

When I would be on a run and be needing a fix I had some really bad

habits. Like, I'd come out of the nod and start to get sick and I'd get really weak. If I didn't fix right away when I began to get like that I couldn't make it. I mean, I would lie there. Y'know. Throwing up all over myself. Shitting all over myself. God! Really miserable and all fucked up. That was it. Until somebody came over with the dope. Or I could get somebody on the phone who was holding dope, and I could get up enough hope to go get it. Otherwise, I would just lay there, dying little by little. Hope or dope. And dope always beats hope.

So, I knew damn well when I'd start to get sick I'd have to get the dope quick. If I went to a connection and he didn't give me the dope right there, sure I'd shoot him. Why not? I needed a fix, I was sicker'n hell. And there ain't no other cure except kicking. And, baby, when you're hooked on stuff, kicking don't come easy.

So, it's either kill or die. And if he wouldn't get up off the horse I'd shoot him dead and fix on his body if I had to, just to get well.

Listen, a dope fiend has to have this "I don't care" attitude. Just to survive out there in that jungle when you're on a long run is going to cost you at least 150 dollars a day. Now, there ain't no other way to con or steal that much bread but to have the confidence that you can do it.

So a dope fiend develops this "I don't care" attitude to survive. Y'know. The way it comes out is the way it's gonna come out. And somehow, it usually comes out right. 'Cause a dope fiend learns to be the best con artist in the world. He is the best simply because he needs money every day. Every day he has to get his hands on 150 bucks, on the average. One hundred and fifty dollars a day, every single day, 365 days per year. You cannot miss. You need it every day.

Every day you gotta find new ways of making money. Or the old ways gotta come through for you again. And you'll do anything. But you'll get it. You come up with the money. It's funny how a dope fiend puts so much energy into getting the next fix. Man, if you could channel that energy into something else you could capture the cosmos. But any dope fiend I ever knew spends every waking hour of his life scratching and fighting for the next fix. Except for the moments of nodding, he is working like hell. Now, nodding is something else. Like a ten-minute orgasm with the most far-out broad you can imagine. Can you dig it? But one way or another, a dope fiend is going to prostitute himself for dogie. So, how did I come to this sort of life? I don't know. Can anybody really answer that question?

It's hard to go back, to open up all of yesterday's experiences and extract meaning from them. Like cutting into a cold corpse, it doesn't bleed. I do remember certain happenings and stages of experience from my past, however, that seem to add up in some kind of loosely defined way to say a lot about who I am now and who I've been along the way.

When I was a little kid it was just me, my brother, and Mom and Pop. We were in the better-offs among the Puerto Ricans living in the Bronx. I can remember Pop running his shop. Kinda like the city version of the old country store. Pop handled a little of everything and his business was good, providing us with a comfortable living. Pop seemed to have a knack for shop-keeping. Just who to extend credit to, for example, and how much. Most everybody in the neighborhood owed my Pop money, and they all loved him. Man, when you got that kind of character, you got something going.

But Pop died, and life changed fast for Mom and us kids. Before, I would have been considered any ordinary middle-class kid. I was patriotic, believed in democracy, and did well in school. Pop had the store and we owned our own house. I didn't do anything much different from anybody else. I remember we used to play stickball, punchball, swim in the pool, and play around the park. I don't ever recall doing anything bad. I did what most of the Puerto Rican kids were doing at that time. Most of the "well-off" ones, that is.

I didn't really start going "bad" as people say until my father died.

That was when I was eleven. We lost everything. There was some kind of legal hassle with the estate and Pop's relatives got everything, all his money, the house, the store, everything. They didn't even come around to see us. They left my mother and us kids with nothing, absolutely nothing.

In a couple of months my mother started getting social security, which would pay the rent and groceries if you adjusted your living standard drastically downward. We moved two blocks north of where we'd been living in the Bronx. Over to Third Avenue, where we could get a cheaper flat. And my brother Bobby, who was two years younger, and I started playing out in the street more. I didn't have much supervision. My mother tried, but, you see, my mother was really small, just a tiny woman with a lot of health problems after Pop died. And how was she going to control two growing boys?

I was eleven and getting kind of wild. At first I wasn't into much of anything wrong, but I had a real temper and when I said no you had to beat me over the head to change my mind. And Mom just didn't have the power to stay with me. So, I started cutting a lot of classes and lying about it until I got caught. I used to have this broad, Becky, write excuses for me and just skip school for days at a time. When they started hassling my mother she'd get real upset. So, I'd promise to do good and stay in school, but I never did.

When we moved over to Third Avenue, that's when I really started hitting the skids. Not stealing anything, but I joined a fighting gang. I became a member of the Young Stars.

Me and my brother had a lot of fun in the gang, I remember that. Me and Bobby were always together. When you saw one, you knew the other was somewhere around. My brother was known as the Undertaker in the Young Stars. And I was the warlord. I remember, I became the warlord in a full council meeting on my thirteenth birthday. And it was my job to arrange fights with gangs like the Scorpions, the Mau Maus, the Seven Devils, and the other gangs.

I was eleven and getting kind of wild.

Remember, this was in the early fifties. It was the beginning of the youth rebellion in this country. Kids in my neighborhood really began to emphasize toughness. Gang rumbles were a way to be tough and a way to demonstrate how to be smarter than others and "outwit the enemy." Also, our gangs gave us the opportunity to be on our own. What went on in the clubhouse was our business. And we made sure it was the most important business for every member.

Sometimes it got really rough. We used to fight in school. I mean, I'd be walking down the hall in school with a sweater on saying "Young Stars." Another guy would be in the hall with a sweater saying "Scorpions." And I'd see him and we'd start fighting. We would fight on sight all the time. This wasn't like black against white, Chicano against nigger, or orange against green. It was neighborhood against neighborhood, territory against territory. My neighborhood against all other neighborhoods. If you belonged to some gang and you came into my neighborhood around Third Avenue and 178th Street, we would fight.

You invaded our territory and it was war. It made no difference if you were rich or poor, friend or foe. For instance, I had friends from the old days who were from really wealthy families, and I'd been over to their houses to parties and for dinner, maybe even fooled around a little with their sisters or cousins. Then, a couple of years later I would fight them "to the death" because they were in a rival gang—guys that used to be good friends of mine.

One gang tried to hang my brother. Really! It was an Italian gang called the Hoods. Their territory used to border ours, and so we were head to head, asshole to asshole all the time. This time we'd went over to their candy store to screw them around. Most gangs used to hang out around the neighborhood candy store. We went over to their store

and took some thirty-gallon garbage cans and threw 'em through the plate-glass window. Some of us had zip guns and we stood outside shooting up the place. We really wanted to down the sons-of-bitches 'cause they would come into our territory and do the same thing. We even used to wait for them on the roofs with garbage cans full of coal ashes. We'd wait for them to walk by and try to kill 'em. It was our thing, and it was really wild.

Well, soon after this rumble my brother, the Undertaker, is coming home from junior high school when these five or six Italian Hoods ambush him. They throw a rope over a nearby tree, put the other end around his neck, and they're trying to pull him up. But they can't get him off the ground.

My little cousin Millie happens by, and she runs over to our house and tells me that the Hoods are trying to hang Bobby. I got this shotgun under my bed that doesn't work. The firing pin is frozen, but I figure that the Hoods don't know that. So, I open it up and I put two shells in it while I'm running out the door. I get over to the park and I see all these guys trying to pull Bobby up in the air. But he's kicking and raising hell and they can't get him up.

They see me running with the gun and they scatter. The rope burned my brother all around the neck and face. Now, the Hoods were not messing around. They were laying to get the Undertaker. But we didn't think nothing about it. No big deal.

Bobby just tells me, "Hey, Manny, it's a good thing you got here. I almost died. Good thing that you got over here in time."

Bobby was known as the Undertaker because it was his job to make the hits. He really played the part to a T. Dressed in black all the time and carried this umbrella with a real sharp point. We would have a war council and decide that a valuable member of some rival gang would have to die. And it was Bobby's job to make the hit. He attempted to fill a few contracts but never actually made a hit. The point is, he attempted. He walked into this candy store one time and fired pointblank at this dude and missed him. Another time he hit a Scorpion from three stories up with an ash can full of wet cinders, but he only broke his shoulder bone and four ribs.

Leadership in our gang was pretty well organized. We had a president, a war counselor, an assistant war counselor, and a hit man. We also had a sergeant-at-arms. He was the dude in charge of all the artillery. We had a pretty good arsenal. Like zip guns we made ourselves or took off other gang members, chains, baseball bats, and tire irons. We even had some real guns, but most of the time they didn't work for one reason or another. And it was hard for us to get bullets for them. But we were building up our arsenal. We really wanted to be gangsters.

But we were just mainly fighters defending our territory and our broads. We didn't steal, didn't use dope. Most of us didn't even drink. It didn't cross our minds to get into this kind of stuff. The whole thing was fighting. The trip was just being a member of some gang. You wanted to be a man and you acted like a man. You're thirteen years old and you're walking around with your chest out, bumping into people and hoping they'll give you a bad time so you can pounce on them and beat 'em into the goddamn concrete.

And sometimes the girls were worse than the guys. We used to have Young Star Debs, Scorpion Debs, or whatever. These broads could really fight. Lots of times they'd stand right in there and punch it out with the dudes. They used to carry all the guns and knives because the cops liked to stop us and frisk us all the time. But they wouldn't frisk the broads for fear they'd holler rape. So, during a fight when we'd need the heavy artillery we'd get it off the girls. But they'd be sure to get it all back and secured in pretty private places by the time the cops arrived. Sometimes the cops would know that the broads were holding the heavy arms and they'd try and get them into the patrol cars. But we'd hassle the cops and create a diversion so that the debs could usually get away.

———————————————————

I remember a lot of fantastic experiences in the gang days. Like, one time I got thrown off this theater balcony. I walk into this movie;

I'm with this girl and we buy some popcorn and stuff and walk up into the balcony to watch the flick. And there's a bunch of Italian dudes sittin' up there. They say, "Hey guys, look at the goddamn Spic."

I thought there would be some of my gang at the movie. I take off my jacket so the Italians can see my sweater, and I holler, "Young Star here!"

They say, "Yeah, Young Star!"

Only one problem. I jump up, but I'm the only Young Star in the place. I was the only one standing, the only Spic in the balcony, and they just pick me up and heave me over. Wow! I woke up in the hospital. Had several broken bones and a bad concussion. They almost killed me.

But that was part of the game. We were just kids playing games. Trouble was, they were dangerous games and sometimes people got killed. When I woke up in that hospital I thought it was a big deal. Guys and debs would come up to see Manny, the kid that defended the honor of the Young Stars against all odds. I was a big hero. It got me elected warlord.

I was into that scene for two years. Always fighting. Learning to down the other guy before he downed you. You'd be walking down the halls in school and all of a sudden three or four dudes'd jump on you. You'd think nothing of it, though. You'd fight back, maybe get beat up. Next day, you'd be sure you had your pack with you. Always go around in cliques if you're smart. Just like

a bunch of wolves.

It turns out that to get confirmed as warlord of the Young Stars I had to survive an ordeal. I had to fight against these five other dudes. And they weren't exactly the gang pansies either! They had me stand against this tree and they tried their damnedest to knock me down. I stayed up for two minutes and so I got to be the warlord. My job was to go around to the other gangs, meet with their chiefs, and decide whose territory was whose. And if we had any debate about it, it was my job to settle on when and where we would fight it out and what weapons we would use.

So, this particular time we were into this big hassle with the Hoods —this big, tough Italian gang up on Braxton Road. I go up to their school—P.S. 118—this one morning and ask to talk with Louie, who was their war counselor at the time. I walk right in like I own the school 'cause I did. Schools had very little control over gang kids.

Louie meets me out in the yard thinking that I want to go duke city with him right there. He's reaching in his jeans for some kind of artillery when I tell him to cool it. "Hey, man, I'm just here to arrange a meeting between our leaders so that we can come to some terms about boundaries."

We decide that the meeting should take place in a candy store over on Forty-third Avenue, which puts it on neutral ground. This is very important, because we ain't about to consent to meet in the other guy's territory.

So, later we gather over at this candy store. My brother, the Undertaker, is there, sitting right up in front all dressed in black so they'd get the message that it's "high noon" for them if they get outa line. Both presidents and leading officers from each gang are lined up across the counter from each other. The candy store owner is playing it cool, selling a little candy here and there and not taking sides because we're all customers. The guy's a real diplomat.

We begin our beef about territory. We're saying that they have two blocks over in their territory that belong to the Young Stars. They're saying hell no! Possession means ownership. And we're arguing back and forth until we see that the only way to settle the hassle is to hold a major rumble. So, we decide to have the fight in a nearby park playground.

Now, we have to lay down the rules. We have to negotiate the style of fighting and how many men on each side should be allowed in the action. Since the argument is getting frantic by now, we decide that the fight should be an all-out war, their whole gang against our whole gang. We check rosters and see that the sides are going to be about equal, give or take a few one way or the other. Then, they wanted to establish what kind of artillery would be allowed, and our gang decided that we were only going to use clubs, chains, and shivs—no guns. We get

all the planning down pat and set the time for the rumble at ten o'clock that night.

We beat it back over to the neighborhood for a strategy meeting. We're sitting in the clubhouse brainstorming on how we're going to outfox the Hoods. We've cased their roster real well and we think they've got more heavies than we have. There were some real good dukers in the Hoods at this time, and they had several guys who'd go all the way gladly. So, we know that we're going to have to cold deck them guys and fix their wagon before their power overwhelms us.

The starting time is set for 10 P.M., so we plan to be on tap at 8. We're going to get all the high ground secured and be ready for the bastards when they come in. Petie and Killer George started to get the pistols from under the daveno springs where we had 'em stashed. One of the members said, "Hey, I thought no guns!"

I told him to dummy up. "It'll take everything we got. Take the guns and everything. 'Cause we're going in there to deal them out. We're going to down 'em and then we're gonna take over their territory."

So all day we're running all over the neighborhood telling everybody, "Get your sweaters on. We're going to down the Hoods once and for all—it's going to be all over."

And I'm not even thinking that in a couple of hours I'm gonna have people shooting at me and trying to stick me with ice picks and knives. It doesn't even cross my mind.

Around five o'clock we go over to the clubhouse and all the girls are there waiting. We start loading them up with guns. Brenda had the rag on so we told her that she couldn't carry nothing between her legs, 'cause we didn't want to get caught with a slippery trigger finger. She just laughed, "I got lots of other places to put a piece besides there, you guys." If we had the guns on us the cops would bust us, because they always used to pull us over and frisk us when we had our sweaters on.

I get my favorite weapon, this motorcycle chain, out and wrap it around my leg and pull it over the top of my pants and let it hang out. So, when we get it on, all I gotta do is rip it out. It kind of fucks up your leg a little, but you can get it out quick that way. I had a gang buddy named Tough Tommy one time that carried his chain that way. One night in a real heavy rumble Tommy went for his chain and ripped the hell out of his balls. He spent two weeks in the hospital and was almost de-screwed. After that, I was a little careful when I had to get my chain out.

So, we're all sitting around the clubhouse just playing cards or making out with the broads—not thinking that in the next few hours we could be dead. Around seven-thirty we gather. We go over the whole neighborhood to everybody's house who is a member of the Young Stars and get them turned out. There must have been over two hundred members. We just walk up and down Third Avenue and 174th making sure everybody turns out.

To get into this park you have to walk up a real long hill and then about four hundred flights of stairs, it seems. There are a whole lot of stairs and then you are on kinda like a plateau overlooking the playground. We walk over to the park and we don't see anyone down on the playground area and we know we've outsmarted them and all we gotta do is bide our time and we've got them Hood bastards.

As we're going down toward the playground to secure our battle stations they come out at us like from nowhere. They'd really out-slicked us. The sons-of-bitches were there way before they were supposed to be. I mean, they hit us from all sides. There were shots going off all over the place.

I'm just standing there and all these people are around me shooting and hollering. Except for the possibility of being downed by a stray bullet I'm not in a whole lot of trouble, 'cause they've got to get through a whole lot of other guys to get to me. I'm trying to get this chain out without ruining myself, and it's stuck on something and won't come out. I pull my shiv, but there's nobody near to stick. Everybody around me seems to have the same color sweater on. I don't recognize all those cats wearing Young Star sweaters as Young Stars, and I think, what the shit, we've really been outmaneuvered.

I could see the cops, who by now had got word of the rumble, at the bottom of the hill sitting in their squad cars. But they don't come in. They just sit down there looking up at us, and kids are getting hurt bad and even dying on that hill. When the fight starts to die down a little bit, then the cops come in. That's just like cops and their dealing with kids, though. They always get there after the action.

There are kids sprawled all over the playground. I'm all beat up. I don't know who hit me or how I got cut up. I'm in a total daze, but I feel good. Because I protected our territory. Them Hoods didn't down the Young Stars.

And the cops come in and pick up all the weapons, but they don't take none of us to jail. They keep everybody there while the medics come in and check us out. The ambulances come screaming up to take the wounded soldiers away. Then the cops hand out their JD cards. Stands for juvenile delinquent. They write out these little cards, kinda on the order of a traffic ticket. Says that you are a bad boy. They give one to your parents, one goes to the school you attend, they file one at the station, and you get one for your wallet. I musta had a hundred of 'em. So, everyone knows that you're a fuck-up and you just continue to rattle around the neighborhood

fucking up. Our gang survived a score or so of those kind of encounters. We became known as the hard-assed Spics around the Bronx and my reputation as a tough leader was well established.

We used to get down with the gang broads all the time. We used to dig the debs regular. Come to think of it, I will never have as much pussy as I had at that time. Sometimes I had sex four, maybe five times a day. And we didn't think of it as unnatural. We didn't do it in hiding. The broads were part of the club and being available to fuck was part of their function. We weren't exactly male chauvinists that way. The broads were in agreement with clubhouse sexuality and thought of it as perfectly nice and natural. They were part of us and we shared everything. It's hard to explain. We never thought of it as sex parties or anything like that. There would be a bunch of us in the clubhouse and two of us would decide to have sex, and we'd go back in the corner somewhere and we'd fuck. It was like, if you wanted to, you just did! And that was it.

I can really remember that experience quite well. And I didn't think of it that way at the time; like, I'm scoring with all these broads, and man, is it good! Anytime I'd want pussy there'd be a willing girl around. I was just beginning to find out what being a man was all about, and I began to dig it.

I had a steady girl friend named Ricky, but she wasn't a member of the gang. She was Ricky, something special. I never screwed around with Ricky. It was really strange. Somehow, I never really wanted to make it with Ricky. It was like she stood for something else. Like, gang girls were fair game, and they were all right in every way, but Ricky was kind of heavenly, if you know what I mean. Really, just because I could make it with the debs anytime, I didn't think they were "bad" or anything. It was just that Ricky was a thing apart from all that, another dimension or something.

On Saturday afternoons I would go over to her house and take Ricky to the movies. Bring her home afterward and sit with her in the living room. She was kind of square from the soda fountain set, if you can dig it. Her folks were upper-class Puerto Rican business people. When I first started going out with her I couldn't wear my sweater over to her house 'cause her parents didn't approve of ganging and didn't like for Ricky to see a gang person. But after a while I got braver and I'd just go over there with the sweater on.

I was very proud of my sweater; it was my most prized possession. It was kind of like a special trophy, only more important than that. I'd die for the club sweater. If you're going to take it off me, you've got to kill me first. It was a great honor when I used to go into another gang's territory, catch some stud unawares, and get his sweater off of him. When you'd come back from a rumble with a bunch of sweaters from a rival gang it was really important.

We fought to destroy each other.

They used to hang in the clubhouse like scalps. It was a big thing. Lots of times people ask me, "Manny, why were you in a gang?" I don't know why. I was in the gang because everybody else was in a gang. "Why do you eat?" Because, if you don't eat, you die. So, naturally, you eat. I was in my gang because it was the natural thing to do. If I wasn't in the gang at this time I would of died socially. And a loner kid on the streets of New York City is really lonely and vulnerable.

If you don't think you belong, then you're dead. You can't make it alone. A guy's got to have contact. And if I wasn't in the gang, I would of been alone. Who would I have played with or said were my friends? I wasn't forced into no gang, I looked for it, nobody looked for me, like to make me join a gang.

We fought to destroy each other. You would beat up a gang and you would get a piece of their territory. In the two years I was involved in gang fighting, the territory kept changing hands constantly. There was never one gang that was dominant all the time. A small gang would get together and beat up another gang and they would get a parcel of that gang's territory as booty. You had six blocks in your territory, and you saw that a couple of adjoining streets were kind of unprotected and you took it. Either you were getting territory or you were getting it ripped off you.

The whole thing was about territory. It was the imperative. I really can't think of any other reason that we fought. Racism wasn't ever the main issue. We just destroyed whoever got in our way. Sometimes when I think about those days I can actually re-feel that experience. We were just angry. We would throw something like garbage cans off roofs at people, and it was a good feeling. Like, it made us feel superior, that we had some stake in that reality, something we had control over, and that was brute force.

It was fun; it made me strong; it blew my head out. I would believe that I was really a tough guy. I used to like to wear this stingy brim, a slick white shirt, and pressed brown khaki pants. And I would carry an umbrella in a tight roll. That was my style, my identity. And, most important, the sweater with the stars.

Everybody in the streets of New York dressed more or less the same. Except the sweater. It was like a uniform, and you could go anywhere in the city and even if you ran into a rival gang, you could still identify with them. You would try and kill each other in a rumble, but an outsider was a mutual enemy.

Sometimes we'd have a truce with another gang, usually for political reasons involving territory. You could be an ally of one gang, and three days later be a sworn enemy. If you belonged to a gang, you were always an enemy to some other gang around the neighborhood. Sometimes we'd gang up together, even with the Hoods, to beat up our common enemy, any kids who hadn't identified with a gang. If you didn't get involved in our gang, you were against us. You were probably a sissy fink.

The gangs ran the schools, and they damn sure ran the streets. People didn't like us because we scared them and they didn't know how to handle us. At first, they figured we were wayward children, so they tried to treat us like little kids. And this didn't work because all we wanted to do was to beat them over their heads. But they couldn't treat us like adults 'cause we weren't adults. So, most of the time they didn't know what to do with us. That gave us a free hand. While all the experts were discussing how to handle the juvenile delinquency problem, we had a free hand, and we knew it!

We never went to jail, and we soon learned that we just about couldn't break into jail for ganging. Like, there would be this big gang war with people laying on the ground hurt. A felony had been committed because somebody had been knifed or shot. And I think it was terribly symbolic that we'd be having this big rumble in the park and the cops would just sit in their patrol cars waiting for everything to calm down. And when everything calmed down, or the guys just got worn out fighting, and they're laying all over the ground, then the cops would storm in. I think this represents the way they treat juvenile delinquency in this country. People wait until the kid is all fucked up. They wait until the kid is strung out on drugs or is an alcoholic. Or perhaps until he has killed somebody or until an open rebellion breaks out in a school somewhere, and then they decide that society is going to do something about it.

Like, if the people were more aware in the early fifties, they could have seen that something was happening with the youth. The gangs started as social clubs. Nobody told us to organize a gang. We just wanted to play athletics with other neighborhood groups to start with. It was mostly over stickball. And our gang started as a social athletic club where we'd go play rival gangs in these ball games. But we would argue.

If you've ever played ball in the streets as a kid, you know that there's always arguments, and the only way we had of settling our fights was to rumble. We would

stand and argue with each other often for half an hour. I wasn't going to give in, and they weren't going to fold either. I would get mad, and they would get mad. So, there is only one thing to do at this point. We get with it, and fight. Whoever comes out on top is right. There ain't no ethical norm or nothing like that. It's just the toughest prevail. And that kind of argument and fighting is how our gang got started.

It got so that we enjoyed the fighting most of all. So, we'd set up a stickball game, but we knew for openers that it was all a front. There wouldn't be no game. That gave us excuses to carry bats around in the streets. The cops didn't see behind our front for a long time. Right from the first couple of games that we played it became evident that we weren't going to play no stickball. We were going to have a rumble. We'd just set up the game and go bust heads or get our heads busted. That's the way it came down, and it got to be habit. It got to be mostly fighting and fucking. Very little else was happening.

I had a cousin named Millie. She used to set me and the Undertaker up with girls. She would tell them what fine warriors we were and how the Young Stars was the greatest gang around. And we'd get these tall, young, thirteen-year-old girls hanging on to us all wide-eyed. And we're playing these manly parts like for real. We're just little kids, at least to start with, but we play it like the big boys do. Fuck all the time; never no hassles behind it. I never once saw an irate father come down on us.

Now, the only thing was, if a broad wanted to fuck someone else, it was cool, so long as she didn't screw a member of a rival gang. If she was caught fucking a rival member, then we would beat her up good. And generally that would touch off another series of gang wars. Broads were kinda like territory. If we went to another gang and snatched one of their broads and brought her over into our territory, that was cool, so long as you could get by with it. But if we went into their territory and made out with someone's broad, man, they didn't like it at all. We would fight to the death behind the honor of our women.

It seems that chivalry was really an important part of our gang experience. We had strict codes of behavior around the notion of "honor the women." But, at the same time, broads knew what they were supposed to do. They were supposed to handle and hide the weapons and front for the warriors before the cops in other ways. We never thought of the women as an object of sex orgies and parties. They shared co-equally in the partying with us. In that respect they were partners, and I never thought about sexism or discrimination in the gangs. Looking back on it, however, I can see that we did have one set of standards for the guys and another for the debs, especially regarding sexual activities.

We used to have a lot of dances. That was during the time of Bill Haley and the Comets. Rock and roll was just starting to break through in the early fifties. We used to skip school and gather at people's houses. Their parents would be away working and we would throw big parties. But it was mostly dancing and fighting, with occasional making out. We'd drink a little, but there wasn't much booze around, and very little dope. We'd get all worked up dancing, and then it would feel good to go home and fight it out in the street with a rival gang member.

We used to have these dances in the school gym with four or five rival gangs. We're all supposed to go there; kind of a neighborhood integration thing. During the day we're trying to kill each other, but just 'cause it's nighttime we're supposed to be nice to each other? The chaperons would tell us that we couldn't wear sweaters to the dance. But we used to put our sweaters on under a white shirt and sport coat. So we had our front on until the shit started. At these dances there would always be an argument come up over something. There had to be arguments 'cause you had these rival gangs there. Anytime you got Young Stars and Hoods together, for example, you had an argument. It couldn't be any other way.

And pretty soon off the shirts would come and you'd see the different sweaters pop out. And we'd just get right down to the nitty-gritty right there. Kids would be busting heads; shivs would flash; tire irons and chains would start rapping. Before long there would be guys laying all over the dance floor bleeding. So they finally stopped having school dances trying to promote peace 'cause they just became another battlefield.

I remember, we used to roam the school halls looking for somebody to fight—anybody! I hear a lot of talk about race riots, and I know they are going on because I've been in a few; people getting killed for their color. But in those days it made no difference what color you were. If you were white, orange, blue, it made no difference. What mattered was the sweater you had on—what territory you were from—especially at night. And we never used to say that we were going out to fight all these "niggers," because a lot of gangs were made up of mixed groups. Even the Mau Maus over in Brooklyn were mixed, although they were mostly black guys. We used to ride the subways over into Nicky Cruz' area in Brooklyn. That was a bad thing to do, 'cause there were lots of warriors in the Mau Maus. All over the streets, and you could get caught short over in Brooklyn real easy. We just barely escaped with our lives once over there.

The gangs we used to rumble with mostly were the Hoods, of course, and then the Seven Crowns, the Scorpions, occasionally the Mau Maus, and then the Fordham Baldies. The Baldies were a group of guys made up of the sons of racketeers from the Fordham Road area. The Godfather up Fordham way used to be known as Baldie. So naturally the kids took that name. They were a pretty tough group so we mostly left them alone.

One all-black gang did emerge as a very powerful gang—like a couple that are going in LA right now. They must of had something like four thousand members. When they would get together they could down anybody. But we were in the upper Bronx and we had our territory. The Seven Crowns, the Mau Maus, and the Bishops were mostly from Brooklyn or Manhattan.

The Bishops used to have a guy called the Batman who walked around with a cape and all that regalia on all the time. He was a stone-cold killer. Everybody was scared shitless of the Batman. I mean, he was fourteen years old and he would kill just for the hell of it. One time Batman walked into a candy store over on Forty-fifth and sat down kind of behind some display cases. In walks this dude that had been making noises like he was looking to get the Batman. So, the Batman just takes this 12-gauge piece out from under his cape and blows the dude away. Killed him deader than a mackerel. He just walked up next to the guy, stuck the shotgun in his guts, pulled the trigger, and walked away. Just like that, no pain, no strain. The dude was dead before he hit the floor, and you know what? The Batman didn't give a shit. He just walked away.

Kids used to give the Batman contracts on other kids. For a few lousy bucks Batman would wipe out anybody. He threw a guy off the Third Avenue El one time for ten bucks. Just threw him off and killed him. They finally give him the electric chair. I don't know how many people Batman killed before that. But nobody thought much about it. That was the thing to do, in a way, for most of us. If you didn't like somebody, if they got in your way, kill them. So, in a sense we were all Batman. And the same way with appearance. We didn't look like most people think a "gang fighter" looks. If you'd have looked at Batman, you'd have never thought he was a stone-cold killer. I mean, he was really small and kind of pale looking. Always reading comic books. You guessed it; he was especially fond of Batman comics. That was his trip. Batman was the only dude I ever met who I was really scared of.

It's funny, but we didn't see ourselves as delinquents or young criminal types. Most of what we were into was fighting other gangs, and if someone got hurt bad or even killed they weren't "murdered" in our way of thinking, they were just a casualty.

Sure, we got into other kinds of scrapes sometimes, like vandalism and petty larceny from a street vendor or a store. Most of the time we thought of that kind of stuff as "just playing around"—never as crime. Our purpose for being was all tied up in territory—protecting our "turf," so to speak.

Another way of looking at it was that when we were in the gang and engaged in ganging activities we were under the control of a leader or warlord. His control over us extended to fighting and methods of defense, but very little else. What individual members of the gang did in their spare time was usually strictly their business as long as it didn't violate any gang codes. Oftentimes, a couple or three guys would be into doing something. The gang leaders knew about it, but we didn't take it into account unless it fucked up our plans for a meeting or a rumble. In my ganging days our principal reason for being together in gangs was it gave us an opportunity to flex our muscles and prove that we were real men. Little else around us contributed to a positive self-image, so we collected together in gangs and contested other gangs in defense of our "identity," honor, and credibility. Our individual "rep" hung on our ability to slug it out or to use a club or a knife—never on how much we could drink or steal.

There was this dude that I used to call Joe Louis because he looked like the fighter. Joe and I had known each other all our lives. His family moved over to Manhattan and then they moved back into the Bronx and he moved into the neighborhood. At this time, the Young Stars were downing blacks because we had just had a big rumble with an all-black gang, and our hostility was up against black dudes. Now, this Joe Louis was my best friend for a long, long time. But as soon as they told me a new nigger moved in down the block, I went along with everybody else and knocked on the door. When he came out we proceeded to beat on him. And it never even crossed my mind that this guy had been my best friend. He was an intruder. And when an intruder comes into the territory, get him out!

I guess that our ganging days just sort of sprung up out of our desire to get together socially. Most of us kids knew each other rather well and were just trying to enjoy life together as much as we could under the circumstances. Although the theme was social clubbing at first, it seems that we soon drifted into an almost sacred ritualistic emphasis on violence. Where we were once just enjoying getting together for sports and dances, now we were finding emotional outlet in fighting. We began to accumulate a weaponry. Caches included guns, switchblades, and hunting knives, as well as clubs, bats, and the usual paraphernalia. Once in a while we would get ahold of a machete or a bayonet, but I didn't often see them used.

I believe that this indicates the somewhat confused, fantasied world view we had. When we rumbled, a lot of times nobody had a clear idea of why we were fighting. Nor was there a good fight plan. We were just in there swinging. Sometimes kids got killed, but usually there was a holding back on the more deadly weapons. My gang years were a confused, sometimes destructive, time of life. And I suppose it was with some measure of relief that I started drifting toward a more organized, if more criminal, behavior.

Chapter 2

A Piece of the Action

As long as there is pain and sorrow and hurt in this world, there's gonna be dopers and robbers and losers.

I think I was about fourteen when I started to get really involved in gambling. Some people just naturally seem to have card sense, and I was one of them. From the first time I ever sat in a poker game or rolled dice in an alley, I knew without a shadow of a doubt that I could win. Now, when I'm talking about gambling, I mean for big money. The guys in the neighborhood would think it was funny to take me to a card game and I would sit there and play like an old-timer. All of fourteen, but I knew when to draw for a straight, when to try and fill up, and what the odds of staying in or dropping out should be. I didn't have the gambling fever like lots of people get. I had the game down

cold. Like, I remember the time when I had three sixes and I knew that I was beat at least once going in. But several players stayed and it was a real good pot—about eight hundred dollars before the draw. I drew two nines. It was as if I knew that I would fill, and I knew I had them cold. I won twenty-six hundred dollars on that one hand. Another time I had three fours and because of the betting I decided to draw one as if I was holding a four-flush or a big straight. Then I had planned to pretend like I drew right and was going to bet like hell. I'd already made up my mind as to strategy. This is important, to get your mind right and not to waver. Well, damned if I didn't catch the outside four and, as they say, I was shitting in tall cotton. I forget what that hand cost them, but it was a bundle.

Although I was Puerto Rican, the part of the Bronx that I grew up in was mostly Italian. Gradually I began to shift from ganging to hustling. By the time I was fifteen I was working for this big bookmaker. Everything was divided up in the New York rackets in those days. And Leo had all the action around the neighborhood having to do with playing the numbers or the pools.

As I was growing up in the neighborhood I used to run errands for Leo and do things like hustle him his coffee from the corner store. I was always around and ready to do him favors. As I got older I started doing him bigger favors, like running book occasionally when someone was jammed up. He thought my gainging activities were "cute" at first but after I grew older he told me to wise up.

So, it was natural for him to offer me a job in his organization. One day, when he had lost somebody important, Leo offered me the job of numbers man. He trusted me, and he knew that I practically worshiped the ground he walked on. He knew that I wasn't about to cheat him. At least, I wouldn't cheat him big. Everybody grifts a dollar here and a dollar there. But only a moron rips off a big piece of the Organization's action.

Leo told me that I would be responsible for all the money that came into the central shop. And I would audit the incoming dough against the numbers being bet as checked out on the slips. I would have to be sure that I had the right amount of money on hand to cover the bets. So, I had control of the books and I was really making money. I was getting a salary plus a big percentage when the rake-off exceeded our operating nut, and it always did.

I had plenty of time to play a lot of poker, rummy, pinochle, or whatever, because my job required only about three hours a day. I was winning a lot of money gambling with guys in their thirties and forties—guys who'd been gambling all their lives. I had a lot of card sense, but above that, I was really lucky. I mean, I couldn't seem to make a mistake, or, if I did, I would get it all back a hand or two later. Everything I did turned out right so I had a lot of money.

I was playing the horses at this time, too. Really lucky. I never knew anything at all about horses. But I'd bet and win, bet and win. Like, I sent my mother to Puerto Rico on vacation one time for a month. Nothing was too good for her. I told her she'd better go first class all the way or I was going to be mad. In fact, I tried to buy her a house, but for some reason it didn't work out, I don't remember why.

I started playing cards in some of the real big-time clubs around New York. Occasionally, when I was short of money guys would be eager to front me and I would play for a percentage. But usually I was clearing about two thousand a week. In my head I thought I was a big-time gangster. I started to dress like all the Italians in the neighborhood. Sharkskin suit, white on white shirts, pinstripe ties, and a derby or a stingy brim hat. Sometimes I'd spend fifty or seventy-five bucks for a hat or a lousy pair of shoes.

And one day I woke up knowing that I had set sail from my youth.

I even started smoking cigars. 'Cause Leo, my boss, smoked cigars, so I started smoking them. I just started playing the part of a real cool hood. At first it was a game. I still felt like little Manuel, the Young Star, acting violent. But soon it wasn't a game any longer. My identity became associated with Leo, the rackets, and big-time gambling. And one day I woke up knowing that I had set sail from my youth.

One thing that always got me into trouble is that I never knew nothing about the management of money. And especially when I was a punk kid making several thousand a month. All this money appeared fast

and I'd spend it just as fast. Easy come, easy go, was the way I believed and lived. I used to order real fine two-hundred-dollar sharkskin suits three at a time. Every night I'd be out spending money. I'd go into a classy bar and order up for the house all night. I don't know how many times I used to put a hundred-dollar bill down on the bar and drink it up.

And my brother Bobby was sixteen and he tagged along with me most of the time. In New York the drinking age is eighteen. But if you got money and are willing to spread it around lavishly, people close their eyes. I was living fast, hanging loose, and raising hell. But I was tending to business and doing real good.

Then, in the building where I was living, a bunch of new tenants moved in; among them was Freddie. Freddie became the apartment super, and I didn't realize it at the time, but Freddie changed my life. Freddie used to pick up the garbage, put coal in the boiler, and do all the odd jobs around the building. He was all the time smoking weed. Bobby and I met him in the hallway one day and he was standing there smoking a joint. He asked us if we wanted some. I had never smoked weed before.

So, what the hell, I tried a joint. Because, you know, Freddie was an all right guy, and besides I just wanted to try it. I tried it and I liked it. About the second time I smoked weed I got higher than a kite. We lived on the third floor and Freddie lived on the second floor, just about under us. We used to go down to his pad every night and smoke weed.

Then Freddie turned us on to a source where we could buy pot. We used to pay five dollars for a whiskey shot glass full, and the connection would measure it out in a plastic bag in five- or ten-dollar lots. Soon I was smoking weed several times a day.

Freddie told me all about his ex-dope fiend life one night. He said he used to have a seventy-five-dollar-a-day habit, but that now he wasn't using any more. Said he'd been doing good for several months. But he was smoking a lot of weed and drinking lots of booze. I mean, he was going to the neck with mucho whiskey. Freddie used to drink two fifths of whiskey a day. Freddie was a young guy too soon old. He didn't have to warn me against heroin, I could see the results in his life. But I really didn't think anything about heroin, about using, that is. I knew it was around, but I didn't think it was for me.

One day my uncle comes around and he's using heroin, but none of us know it at the time. He came over to see my mother, but she was downtown. So, he throws this three-dollar bag of dogie on the kitchen table and says, "Try some."

I say, "Eddie, I ain't about to put any of that shit in my arm." He acts real surprised. "Hey, Manny, I'm not talking about shooting. I mean, you can snort it and get drove into the next county."

So, he shows me how to take a book of matches and cut off the end of a paper match and mash it between my fingers till it's like a spoon. And I stick it in the heroin and hold it up to my nose. I close off one nostril, hold the other one, and breathe in. Shit o'dear, man! I just got fucked up. My head starts to spin, I start to throw up, and I say, "What the fuck did I do, Eddie?" Man, I really got up tight. I was really sick; I felt terrible. And I tell Eddie, "Man, I don't want no more of this. That's it, I've had it!"

And he says, "Okay, Manny, I ain't going to force you to use my stuff."

A couple of days later he comes by the house again and he is holding some more horse. I say, "Eddie, maybe I'll try it again. Will it be any different?"

"Sure," he says, "Oftentimes the first snort is a bummer."

So I snort again and hey, it's really something else. I mean, it's like the shit really hit the fan . . . you can't describe it. All the colors of Times Square tumble right over your forehead and explode in your eyeballs like a million, jillion shooting stars. And then, each one of them goddamn stars novas in a cascade of brilliant Technicolor.

And the world levels out. You know what I mean? There's no

right, no wrong. Everything's beautiful, and it's like nothing's happening baby but clear, crisp light. The mambo beat is like hot fuck notes bouncing off lukewarm street scenes. The drummer downstairs in the park is onto life's whole fucking secret, and the primitive urge of his swinging soul becomes a mellow sharpness in your ears. And you want to gather all of creation inside you; maybe for a minute you do. What a perfect Manny Torres you become for a moment!

But I was real scared of the effect, although I think that I wanted to experience it again. So, I went a couple of months and didn't use any more. Until one day when I went back into a shoeshine parlor in the neighborhood where I used to go to get my shoes polished every day. I changed shoeshine boys, and that cost me a life on heroin. I used to spend two, three bucks each day to get a spit shine. Seeing my face in my kicks would make me feel real good. But that was the trip I was into. Different suit every day; fifteen-dollar ties by the dozen; the hats, the shirts, the whole bit. Anyway, this shoeshine dude was selling heroin on the side. I didn't know it until I seen him passing a bag to somebody and I say, "Hey, you know what? I want one of those."

And he says, "Two dollars."

"Sure, that's no problem." So I give him the two bucks, stick the bag in my pocket, and I'm real happy. I go home and I snort it all up. I really got loaded. And you know what? For the first time I begin to relax a little in my obligation to Leo and my work. Now, I get so I'm going over to the shoeshine parlor every day after a bag or two and snortin' several times a day.

Then my uncle comes over one day with an outfit. And he says, "You wanna try fixing it?"

"Hey, man, I don't know. I'm scared of needles." I'm still thinking that you can get hooked with needles, and that there ain't the danger to just snortin' the stuff.

"Well, look," my uncle says, "you can go halfway and skinpop it."

Okay. I decide to go 'cause what the hell. If snorting is so good, maybe popping is even better. So, we draw it into the syringe and he shows me how to just break the skin and get the stuff into the muscle, just underneath the skin. And you get the same reaction as snorting, only better because the kick hits you faster.

I thought that I'd be satisfied with skinpopping forever. But everybody else around was mainlining it, sticking it in the vein. I go for about a month popping. Now I'm scoring every day, and some days using a lot of stuff.

It gets to be easier and easier to think about mainlining, until one day I decide to try it, just once. Hell, yes, just once! Shit, man, from that day on it was straight shooting for me. 'Cause you stick it in your vein, and the blood comes up working its way into the syringe. And when you see your red river of life well up in the glass, you press in that hellborn liquid fire and the whole universe rushes on you.

You know, it's hard to explain the rush. It just knocks you completely into another dimension. The nod is like—you know, it's not describable. There's not words to express the feeling. The feeling is *that* good. So good that once hooked you never really live the feeling down.

And from that day on, scoring and fixing, nodding, puking, scoring and fixing became my song of life. Everything else was marginal to my major concern—dope, shit, heroin.

Okay, so I still got money. I'm still hustling the numbers. I'm still able to front as a big shot, a guy to reckon with in the neighborhood, a guy who wins big at the poker tables. But I'm beginning to get hooked. The physiological must is beginning to inhabit my guts until I can't stand it if I don't have shit in my system constantly. So I'm beginning to fix—instead of once or twice a day, or even missing a day now and then, I'm beginning to have to go four times a day just to maintain.

I try to hide from my friends, Leo and the guys, the fact that I'm using but I'm spending more time with dope fiends than I'm spending with my job. You can just front and cover for so long and then it all breaks down. The explanation is

simple. You gotta have dope. To have dope you gotta score. To score is sometimes easy, sometimes very difficult. But it usually always takes time. And then, the fix and the nod. Like, your whole damn life is shit, man, shit!

See, once you're hooked you're not your own boss any more. You belong to your habit. Plain and simple. You plan and scheme, and con, and lie, and hustle for your habit. Anybody and everybody becomes fair game. Look, you leave mother, brother, sister, father, friend for heroin. When you're hooked you gotta score. It ain't maybe I'll score, maybe I won't. It's, man, I'm gonna score and all hell ain't gonna stop me! And scoring can take time; it can be downright frustrating and uncomfortable. I've waited for over three hours on a street corner for a cat with the bag to surface. And you don't leave, 'cause he's the only one holding and if you miss him someone else will get the stuff and you'll be left holding air.

So, a lot of time I used to spend taking care of business for Leo on the job I now am spending feeding my habit. It begins to get obvious. 'Cause I gotta hurry with the collections and such, I start making mistakes. I even miss pickups and tallies, and this is really unforgivable in the business.

Leo calls me in to his office one day and says, "Liston, Manny, I've heard. No use lying to me, man, I hear that you're hooked on heroin.

Now, if you're using dope, you've gotta stop now! Nobody in this organization uses any kind of narcotic. A doper becomes dependent on that shit, and then we can't depend on him. If you're using heroin, you gotta stop now."

I started to run it down on him. "Listen, Leo . . ."

"Kid, I'm saying that if you are using I'm going to give you two weeks off and the number of a private hospital. You don't have to tell me if you go in or not. You just go. I don't even want to know if you're using or not."

Leo was really trying to help me. It wasn't only that I was missing collections and making mistakes that bugged Leo. He really liked me as a person and wanted to keep me from getting blown out. He'd arranged the hospital bill already whether I went or not. This is typical of the Organization; when its people need help, they'll front you all the way.

So, I went. And I kicked. Rather, they reduced my habit gradually with the use of morphine. They had me on maintenance therapy using morphine, hoping I'd be able to finally kick the morphine easier than the heroin. But it doesn't make it. All that happens is that the hospital mothers you along until you can get down.

Although there are some differences in effect, morphine and heroin are a lot alike. Only, I can tell heroin every time when I mainline the shit. It just works best for me. Like, I die almost, sort of all heavenly fucked up with a good fix. It starts deep in the gut and radiates out onto the furthest rim of consciousness. And the nod! Man, the only supersatisfactory nod for me is behind some good scag.

Scag is the only way into the real deep nod, that state of near oblivion when you lose touch with the reality of hurt and necessity. Where nothing is urgent, and for a little while it's as if you can walk on tiptoe with the gods.

So, I was just maintaining on the morphine in the hospital. But when I came out I made a beeline for the connection, anticipating the rush like being drop-kicked in the belly. As soon as I got fixed up with some sweet bonita dogie—like, a bag of scag—man, I was all right. I walk out of the hospital loaded on morphine, and I am in the neighborhood maybe ten minutes and I get down with heroin. It was no problem to find the ounce man, look up one of my kits, and take care of business.

Leo thinks I've kicked. 'Cause I told him so. He believes it 'cause I said it. Why not? After all, I had a boss rep from a long history of straight shooting with him. So, for the next two or three weeks I'm doing pretty good. I mean, I can manage to come down to the buzz level long enough to take care of Leo's business. The work requires perhaps three hours a day at the most, totaling up the tallies and keeping the books straight.

But it is only a matter of time and my habit begins to grow. And my front falls apart. Finally Leo says, "Manny, we gotta let you go. If you ever stop using, come back. You got a job forever. But scag and the business don't mix. Even if I would, I couldn't handle it. My boss would have my ass uptown in five minutes if he heard I was stringing along with a user."

I got a couple of personal things out of my desk and started to split, knowing inside that I'd really fucked up. But I didn't care. Not really. All I cared about was scag. Leo told me as I was leaving, "I'm giving you a month's pay and you're on your own. If you get into any trouble connected with dope don't bother to call. Because I'll hang up on you. If you get behind any scam besides stuff, call right away and we'll help. But with heroin you're on your own."

You know, I didn't even think of what Leo had done for me. All I thought was how much dope I could buy with the bread Leo had given me for separation pay. I didn't care because I got several thousand bucks, and that will buy a lot of shit.

I really gave up a good thing for heroin. Leo trusted me. He knew that I wasn't going to cheat him. He's told me since that they had big plans for me, maybe even to take his spot in a few years when he moved up. That ain't bad for a poor Spic kid! They liked me 'cause I had real good sense. I knew how to keep my mouth shut. I never said nothing. No matter what I heard about the Organization or the man I'd never repeat it. Even party talk, when the big bosses got a little mellow and said some kind of scary things, I'd dummy up like I never heard. They really dug that about me.

Getting down was life . . .

And I would ask questions if I didn't understand. But never get nosy or up tight if they put me in my place. I was on the bottom of the pyramid in the rackets, but that was all right. 'Cause there was lots of money trickling down. There was plenty of scratch for everybody. That was part of my problem. All this dough and you can only get rid of so much at a time.

I even asked them for more money just before the end—and got it. I figured out that they were making much more money than I had thought, and I asked for a higher percentage of the collections. You know what? They gave it to me; no hassles. It's clear as I look back on my days in the rackets that they were beginning to groom me by increasing my responsibilities and giving me more money. And I was good at it. I could have made it big, but I broke it instead. All for scag fever. Getting down was life, and nothing else even made good sense.

By now I had a constant urge in my throat for junk. I could taste it, touch it with every angry nerve ending in my body. Nothing else mattered a damn. All the good intentions in the world fall before one cap of scag when you're using. Promises, once important, evaporate when the stuff is there. When you're yenning, nothing matters but scoring, fixing, and nodding. That's the way it comes down.

The white lady sucks, man. You think that you're sucking her up into the glass and mainlining her radiant ass. But the white junk lady sucks you in, man, until you belong. At first she's just a pretty little monkey; before long she's a shaggy gorilla. I've heard junkies say that you may be a weekend warrior when you start to flirt with her, but you soon get your wings. And that's the truth!

After I left the Organization I just used. Didn't have to hustle for a long time 'cause beside all the bread I scored from Leo as separation pay, I had a lot of markers out in the neighborhood. I started collecting what people owed me and living on that. But day by day it takes more scag to maintain, to stave off the cramps and chills. I go from a thirty-dollar-a-day habit to the place

where it takes a big bill to score enough shit. Now I'm pushing and scraping myself. I'm trying to score from the kilo connection to get behind enough scag to push for profit. But this takes money in front.

For a while I get by on the touch. When you have a good solid rep, when you're *people*, other people will loan you bread no questions asked. But living on your reputation lasts just so long. You run out of gas and good will. You can only burn the best friend once or twice and it's all over between you. And the word gets around. "Watch Manny, he's slipped. Piece him off with a buck or two, but don't let him get into you for any long green." Then all you're doing is blowing in the wind. Your friends know that you're hooked on junk. They're sorry, of course, but they put you down.

So, you go back home to your family. (I had several aunts and uncles around New York.) 'Cause the family is always willing to give you the benefit of a doubt. "Oh, Manuel can't be hooked, not him. Maybe if we favor him some he'll straighten out." I remember working Aunt Rea and her old man for every nickel I could get. It didn't matter if it was food money, rent money, welfare money, doctor money. It wouldn't have mattered if it was burial money for my old lady I was stealing. Any money at all buys scag and that's all that counts.

Pretty soon the family is burned out and won't lend me any more dough. I hassle them, but before long they won't be hassled. So, I start stealing from them. I go over to my sister's house when they're all downtown and I walk off with anything that I can hock. This happens a couple of times with relatives and pretty soon they put out the word. "Manny's hooked like a dog. Turn him out like a mad dog."

So, they turn me out. Nothing else they can do. You can't have a dope fiend around the house, mainly because he'll steal everything in sight. A lush's behavior may be undependable and raunchy, but a doper is five times worse than a lush. Once you are wired behind scag, it is *life,* nothing else lives. A lush flops, passes out, quits. But a dope fiend hustles, scores, and fixes so he can get down. And he has no regrets. He doesn't care at all. If somebody gets wasted in the process of hustling, scoring, and getting down—so fucking what? The doper is a true isolationist. He doesn't give a damn for others. Only insofar as they are a means to score.

So, I've blown a good position in the Organization; I've burned all my old friends to a cinder; my relatives have put me down from self-defense. I'm out in the street. Only I still got my apartment 'cause I have paid up my rent for months ahead. I've got a pad to lie down in, but I don't have lights or gas. They're turned out long ago because I didn't pay the bills.

But I am still able to front because I've got clothes. The shark-skin suits and the million shirts I bought in my big-money days are all I got. Although I'm still dressing good, I'm running out of people who will believe my story. Everybody now is onto the fact that I'm a dope fiend. So I give up on trying to pretend. I pass over into the dope fiend world. I might as well. I'm wired, I'm hooked, and I better quit pretending to be something I'm not.

I start selling my clothes. I had racks and racks of them. I paid over two hundred bucks for lots of those suits and I sell them for like thirty bucks. Brand-new tailor-made suits. But I don't care. You don't have to look good to use. The white lady will take you any way she finds you. I went through about thirty suits and pairs of shoes in thirty days. I needed a hundred bucks for dope, so I'd get rid of a hundred bucks of stuff. When I run out of stuff to sell my act really starts to fall apart.

In fact, I ain't got no act any more. I'm starting to wear the same threads over and over. Sleeping and walking around in the same clothes for days at a time. Not showering, not bathing, a real filthy pig. Now I'm in the center of the dope fiend world. Before, I was a big shot. I used to look down at the dope fiend, even when I was using. Because scoring was no problem. Just peel off a few bills and get down. When I had influence, the Organization, and money, I used to sit high in the leather down at the shoeshine parlor and sneer at the filthy dope fiend. But now I got to go down to his world and call him brother. No problem. Anything for scag.

Before, all I did was buy my way down. Now, I gotta learn how to hustle. I gotta learn how to get dope. That means I gotta learn how to make money. Because I got no front, I'm automatically going to be a low-class hustler. I got no clothes, no wheels; I ain't exactly sharp. And I don't know how to be slick. But I learn.

I'm flat broke this particular morning and I really need a fix. 'Cause if I don't score soon I'm going to come down hard. I try to get a dime bag on the cuff, but the connection just laughs. So, I'm standing around on this street corner and I meet this dude. He's just a little kid, but I can tell that he's got something going. I tell him that I got to make some fast money 'cause I have to score some dope. He says, "Look, why don't you go boosting?"

I say, "I don't know how to boost." Remember, I always been pretty honest. Because I never considered work in the Organization as criminal. That's the norm around my neighborhood; not deviant or criminal. And dope, too. That's the normal kind of behavior that everybody's into. But boosting is something different. I started out in markets and drugstores boosting cigarettes.

Me and this kid worked as a team. We'd find a store, usually uptown, that didn't cover their cigarettes but left them out in open racks. One of us would stand point while the other would go under the coat and shirt with three or four cartons of butts.

Like, it's easy. You get a grocery cart and put a few items in it. You have an old envelope or something in your hand like a grocery list from the old lady. This is your front. You act like a legitimate shopper; you *are* a legitimate shopper in the eyes of people around you. When you learn how to arrange your clothes right, you can get maybe four or five cartons underneath your belt. Each carton was worth a buck then, and usually the connection would take them for dope. So you boost cigarettes and get down.

You don't eat much, don't pay your lights or gas. You just buy dope. I'm sleeping on a dirty mattress and I got no sheets, no lights, no food in the house. It's cold and I'm always hungry because I can't spare much scag money for Hershey bars and hot dogs.

I've always got a connection and that helps me score. 'Cause like, when my friends would come over from Yonkers, or other friends from Brooklyn, and we're looking to score, I would steer them to the connection. And they would share their scag with me. But this kind of nickel and dime hustling wears me out and is a drag, so I'm looking around for other angles.

One morning I decide to get a little further into this boosting than cigarettes. I wander over to Macy's Department Store, because I figure they've got everything at Macy's. I kind of walk around looking for a good touch. I'm not exactly hip on how to do it, I just know that I'm going to rip something off. I must have been in there three or four hours, wandering around all the floors playing with toys, looking at clothes, and such. That ain't the right way to operate and it's a wonder I didn't get busted by the floorwalker. 'Cause you're not supposed to do that. You're supposed to identify the article you're after, make the hit, and walk right out like it was legitimate business. I finally decide that I'll take a TV. And I locate the biggest, most expensive TV on the floor. I figure that the bigger it is the more money I'll be able to get for it. And this one is on little wheels. It's sitting right in the center of the display area . . . with posters on top. I just walk over and take the posters off and start rolling it towards the escalator. I don't have the slightest idea of how to get this big box down the escalator, so I ask one of the salespersons, "Do you have a dolly handy, 'cause I have to get this thing down to the next floor?"

He says, "Sure, right over here. Let me help you strap it on." So he ties the TV on and we get it down to the ground level. I thank him for his help and he takes the dolly upstairs. Evidently, without forethought, I have successfully fronted as a legitimate store employee, as he wasn't suspicious at all. I just walk out of the store through the double front doors rolling this TV.

I have no car. And this is on 149th, Street and Third Avenue and I gotta get up to 174th Street and Third Avenue. It's starting to rain and the top of the TV begins to get wet and it's running down the sides onto the fabric covering the speaker. I go about two blocks, lifting and bouncing the TV up and down the curbs and I think, "I'm going to ruin this set before I get a chance to sell it."

So I hail a cabbie. I have no money, but that doesn't bother me. I tell him I gotta get this TV up to 174th Street and Third Avenue. We rassle the TV into the back; gotta leave the trunk open 'cause the set sticks out a couple of feet. We hop in the car and go to 174th Street. The cabdriver helps me unload it and carry it up a flight of stairs to the connection's pad. The cabbie doesn't know if the TV is a stolen item or not; evidently, he doesn't care. He just helps me push it and carry it up to the connection's door.

I knock and tell him I got this TV for which I want some dope. "And, by the way, I need some money to pay the cabbie."

The connection isn't a bit shook. He says, "I ain't carrying too many bags at the moment. But I'll let you have one bundle of five-dollar bags and fifty bucks for the piece."

I figure that 125 bucks is a little light, but I'm not in a position to argue so I say, "You're holding and I'm hurting so it's a deal."

So he gives me the money, I pay off the driver, and I get my dope. That is the only time I did anything as foolish as that, but I figured that was boosting—just walk in and take something of value. I didn't know at the time that there was all these fine points to the shoplifting trade. But this is a good example of how an addict can't seem to do anything wrong. He just gets out on a limb time after time when he's hustling, and he scores and gets away with it when others get ranked and busted. It's a little like the drunk getting by without a scratch in a real brutal auto wreck. He's just so relaxed and unconcerned that he comes through a terrible accident smelling like a rose. The addict who hustles for his daily fixings has his eye on one thing alone, the dope and getting it into his veins. He knows he's gotta steal to score to fix, so he's just relaxed about the whole thing. It's a fact of living, like breathing.

It isn't long until I run into some other dope fiends who are boosting in a more organized, systematic way. And for a while, we had a real cool number going. We used to have four or five department stores that were pussy for organized boosting schemes. TVs, expensive radios, broilers, small appliances, anything in cartons stacked in the storeroom were fair game. But usually it was the nicer TV sets that we were after. 'Cause they moved real well and our fences couldn't get too many of them.

This kind of a caper was planned out in advance. We would lay out our strategy and movement like on a football field. We'd get uniforms; like, at Macy's they were gray at this time. Just a gray pair of pants and a gray shirt with the Macy emblem above the pocket. A favorite modus operandi was to back a commercial panel truck up to the warehouse dock. Guys fronting as Macy warehousemen would roll out appliances stacked three or four high on dollies. We'd have the caper down pat; when certain supers were off for lunch, so our front men wouldn't be recognized as phonies. We'd have fake bills of lading and manifests, the whole bit. Several times when I was with this organization we got away clean with like ten thousand dollars' worth of goods. The only reason I quit that business was that Macy's changed uniforms on us and came up with extra security measures that made dock boosting sort of hazardous.

We figured that other stores were getting wise, too, so it was time to find another hustle. We broke up and each dope fiend went his own way. The only time you team up like that is to cream out a deal. When there is cinch bread to be had and it takes more than one to get it, dopers will combine efforts. But it doesn't usually last long. When the scam peters out, you go your own way. Usually dopers are pretty careful, 'cause when you get busted and go to jail, you have to kick.

One other bit of organized capering I was in for a while was checks. I don't mean personal checks. Almost every dope fiend will get in a corner sometime when he will even cash his own personal bum checks or forge his sister's or mother's name on her bank checks. But I'm talking about organized payroll check cashing. This is usually not dope fiend activity because it takes too much discipline. It's like carrying a lunch bucket from four to midnight. And that's too much of a hassle for most dopers. But it was good bread and I tried it for a while.

I ran into this couple who had a good thing going and solicited my help. There were four or five people in the organization. Fred ran the business and Mary, his old lady, was like the secretary-bookkeeper. We were mobile, going from town to town around the East. Fred liked to pick towns of about a hundred thousand or so. Just big enough to have several shopping centers and banks but not so big that the police were swarming.

Fred would set up the caper. Usually we liked to pick on gas station chains. Maybe a town would have fifteen or twenty stations under one franchise. That would mean that one head station would pay all the bills, handle all the ordering, and make out a central payroll. We had a burglar who could get in and out without leaving a trace. He'd go into this head station, get into the filing cabinet where the checkbooks were stored, and take checks out of sequence from the middle of several books. Most commercial businesses have several books ahead and it is easy to clip a hundred or so checks so they won't be noticed for a while.

Fred would already have identified the amount of an average payroll and payday for the individual company employee. He studied this down to the most minute detail, including the various payroll deductions and so on. Mary would make up the checks so you coudn't tell a phony from a genuine article. She was the best forger I ever knew, in prison or out. That broad had class. Sometimes we would get a real check off an employee coming out of a bar. That's how we'd know the right signatures. Regardless of how we got the signatures, Mary could duplicate them till the owner himself wouldn't know the difference.

Now we're ready for the hit. It's like Friday afternoon when we get set up. Usually we go out to cash the checks in teams of two. Fred has done his homework here, too. Stores that have special alert systems are avoided. We keyed in on big-volume grocery stores. They were the easiest marks. But we'd really have our act together. Fake ID packets had already been obtained for every name we planned to use. Sometimes we'd use real employee names. Then we'd be sure to cash those checks away from where they lived. There's pros and cons to using real or fictitious names in this business. If you use real names and real addresses, the store owner can look them up in the directory. You can say, if he doesn't want to cash your check, "Look, I do business in here all the time, buddy. Check me against the directory; if you don't want my business, just say so and I'll take it somewhere else!" Sometimes, with real names the store man might know the guy, and then you have to take out of there like fast.

When we'd go into the store we'd be dressed like we should. If it was an oil company, we'd have on their pants and jackets; a little grease here and there; a lunch bucket in our hand. We'd get a basket and pick out some stuff we needed back at the motel. But the object was to make it look realistic and not contrived. Good realistic items would be like a box of Kotex, two dozen eggs, a six-pack of beer, three loaves of bread, a can of tomatoes, and a roast or package of steaks. My fifteen dollars' worth of merchandise.

Usually we'd go right up to the check stand in pairs, each with our basket of stuff to take home to the old lady. We'd pick the toughest, sharpest checker in the place; the assistant manager if possible. We've got our shit together and we want to start at the top and not mess

around with some green broad who will be asking a lot of questions to protect herself or make points with the boss. When he'd check out our stuff we'd pull out the check with the stub still on it. We'd tear off the stub and shove it in our jacket pocket. The ckeck would be made out usually for like $238.47 for a two-week pay period. We'd sign in front of the guy and hand it to him. Almost no questions asked. Sometimes he'd look at our ID and record a driver's license number, but usually we'd get our change and the time of day without any problem at all.

If you got your act together, payroll check cashing is easy. Providing of course that the checks aren't hot. Sometimes Fred would have to shag us out of a place 'cause he just found out the cops knew about the checks. But usually we'd have all day Friday, Saturday, even Sunday to cash the checks. Passers would get 40 percent of the action from Fred. He provided the front and paid all the bills except food. What we didn't steal, we split the cost. It was a good racket for several months.

Like I say, though, I don't like nine-to-fives anyway. And I sure didn't have time for a regular job and get it on with Miss Heroin, too. I started sloughing off and kicking back because I was rich again and thus loaded all the time. So, Fred and me parted company. It had to happen. I had to get back to my love affair with Miss Heroin.

I went back to the city, where I still had my apartment 'cause I'd paid up the rent for a long time in advance. Soon, I didn't have nothing else but this sleazy pad, and I was back to nickel and dime boosting.

I was hanging around Anita's Restaurant one night, just watching the Bronx light up for the evening. I was just standing there, eating a hot dog and drinking a soda. Actually, I was trying to figure out where I was going to get some money for a fix. Just hanging out 'cause it was warm in there and I was temporarily at a loss for a moneymaking scheme.

And this broad walks in. This real foxy piece walks in and comes over and stands by me and orders something . . . but she keeps staring at me like she's interested. So I figure, oh here it is, man. Like, I might be able to get some money off this bitch. You know what I mean. The first thing that crosses my mind is that I can turn this encounter into some bread and get down. So I start talking to her nice and easy, and she invites me for a ride in her car.

I say, "Oh yeah, why not."

So we get in her car and we're just driving around . . . not going anywhere in particular, just driving. And she asks me if I know anywhere that I can score some dope. Shit! It never even crossed my mind that she was a dope fiend. I mean, this broad was together, man. Usually you can spot a doper broad right off because they are so strung out.

You know, their clothes don't hang right, their hair looks like hasty pudding, their make-up is never right because they water from the eyes and nose. But this Fran was like real silk, with every seam and hair in place naturally. And there was nothing artificial about her. She was a right-on piece of machinery.

Anyway, I say, "Sure, I can get some herion. No problem, all I need is the bread."

So, we go to the connection's house; she gives me the money, and I score two half-a-loafs of stuff. A half-a-loaf is ten three-dollar bags of dope and I score two of them for thirty dollars apiece.

We go back to the car and head for her place. It turns out that she's got this nice pad in the upper Bronx. Man, it's even got the red canopy and carpet, with this bald-headed black dude dressed to kill doing the doorman routine.

Soon as we get inside and up to her room we fix and get down. I mean, I really got fixed. That dope was extragood stuff, cut with just the right amount of milk sugar, so when the junk spread in warm, relaxing waves through my body it lapped over all the shores of consciousness in me, protecting me from a world of pain and hate and the sorrow of not belonging.

When I come out of the nod Fran's cooking dinner, complete with steak and baked potatoes. After dinner, we're just laying around fixing dope and really feelling good. And I'm thinking to my-self, I may stay here tonight. Yeah, man! Now you have a real neat place to stay.

I'm trying to figure out how I'm going to get around to letting her know I'm planning to stay.

And, she says, "Why don't you get comfortable. Go take a shower, Manny."

That did it! Right? Man, I'm staying! And I went in and took a shower. Got all sweet-smelling and stuff, rubbing Brut all over my bones. I didn't even notice how skinny and out of shape I must have looked. When you're in the middle of a long run on dope, you're really out of shape. Short-winded, no muscle structure, bones jumping out of the skin almost. But it don't matter. It don't matter at all. All that matters is the moment of truth. Holding the dropper poised between thumb and fingers; feeling the needle slide into the vein; watching as the dark red blood spurts up into the dropper. And then, letting go the tie and feeling the balm of nothing-ness softly relaxing the tension and covering reality.

After the shower we tried to ball. And I couldn't get it up. I was so loaded I couldn't get down sexually. And I thought to myself, It don't affect broads the same way. 'Cause they can do it whether they're loaded or not. All they got to do is spread 'em and take it in. But a man has to get it up. A man has to be prepared and feel ready, and be ready to do the thing.

So, I felt kind of bad. But, you know what? She didn't care. Y'know. We just nodded out and went to bed.

In the morning there were no re-criminations. Everything was smooth, 'cause we had dope. So, the first thing we do is fix. We're sittin' around just feeling good and Fran wants to know what my game is. How do I get by? What do I do to support my habit?

"I don't know. I just do whatever comes up. You know, a little here and a little there. Sometimes a pretty good score and sometimes it's get by on cotton inhalers. But I usually make my hundred or so a day to keep in dogie."

We fix again and really get to feel-ing cosy inside and out. Then she runs it to me nice and easy about her steady rip on fur coats. She's into boosting two- three-thousand-dollar fur coats from the whole-sale-retail houses in the fur market district down by Delancy Street.

Next thing I know, Fran is offer-ing to cut me in on her caper. She wants me to be her partner and operate as her cover, or front man.

I tell her, "You're crazy. I'll never look the part. I mean, I've been short-grifting for a long time and I can't go in there and act like high society."

But Fran says, "Look, Manny, if you had a lot of money could you feel like it was yours?"

"Sure," I say, "if it's my money I don't have to act because it's my money. It's that simple."

"Okay." So, she takes out ten one-hundred-dollar bills and says, "Here, the ten big ones are yours."

And that just . . . it really blew my mind. I was standing there with one thousand bucks and the only thing that crossed my mind was, All that dope! Do you know how much dope that could buy? All the dope I could use.

And she asks me if I have any decent clothes. Anything that I could front in, that looked respectable.

"Hell, Fran, I'm just like any other dope fiend lookin' for a score. The only clothes that I got are on my back. That's all. I sold the last wardrobe my mother bought me for dope."

So, we go down to Macy's. She waltzes me right into the toney men's department and starts buying me these clothes. I mean, nothing's too fine. She don't pay any attention to the tags. All she's looking for is quality and how it looks on me. You know, the cut has to be just right, and the pleats and creases have to be just so.

I'm just standing there, you know, and I just can't believe it. Shoes, shirts, suits, scarves, the works. And she puts all this stuff—it must have come to six, maybe seven hundred dollars—on a charge card.

At that time charge cards were fairly new. It was the in thing, to have a charge card. But when they checked her out after the stuff was all written down and wrapped up, this crazy broad came out clean as a Dodger shutout. And they even call a stockboy over and carry all the goods out to our car.

Now, all this time I'm not saying anything but, "Yes, Fran; no, Fran; all right, Fran." I don't care, you know what? She's got the dope; that's all that counts. If she wants to play at fun and games, that's great! Already I'm planning on burning this broad sooner or later. But meanwhile it's a real good ride, and so just hang on, Manny, and don't knock it.

We go back to her pad, which is now home. I put on some of those fancy clothes and look pretty neat. I feel good. You know what? It's a long time since I've had on good threads. As I stand in front of the mirror I begin to feel really good. I have dope, all that I want. I have money, all that I need. I have clothes, all that I can wear. And I have this crazy broad.

So, I really feel that I'm beginning to play the part now. I think, "Oh, what the fuck, I might as well play the part."

I just begin to naturally act like Manny the front man, Manny the hood.

Fran senses that she's built some confidence in me and she ways, "Let's go down and look at some of the fur shops."

But we gotta fix first. So we fix, and I get loaded up on all the confidence I need. And we get in the car and drive downtown to Delancy Street.

We started going in and out of these fur shops, kind of hanging around looking like customers. I would just stand there and look at her and she would talk to everybody and smile and try on fur coats, you know, and giggle and act kind of silly. And every once and a while she'd come over and kiss me on the cheek and go through a weird trip about me being her "honey pie all ready to buy her annnnything, aren't you, darling?"

And we leave.

We must have gone in and out of five or six different fur shops. And always the same trip. Then we go home.

Fran tells me, "See how easy it is? I could have walked out of any of those shops with a piece of fur anytime, if I would have had somebody cover for me."

So, now I'm beginning to get the message. I'm feeling the part. Like a real, genuine hustler. Look, man, I gotta be a hustler. 'Cause I look sharp. I got a real good front, and I got lots of long green in my pocket.

I tell Fran, "Sure, I could do that. I'll cover you. No sweat, baby. 'Cause just one of them fur coats is worth many pieces of dope."

So, we spend the next three days just fixing and laying around, talking about how it's going to come down. Fran's real good about schooling me in the right moves.

First, the morning of the hit we go down and rent a Lincoln Continental. Like, it costs us about thirty bucks for two hours. And we drive down to where the fur warehouses are. We drive right up to the door of one of the fine shops, and someone comes out to the car to help us. Fran would start right out talking about what kind of a fur she wanted. Man, that broad had class. She really knew her furs! She would run it down to them about how she had to have a certain cut and just the proper grade of fur. That kind of stuff I never could figure out. I didn't understand what they were talking about.

Look, man, I gotta be a hustler.

So Fran would go off with the saleslady, who by now was conned into "knowing" she had a sure sale. And I would just start talking a blue streak to whoever it was—the manager or one of the salesladies. And tell them that I didn't know anything at all about the fur business or the product. "But my wife here wants to buy a coat, and she knows about it, so, you know, I just hope that we don't get taken. . . . 'Cause whatever she decides on, I'm gonna have to buy it for her. I promised her for two years that I'm gonna do something big for her, and this is sort of a present."

I'd just keep on talking like I don't know much. I'm a poor slob who happens to have a little bit of money. And the wife is spending it all up, y'know, running around from shop to shop. This is all part of the scam. And I just keep on running it down to them. I just rap on and keep telling them stuff like, "My wife can never make up her mind. This is the third time we've been down here. We keep going in these places and she keeps walking out on me. You know, leaves me stranded half the time. I'm liable to look up and that crazy broad'll be over in the shop next door or someplace."

This effectively sets up in his mind that me and her might not necessarily leave together. That when I leave my wife might not be with me because she might have just walked out. So, I just keep on rapping like that, usually for ten or fifteen minutes. 'Cause Fran would have to be out of the shop with the goods within five minutes after she had walked in. Time is of the essence in a caper of this kind. You set the mark up, lay your story on him, and then engineer the play before anybody gets wised up that things might be different than you've represented them to be.

"Hit 'em while they're still believers," Fran used to say. Our front looks good to them, so they proceed to show me around and Fran is trying on coats as if nothing is quite good enough for her. Most of the time the salesladies would get tired of standing there and they'd go do something else that had to get done.

So, when Fran found the right coat (often she had an "order"

from our main fence, Mickey, or some other fence) she would just walk out. If problems were developing because the store personnel was hanging out too close to her or the door, I would create a diversion by asking about a coat or some product in the back of the store.

After Fran split with the fur piece, I would just keep walking around acting as if I was intensely interested in the furs until I heard someone say something like, "The last time I saw her she was over here."

And I'd say, "Aw, shit, she must have left me again," and I'd do the irate husband trip and act like I was very fed up.

You know what? We never got ranked on that caper. We didn't change our scam hardly at all for over two months. Sometimes we'd hit three or four shops a week. Sure, sometime during the day, they'd take inventory and find out that an expensive fur was missing. But who cares. 'Cause we're gone, and the fur's gone. Probably all cut up and being remodeled by that time. And we're sitting up in the apartment full of dope, nodding away and having a hell of a time.

Our principal connection for the coats was a stud named Mickey. He'd take all the fur coats or stoles we could steal and carry over there. No matter how many. If we had a hundred, he'd buy a hundred. But we usually would bring him like one or two a week. After all, even New York is only so big and we didn't want to run a good thing into the ground.

Mickey'd check the coat out to see that it was the genuine article and then he'd give us half the agreed-on price in money and half in dope. So, we'd get like a thousand in cash and a thousand worth of good, 15 percent heroin. In fact, we had to be careful of an overdose from the dogie we got from Mickey. He had a steady connection for good stuff, and if we used regular street dope, Mickey's stuff would be strong by comparison.

But Mickey had it good. He made a profit off of everything. He dealt in furs and dope and was raking in the bread in both directions. But we didn't care. Man, I sure didn't care. Mickey was right on! See, I'd have a thousand dollars in one hand and a hand full of dope in the other. Now, who cares? You know what I mean? When the dope runs out, I can buy more dope. 'Cause I got money. And besides, I got a big charge out of actually being a con man. All I was was a glorified booster, but it paid well, and it was good work that took some intelligence.

The whole game was to set people up and get them off guard, and they'd walk right into it. See, like I could never play the part of a really educated, high-society person, 'cause I'm not put together that way. But I could play the part of the new-rich slob who somehow had

ended up with lots of money and a good-looking crazy broad. Shakespeare had it right a long time ago when he said that all the world's a stage and all people are actors. All you gotta do, man, is find your right part. The way I saw life in those days was that a man's either a mark or he hustles the mark. You either make it or you're made. Sure, there is a sucker born every minute, but you gotta be there on time. 'Cause, especially in the city, hustlers come by the bucketful, and you better have your act together if you want to get in on the action.

I had it real good with Fran while it lasted. She was really a slick hustler. She had a lot of confidence. She taught me how to lie and believe I was telling the truth. That's the first sign of a good hustler. But all good things come to an end, especially for a dope fiend. Because sooner or later a doper gets in a bind and burns everyone around him—even the goose that lays the golden eggs.

The point is, I didn't have this good hustle on furs for the hustle's sake; that wasn't where my head was at. My meaning, the way I saw myself as a criminal, was filtered through the drug effect. Criminality, for me, was a convenient means to get dope. It was scoring bread so I could score dope. Nothing else made sense to me.

M y whole life was drugs. All my friends were dopers. Our very existence was 100 percent related to drug use. What exists, what is happening, what is real at this time of my life is dope, horse, shit, dogie, heroin.

I'm twenty, it's 1962, and nothing makes any difference but the next fix. Where it's coming from, making sure the paraphernalia is handy to get the stuff into my bloodstream, and how good it feels when the shit hits the fan is all that counts, man. Don't ask me to attend to anything else, because I'm altogether busy scoring, fixing, and hurting; scoring, fixing, and hurting in that order.

Often, when I was around my apartment, people would come over to visit and sometimes they would share their dope. I was stealing a little, not too much, just barely keeping my habit going. I was just coasting along without too big a habit until I ran into some money, a lot of money, in fact.

In this place where I lived there were rats. In the back yard they ate and scratched their way into the brick and stone of the next building. The rats, big as alley cats, used to hang out in these holes. So, at night when I didn't have nothing better to do I used to sit there on my fire escape and plunk at rats with my .22. I'd flash my flashlight at the wall and if I'd catch a rat with its head out of the hole, I'd fire at it. Occasionally I'd get to practice at a moving target as the rats tried to negotiate the strip of no-rat's-land between the wall and our house.

One night I'm playing my game of war on rats when I notice this guy slide around the corner of the wall and stash a brown paper bag in one of the deeper crevices. I just sit on the fire escape and dummy up because I have a real warm feeling in my gut that something out of sight is happening. He splits, and I go downstairs and pull the bag out of the hole. I glance in the bag as I'm making it back to my room and there's nothing but bills—good, legitimate long green. I run upstairs and lay the money out on the bed and count it; I got over six thousand dollars in cash.

Man, shit! I don't care where it came from. So somebody got robbed or knocked over behind the money. All I know is that I have six thousand dollars in front of me and all I can see is mounds and mounds of scag. I can hunt up the kilo connection and find out where he's getting his stuff. I mean, all I think is, No more smalltime scoring for you, Manny baby. I look at the six thousand dollars before me on the bed and all I can see is mountains and mountains of scag, smack, lovely, lovely heroin. That's all, just dope. It doesn't even cross my mind to pay up the gas and light bill so I can see and be warm. I don't even think once about getting my threads out of the cleaners. It doesn't dawn on me to pay up some more rent. All I see is dope.

I go and call up a connection and I say, "Listen! I want to buy a lot of dope." He asks me how much and I say, "I don't know, maybe a piece of dope." This means a whole ounce of almost pure scag. He says he doesn't know if he can get me an ounce. It's very hard to score ounces in New York. Because you have so many guys dealing and so many dope fiends, everybody is looking to support their own habit.

But I finally score the ounce by convincing him I'm not into chippying and offering him a good price. He treated me real good. He pieced me off an ounce of boss scag, about 25 percent pure. This meant that I could cut it four times again and still have good stuff. What I had to do was to buy him a half an ounce. This did it. The dope fiend never turns his back on free dope.

I get this piece of dope in front of me in my room and I'm happier than a kid with six grand. Money is just money, no more. You can't smoke it worth a damn, and you sure as hell can't shoot it. But scag, man, is the cool cool cool of the sunlight, that stone-good feeling, the ultimate kick! And I open up the package and I got the white lady in front of me, fluffing her up and playing with her. And the more you fluff heroin the bigger it gets. It's almost like fondling a tit. It gets nice and firm and begins to swell under your hand in anticipation of the final thrusting explosion.

In much the same way as a lover plays with his delight, I anticipate the fix. I just can't believe that I've got this much dope. But I fix, and I really go into the nod. The universe becomes void of all hurting. I step outside myself and forget for a moment the sadness of birth, the regret of youth, the looking forward to a withering away. And I only not-think of many mere dreams and possibilities groped for a century ago, it seems, in my family when Pop was alive. Like, poodles instead of rats, sunflower seeds instead of roaches, farmhouses instead of dirty stinking tenements. We always dreamed of a farm in the country. And all these history hassles are cinched under the belt of my white lady, where the many shitty worlds of Manny Torres fade into one fine, quiet vibration.

I fix a number of times that first day and I'm really riding high. I'm abusing, even by my standards. But you know what? I don't care. 'Cause I am smack-rich, man, and I'm going to continue to use this shit until I want to stop using it. So, I take a quarter of the ounce and I put it aside, knowing that I'll have a supply for a while. And the rest I start cutting. I had three quarters, which cut up to almost two and a half ounces of really good heroin. I used to cut scag with quinine, which is popular in the East. Out West milk sugar is the most popular cutting agent. Actually, scag has to be cut 'cause you would overdose immediately on pure heroin. Pure gold is a myth 'cause it won't hold together. Same way with stuff. When a doper talks about "pure heroin" he means stuff that hasn't been cut away completely. Sometimes when there is a lot of stuff around it won't get cut enough, and guys will OD right and left.

So, now I'm a big dealer; I'm the bag man and people have to come down from Yonkers and Brooklyn to score off of me. I develop a clientele of mostly middle-class kids who don't have a regular connection. They come to me 'cause the word gets around that I'm holding the bag. And I have them all in my hip pocket, which makes me feel kind of good, like I'm a rung above the common dope fiend who has to hussle his buns off every day to score.

For a while I'm really wheeling and dealing; using all the dope I want; having money all the time. I still haven't paid the rent, gas, or electricity. I'm still staying in this house lit with candles. Staying high all the time and surviving on hot dogs and Hershey bars washed down with Pepsi-Cola. But it don't matter what's on the outside, inside, where it counts, I'm a big-time dope dealer. I've got visions of becoming the area ounce man, who holds the bag for the dealers. And I live in a fanciful, free-floating world where dreams are the stuff identity is made from. And reality is either real far away or right in tight, depending on how you look at it.

This scene goes on for quite a while; maybe six or seven months. And then my connection gets busted. I begin to look up out of my nice comfortable little hole and I see that the heat's really on. And I can't score any dope in quantity anymore. Now I have to buy dope in the street like anybody else and I begin to lose control of both quality and quantity.

And I'm hooked. I mean, I'm hooked like a dog. At this time I was using something like two hundred dollars' worth of shit a day. That's a lot of scag to shoot into your system just to keep even. And it leaves tracks on your body and tracks in your mind. And I was into that vicious syndrome where the more you have the more you use. I had scag, man, and as long as you have scag, you use. That's the formula. But since I'm no longer able to make the good scores my money is going mostly to support my own habit. I begin to slip back rapidly into a lifestyle where the central act is a constant frantic run for the pusher, nerves jangling for another boost. And after the scoring comes the fixing. Never mind that your factory is still dirty from the last time. Just melt that medicine down, Manny, and get it into your arm where it will do some good. And the monster grows and grows deep inside your guts, and there's nothing you can do as the craving for junk—and more junk, and more junk—drives you nearly insane.

I try to stop. Kick! Reduce my habit. I even try to cold turkey. Any way at all to get Lady H off my back for a while. But this time it don't work; I can't get well. 'Cause I'm in the streets, and the stuff is available one way or another. And though now I'm broke, that's only a problem by degrees. 'Cause as long as stuff is around, money can be had. It just depends on how desperate you are what methods you'll use to get money for stuff.

I'm barely surviving from day to day now, and even a freak in my condition knows that this act has got to close. There must be another way. I'm reduced again to nickel and dime hustling for my daily junk. I think I'm dying. I know that I've got to get some real money quick. A few weeks before, somebody had traded me some ammunition and a gun for some dope. So, I say to myself, I ought to hit a connection for a piece of dope. That makes sense. That's where the dope is at. Why go to all the hassle to get bread and then spend that bread to get dope? Why not just hustle the connection? That's where the dope is at. Right? Makes sense! Right? Like, you go to the bank for money; you go to the grocery store for goodies; you go to the connection for dope. If you take money to get dope, why the hell not just take dope?

I get the gun from where I have it stashed and I don't think no more about it. I just stick the gun in my pea coat and walk out the door knowing that I've hit on the perfect formula. Why nobody thought of it

before is a great mystery to me. I go over to the connection's house and knock on the door. I say, "It's me, Manny."

He says, "Come in, old buddy." He's a real friendly guy, and for a moment I'm a little sorry, but only for a moment. 'Cause I've been buying three-dollar bags off him for a long time, about fifty or a hundred at a time. And he's never given me any special deal 'cause he knows I'm wired behind stuff and have to have it.

I walk in and he asks, "Okay, Manny, how much dope do you want this time?"

And I say, "All of it, you bastard! No hassles, no story, just the dope."

He goes and gets the bags of dope and I stuff them in my pockets and I say, "The money!"

No hassle. He gives me all his loot. I tell him to sit still in one place nice and quiet like until I'd had time to split. So he sits down and I leave.

When I get home I'm really sweating. I think, What the hell did I just do? Now it dawns on me that I robbed somebody. I went and took something that wasn't mine with a gun. And I realize that it wasn't just an everyday, garden-variety robbery that I'd done. I had held up a connection who had connections in the Organization. Man, I could have the whole damn subterranean underworld down on my neck in a minute. I start to shake all over. I got the gun in my hand, kind of looking at it, and I drop it on the table. But all of a sudden it dawns on me that I got all this dope in my pocket. And, All things work together for good, Manny, I think to myself.

So, I start fixing. I go to the arm with all that scag and use all that money to buy and shoot up more scag. I'm running around trying to steer clear of the guy I robbed. But you know what? I finally run into the guy and he don't say or do nothing! And there was no word out in the street that I'd hit the connection. So, I'm figuring to myself, Boy, this is an easy mark! What a way to go! I happen to know a lot of connections, because I've been to them all, shaking and biting my nails. So this is my game for about two weeks—hitting connections. I guess I got a little thrill deep down inside. Besides the dope. I can knock off the connections that made me sweat. Never mind that I've been a connection and made dope fiends sweat before. It's always dog eat dog in the dope fiend world, and an addict is the most undependable, irrational freak in the world.

However, the word soon gets out, "Manny's hitting connections, watch out for him." And I know that the heat is on so much that soon I won't be able to move. I need a big score. So, I remember these two black dealers in Harlem who are supposed to be really tight friends of mine. Like, they thought that I was their good friend. And I go out to their place and they're partying, both higher'n a kite. I'm coming on the scene meaning to make a hit 'cause I know that these dudes carry a lot of dope. They're what's known in the trade as ounce men. And usually they deal strictly with blacks. But they used to deal scag to me when I had the money because they knew I was people and that I represented power.

I go on into the party. Like, they don't ever keep the dope in the house, they keep it at the stash pad. I say to my friend, "Louie, listen. I want four ounces of dope and I got the money and this dude is waiting at the house for it. I need it right away 'cause there's half a piece in it for me and I can't wait."

I don't show him no long green, but my word is still good up in Harlem. He says, "Well, wait here and we'll go to the stash pad and deliver the bag."

"No, man. I'll go with you to the stash house. Then you give me the dope and drive me home so I can supply this dude before he splits on me."

So, they say they'll do it my way. We get in their car, and I'm in the back seat. When we get to the stash pad they run upstairs while I wait in the car. They're only gone for a minute and they're back with the four pieces of dope. Right there I stick the gun on them and say, "Hold it nice and easy, Louie. You been had."

I take the dope, stick it in my overcoat pocket, and order them upstairs. Now, this is in the street during a busy time of evening, with people walking and loitering around. I get the gun out, kind of hiding it with my sleeve. I get my dealer friends upstairs and take all their dope. There were like ten or twelve pieces. There was only one piece open already, but there was lots of heroin. I march them back to the car and order them to take me back to my neighborhood. I tell Louie to open up his glove compartment and I get the heater out of it and put it in my pocket. I knew they were heated all the time. I get them to drop me off near my house. I know that they know about where I live, but not exactly. So, I have them drop me off in the neighborhood and tell them to split. I run to my pad, throw a few things into a couple of suitcases, and take off.

I have to hide out clear over on the other side of the Bronx. I know that they're really looking for me now. The Organization didn't care much one way or another when I was knocking off the little street pusher, but when I went for the kilo connection I was hitting them too hard. So they put out a simple contract on me. "Get Manny out of the way, even if you have to hit him hard." I'm hiding out in one sleazy basement apartment after another. I got this dope, which I've cut up into a whole lot of nickel bags, but I got to be real careful about selling it because the word could get back to the Organization. So the only ones that I can sell to is people I don't know. 'Cause you can't trust a dope fiend, even if he's your best friend; especially if he's your best friend.

Now I've hit the bottom. You can't get any further down. That's it! I've got guns and dope, but that's all. I'm holed up in this dingy little apartment, strung out on dope, starving to death 'cause I'm afraid to go out and hustle food. I'm scared of the cops and scared of anybody connected with the Organization people. But I get bailed out of my predicament by sheer fate. Louie gets shot down walking out of his house. Somebody just blows him away with both barrels of a 12-gauge shotgun. I mean, they cut him in half. Nobody knows for sure who is the trigger man or why he is wasted. But since the word is out that he was after Manny, there's strong rumors to the effect that I got to him first.

Now, I know I didn't touch the guy, but I'm going to play on these rumors. I let it get around that I'm not taking any crap. "If you fuck with me, you're dead." Louie's brother got the message and quit looking for me. The truce with the Organization was formed when he quit looking for me. But even to this day if I go around the neighborhood, some of these people will ask me if I did it. I could tell them now that I didn't do it, but at the time I never admitted or denied wasting

Louie. I'd just act kind of noncommittal, like I didn't want to talk about it. These kinds of games is what survival in the life is all about.

It never really dawned on me until then that if you hit connections they are going to try to wipe you out. But now I wake up to the fact that I better leave the vicinity. My welcome is really getting thin. I know that if I persist in hanging out in the Bronx that someone is going to blow me away. So I'm still hiding out in this old boiler room, just hustling enough to maintain a weak habit. Really sick most of the time and barely scoring enough to keep alive.

But I still have the gun, because that is my insurance. If things get too bad I can always use the gun to get money. I was hungry one day, really hungry. I hadn't had much of anything to eat for days. And I went into this little grocery store to steal something to eat. But I was so sick and spaced out that I couldn't even take care of business, and this clerk caught me in the act. He made a grab for me to try and hold me until the cops could come, but I got my gun out and threw down on him. Now I was committed. You know what I mean? They just froze, and I said, "All right, just stand there while I just take what I need." So I took it. I walked the clerk around and had him fill up a shopping bag full of cigarettes, candy, and stuff to eat. I got the money out of the till, made both clerks empty their pockets, and even looked under the counter to see if they had any large bills stashed. I made the clerks go back and get in a walk-in freezer. Then I took out of there fast. I got me a hotel room not far away. I washed up, ate, scored some dope, and relaxed. I said, Okay, Manny, this is it. I'm going to steal what I need, take what I want, and to hell with it from now on.

Right there my life changed dramatically. I met up with four or five guys that were heavy into robbery on almost a daily basis. There was Izzy, Fred, and Alan mostly who I worked and associated with. Izzy and I were the only dope fiends. But all of us had been "in the life" for years, and they just accepted Izzy and me because we handled our habits pretty well and made a valuable contribution to the organization, if you could call our outfit an organization. We worked in a sort of loose, unstructured way. Each one of us finding places to hit; casing the layout; setting the job up. Then we would solicit as much help from whoever was available as we needed to pull the job off.

Sometimes Izzy and I would need to up our supply of scag, so we would just go out and hit the first likely cleaning shop or grocery store around. I remember that Fred used to get sort of hot at us sometimes because we would run out and heist some store on the spur of the moment for dope. But he liked the way I operated. He liked the cold, businesslike approach I had to armed robbery. So he put up with a lot of shit to keep me available as a hit man.

I used to carry a double-barreled shotgun, 12 gauge, on a string around my shoulder slung between my arm and my body with this trench coat or army overcoat covering. My front consisted of sunglasses and a slouch-brim hat. We'd park around the corner from the mark, put on our hats and glasses, go in, and just line everybody up against the wall. Or, if things were too visible from the street, make them act perfectly natural. When I threw down on people with my double-barreled 12, they would almost always get very scared and very quiet. Hardly ever any trouble. Looking back from where I am now, I guess that I would have blown a dude away many times if he hadn't froze. Sure, I was there 'cause I needed dope, but I was also there 'cause me and my righteous piece were king, and I liked the overwhelming sense of potency I got from being in that situation.

I remember when we held up this butcher shop owned by a real crazy Dago. We went into our usual number, storming into the place with overcoats, sunglasses, the whole bit. Izzy and I threw down on the Dago and his two helpers. There were three or four customers in the shop,

no problem. Everybody froze and was following orders real good except the Dago. He just stood there hollering at us, "You mothers, nobody is going to take this money I sweat my balls off for. I die first!"

I say, "All right, die, you son-of-a-bitch, if that's the way you want it." And I put the gun right up in his nostril, meaning to scare him into submission. He just knocked it away, grabbed up a cleaver, and backed up against the wall hollering for the others to fight back, too.

Izzy and I were hollering at Frank for directions 'cause neither one of us wanted to let go. Frank said, "Shoot the bastard, for Christ sake, before we all get ranked! Shoot him, Manny! Blow him out!"

. . . me and my righteous piece were king . . .

But Izzy had the presence of mind to step over and drop the crazy Dago with a barrel up alongside his hard head. Frank said, "Hit that Dago mother a couple times for me."

But I got kinda mad at Frank and told him to get busy and pick up the money. "That's what the hell we're here for, isn't it?" Sometimes now I wonder if that's all we were there for. And I know it wasn't. Fred laughingly confessed to us after the butcher shop caper that he'd "creamed my jeans during that one." I never actually went that far but I know the feeling of getting my kicks by holding up four or five places in a day. It was more than just to support a habit.

One time I remember we'd made two good "withdrawals" in one day, both chain grocery stores. When we'd divvied up the take we each came away with over three thousand. That buys a lot of dope. Besides, I had over an ounce on me at the time. Not actually on me, but stashed. So I didn't need to do any robberies for a while to score bread for dope. But that very same evening I went out with Izzy and we hit two candy stores. Now, what the hell you going to get outa candy stores? Money? Not much. There's the same thrill though when you back those people off and stand there like god and demand that they move like you got them on the end of a string.

Wow! That wigs me, come to think of it. A person's going to find their competencies in those areas open to them. And I didn't need no license or diploma to wear a gun. A guy's going to find a sense of belongingness where he is accepted. And when our group went into our number, or even when we were planning a caper, we *belonged*. We worked together like machined parts, we respected each other's abilities and talents, and we accepted each other to such an extent that we would die for a brother if need be. For almost two years Izzy and I and Fred and Alan were like that. In a strange, perverted sense it was

almost like love; not sexual, but *being tight* together.

The thing about power or a sense of personal potency, though, is important. I think it was the power-seeking thing that got to be a habit right alongside of the heroin. I was hooked on dope, and hooked bad, during this whole period, but I was also hooked behind robbery.

When you're on a heroin run, you stay loaded so long as you can score. When you're loaded you are not good for regular employment. Now, I know you hear about these users that can maintain on heroin and work at a nine-to-five job. I believe that this may be possible on smack, where I know damn well it isn't on crystal (speed). But it wasn't possible for me behind any drugs. You see, I'm a pig for heroin. I'm a real scag freak, a heroinic, if you get the picture. And I think that most people that have put that shit in their arm over any period of time are both psychologically habituated and physiologically addicted. And when you're in that shape, you are spaced out and unglued too much of the time to hold down any kind of important or significant employment.

Robbery worked for me for such a long time for two basic reasons. First, I was lucky. God must take care of dope fiends. Because for almost two solid years, while on a constant heroin run that cost on the average of 150 dollars per day to maintain, I pulled off robberies almost daily. Seldom a week went by without at least one or two major robberies. In all this time I was only busted once—at the end of the run. The sun shines on the just and the unjust; I believe it!

Second, robbery worked for me because it is a swift, and relatively sure, method of criminal endeavor. I mean, in between fixes and nod-dings I could venture forth from my apartment, meet my partners, pull the caper off, and return to my pad—sometimes within fifteen minutes! New York is wall-to-wall people, sidewalks are crowded with folks doing their thing. It is a simple matter to step out four or five blocks, step in to one of a thousand or so neighborhood shops, score, and go home. People don't have the slightest idea how simple it is. How you gonna stop it? Are you willing to put a policeman at every store-front? You can't apply enough force to stop street crime. It's too costly, and besides, who wants to live in a police state? Whenever you got people who are economically and psychologically fulfilled more by crime than by the straight life, you're just naturally going to have criminal endeavor. We provide the opportunity for crime in our white racism, our establishment economics, and in our social materialism. Any-way, what the hell, live fast, die faster, and have a beautiful corpse! If you can't beat the Joneses one

way, beat 'em another. That's what I used to think.

I read in the criminal justice literature about modus operandi, and I laugh. We used to have so many modus operandis that we didn't have any at all. Variety was the spice of our life. About the only consistent thing in our opera-tion was the shotguns hung on the shoulder. Sometimes we'd plan a caper right down to the last gnat's eyelash. We'd case the place out and get a time and movement study that'd make some efficiency expert look like a lollipop salesman. We'd spend a week getting ready to hit a grocery store at the right time.

Other times we'd just walk out the door, find a likely place that had cash, hit it, and hole up for a few hours until the local cops changed shifts. When nobody is killed on a robbery, shift change at the station house usually kills the investigation. They got so many un-solved robberies in downtown New York they could paper the county with them. Sometimes people don't even report it when they're hit, es-pecially if they don't carry insurance or haven't paid it up.

After we'd been together for a while I turned my friends onto robbing connections and bookies. I figured, what the hell. The bookie's money is just as good as the grocer's. And I knew where a thou-sand nag parlors and numbers shops were located. Sometimes there's more money in cigar stores and shoeshine joints than in the local bank. And they bend easy. They don't want to get blown away for mere money. You can always score money in the underworld, but you only live once regardless of your game. Bookies don't like to get hit, but what can they do if they can't kill you? Can they call the cops? No. Can they spend a lot of time looking for you if they don't know who you are? No. So they usually just mark it off and go on taking care of business.

Wild! So we run around town hitting bookies and connections for a while. Sometimes we'd score ten grand. A lot of money? No, not at all. When you cut it four ways it's only two bills. And when scag is running five hundred dollars an ounce, you're right back out there sticking a gun in someone's face. All that time we were hitting bookies I figure we're doing society a big favor. We're taking from rich criminals to support poor criminals. Like, we're the Robin Hoods of the underworld! Ain't that a kick!

Yes, it's a kick! You know, it's really a choice thrill to pull off a caper against the other underworld operator. It's like a game. It doesn't do violence to the "underworld code of honor" either, the way I figure it. It's like legitimate competition, sort of like manifest destiny or the survival of the fittest. But it draws heat after a while. I even started nicking on the edges of Leo's territory. As long as we were

holding up the independent bookies Leo could care less. Then we were just weakening the competition for him. But when we started to feel our oats to the extent that we held up franchised syndicate bookies, we were hurting. Somehow Leo got the word that I was involved and he got word out to me that I'd better knock it off or I'd be dead!

So it was back to supermarkets, butcher shops, hardware stores, and an occasional loan company. By this time we were becoming proficient at the business of robbery by force and violence. We seldom had to use violence 'cause looking down the barrels of Mr. Twelve is a very forceful experience for most people. Private finance companies and loan companies were good capers sometimes. But you never could depend on them having a lot of cash available unless you could get inside information. They often deposit their cash in their parent banks on an unsystematic and frequent basis. We used to get frustrated when we didn't score much cash in a loan company heist and we'd try to carry away a lot of merchandise instead. But that's a hassle. There's nothing like good, clean cash. You don't have to turn cash. Even fairly high-class merchandise has to be fenced, and that's just another operation to be bothered with. It compounds the action. You take a risk in the stickup in the first place, then you got to carry the hot goods around to your connection to drop them.

So we liked to think up capers that promised large sums of money. Sometimes the big score takes real calculated planning and real cool operating. Like I said, the four of us could depend on one another to take care of business. Even in that butcher shop caper that almost went sour, Frank never completely lost his cool, Izzy was real cool and took up the slack. The rest of us just hung in there and brought the job off.

One thing about our outfit at this time was that we all fronted real well. We didn't try to be overly big movers, always flashing our roll and acting like big-timers. By fronting well I mean that we had our act together and could mix well with customers and not draw the heat. Then, when it was time to get it on we would drop our front and do the Dillinger bit convincingly and walk out real cool and collected. In one minute and only a block or so away we'd have our righteous front up again and be home free.

I guess the fly in the ointment was Izzy and me. We were trying to live in two different worlds. The dope fiend world and the thief world are not congruent. In fact, features of each are diametrically opposed to the other. For example, some days "taking care of business" would mean nodding to me, but it would mean casing a caper to Frank and Alan. You can't nod and case at the same time. And for a dope fiend there is no contest; heroin always wins. If you got stuff, you use. And there's always periods of time when the user is just no good for organized, systematic business.

Also, the world views of the doper and the thief conflict at most points. Character and solidness are important to the thief. It is important for him to be on his toes. The world exists to be had and can be an exciting, adventuresome experience. For the dope fiend, however, "rightness" is sacrificed whenever necessary for a fix. The world is often not exciting at all, but a dull, gray place from which to escape into the nod.

In essence the only real solid commitment the addict has is to junk. Robbery was a way to get the revenue to sustain a steady junk habit. But the doper doesn't look ahead and rationalize everything. Robbery can also be a hassle and take up a lot of time. Along toward the end of our lives as the "Fearful Four," Izzy and I turned more and more back toward the junkers we were. I remember, there at the last, when I had lots of money, that I would shoot up over an ounce a day. That's a lot of stuff. Sometimes I'd get the needle in in the morning and shoot syringe after syringe of scag into my system. That's a five-hundred-dollar-a-day habit, and it is time-consuming. It is also debilitating and tends to make one scrawny and nervous. Good thieves are healthy and calm.

But the cops didn't every really catch us in the act. I suppose if they hadn't got me the way they did, they might have got all of us, because I was falling off bad. I think I was dying of scag fever. Somehow or another the cops got wise that I was one of the robbers. They came over to the house and rousted us out. They said that someone who was in a drugstore that was robbed a couple of days before had identified our car. The car hadn't even belonged to me, but we had borrowed it to use in this caper and the cops had traced it down through this friend.

So, they had enough evidence to make a pinch. And while they were at the house they found one of the guns hidden in my closet. They took us down to the station and put us in the line-up. None of the owners, clerks, or customers were able to identify me at all. Boy, was I glad! Here I was, just a little over twenty years old, and so close to being busted on a major felony. Just close, or so I thought.

I figured for sure that they'd have to cut us loose, 'cause all the witnesses could identify was the car. And since we hadn't copped to anything, the car was far too circumstantial to build a case on. I thought that any time now I'd be going home. And I was beginning to get sick. I'd just used that morning twice already and now it was afternoon and I was feeling the effects

of early withdrawal. Nothing heavy yet, but I was beginning to get fidgety and nervous. You know, like pacing my cell and skinning my knuckles on the bars in frustration. I was starting to get a runny nose too, which is a sure sign of early withdrawal.

So, I started raising hell. Hollering at the jailers that I wanted out and that they had nothing to hold me on. It wasn't ten minutes until one of the jailers hollered down to me, "Shut up, you goddamn Spic. The DA is sending someone down to talk to you."

I thought, Here it comes, I'm getting sprung! So I started rolling 'em up and getting my stuff together for check-out.

In about an hour the deputy DA comes down and I get called out to the counseling room. The guy says that the State of New York is busting me for violation of the Sullivan law. I didn't know that there was such a thing as the Sullivan law. He says that in New York you cannot have any small arms in your possession without a valid permit. And they said that conviction was automatic once possession was proven.

Man, I hollered rape! "You guys are nuts! You can't hold me on any goddamn trumped-up charge as that. Just because you can't prove me guilty of your armed robbery, now you're going to fuck over me with some phony charge. You can't make it stick, and you know it."

But they sure as hell book me in on violation of the Sullivan law. I'm flat broke 'cause I've been spending all my money on dope. My friends are not going to help me out 'cause they're too busy tending to business. Either they are strung out on dope themselves and can't worry about old Manny, or else they're afraid to touch me with a ten-foot pole, 'cause they been close to the caper themselves.

So, I'm wasted, man, really wasted. I can't make bail and so I'm booked into the felony tank. Now I know that I'll have to kick. Cold-turkey kicking is no fun. I'm trying to puke out my guts and nothing but a feeble moan will come up. I see all the demons of hell parade before my eyes, screaming and making fun of me. I can't hold my mud and so I have to perch on the shitter like a bare-assed bird on a telephone wire. I really got the miseries.

But I know that in a couple of days I'll be all right physically. The thing that's got me really worried is this beef they've throwed at me. It's like they're coming from the moon, or somewhere beyond reality. And I'm in complete ignorance. I feel deep down inside of me that I'm going to prison and I'm scared as hell. Not so much physically scared, that too. But more like scared of the unknown world that's been told of only in whispers and fragments. Drifting into my consciousness like unreal sounds and sensations from the lives of friends and relatives who've experienced it, but never taking on form or sub-

stance until now. Now the reality of prison begins to crop up in my being like a rock wall. And I know that I'm going, but I still want to fight it off. I wonder if a fish feels much the same way when he's hooked.

The next step in a few days is court. I go to court and get assigned a public defender. What a laugh. He listens to me for about three minutes and says right off, "You're going to the joint."

I say, "Well, wait a minute, ass-hole! Don't talk to me that way. You're supposed to be my lawyer. Aren't you representing me? What the hell, are you the district attorney's brother or his punk or something?"

He stays real calm in spite of all my cussing, like he's been through this scene a million times before. "It's an automatic three years, Manny. You can't beat it, especially since you're a street person. That's what they made the law for."

"Look, I'm not going to the joint behind this Mickey Mouse charge. Get that through your head, dummy. Now, get the hell out of here and find some ammunition to beat this rap and I'll work my ass off to get you some extra bread, like mucho bread!"

He says, "The gun was found in your apartment; in your own personal room. It's got your fingerprints on it, plain and simple. You

don't have a license for it. Therefore, you are going to the joint for
three years."

How right he was! It wasn't no
time until I was before the judge. I
got busted in May and I was in the
joint July third. I had been in jail
maybe an hour or so twice for
bookmaking before this experience.
And now it was beautiful July in
New York, I was twenty years old,
a dope fiend, all screwed up, and
on my way by boat to Sing Sing
Prison.

Chapter 3

Sing Sing Prison

Get up, stand up, line up, shut up, and lock up.

The very first thing I remember about being in prison is walking up a long, long flight of stairs with all of us chained together at the waist and around the legs. We were half pushed, half dragged up this forever flight of stairs to the Admissions Center. I'd been really spaced out all the way up from the city because I still couldn't believe that this was happening to me at all. Several older and wiser cons, coming back for another dose of the steel womb, assured me, "You're damned right, Manny! This is it; Sing Sing Prison! Ain't it beautiful?"

And I come outa the fog going up these stairs into the main prison. We all crowd into this little room and somebody yells at me, "Drop your laundry, Fish! Get them goddamn threads off! Let me see the crack of your ass pronto!"

What the hell did I get into? Man, this is insanity. Am I in Sing Sing, or in some sixteenth-century asylum? It's still not real to me at all—like I'm dreaming. I just barely kicked the habit, and I'm weak. There's nothing I'd like better than a fix. But I can see that's an impossibility, so I'm really up tight.

They don't give a damn. The guards, assisted by white-shirted trusties, are processing us like so much merchandise. No! It was much more personal than that. They were seemingly intent in getting across the idea that we were not men any longer. I, personally, felt like shit being flushed. And this was the end of the line.

We were standing there naked; they'd taken our street clothes away and didn't seem to be in a hurry to dress us. While we were stark-assed naked they phtographed us. Just sat us in a chair, draped a coat and shirtfront over us, and hung a board with our number around our neck. One by one we got this treatment. I really felt crappy when the cheeks of my bare ass hit that cold chair. Like, I'm sitting there in front of God and everybody, can't even cover myself up, the man hollering at me, "Look into the camera. Not like that, asshole! Over here! That's right. Okay, go on over there and get fingerprinted."

Still naked as a jaybird, I parade over to the inking table and go through that routine. I think, These dumb bastards. On this beef alone already I been fingerprinted three, man, three times. Why don't these freaks get it together? I get the ink treatment at the precinct station, at the courthouse, the FBI has to have their own set, and now again. No wonder these bureaucrats got jobs. They just duplicate each other like mindless robots stamped outa the same mold.

When he gets done fingerprinting me, I go over in line to wait for the "skin game." Ever felt useless? Just try standing naked in a line, with all the lights glaring overhead, for fifteen or twenty minutes. What do you do with your hands? You want to put them over your parts, you know, but that looks kinda foolish, so what do you do?

The skin game is where they check your person out for contra-band. Now, I think, Ain't this foolish. What in the hell can I carry around in this condition? But I soon get the idea, and I don't like it. One by one they make us go in this little room, bend over, and get the treatment. Even the older, wiser cons look a little sheepish and undone coming out of that cubicule. Then it's my turn.

I go in and this screw inspects me under the arms, in my hair, around my pubic region for mites, lice, and whatever else he thinks he's going to find. Then the doctor steps up. He's a nasty-looking pot-bellied guy, old and almost senile. He does a preliminary medical checkup, like the eye-ear-nose-throat thing. Then he puts on a pair of powdered gloves, kinda grabs me by the neck, bends me over a little table, and before I know it sticks two fingers about eight inches up my ass.

Now I realize where I'm at! And I really blow it. I try to push this dude away from me. "Get your fucking hands off me and leave me alone!"

I couldn't believe what hit me. All these bulls came outa nowhere, like through the walls, and proceeded to beat on me. I'm on the floor and they're kicking and punching me, called me all kind of names. I mean, they're using me as a ball like in some kind of weird, unreal game. And I pass out cold.

When I come to my senses I'm in bed in the prison hospital. Now I really understand what's happening. I'm hurting, not only outside, but way down inside at the heart. I understand, finally, as I'm laying there, I recognize that I've been through the ceremonial process of depersonalizing the new inmate. I feel all cold inside as if it's just me against the world, and Manny is so tiny and insignificant that he just shrivels up until he's a dot in the center of the bed. Now I know that I'm absolutely powerless in my present condition. There's nobody to stand by me like in the old days in the Young Stars. I'm all alone now, and I feel the terrible weight of the Man on me, and the three years on me.

Then I started thinking about all the stories I'd heard in the street about doing "big time," about the joint and all its hassles. Aside from casual conversations and rumors, I didn't know anything at all about doing time and I really started worrying about what I'd gotten into. I was really depressed. But, like people say, when you're down something always happens.

This con comes wheeling in the lunch cart and lets me know outa the side of his mouth that he's got a word for me. The bull is busy supervising the feeding to insure that meat and desserts get distributed equally. My newfound friend leans over me and says, "Hey, there's a homeboy of

yours that wants to see you."

"A homeboy?" That shows you what a daze I was in. I knew perfectly well what a homeboy was. "Far out! Maybe I'll be able to link up with somebody from the neighborhood."

So this guy says, "When you get out of the hospital Raul will be waiting to see you in the cellblocks or on the yard. He'll clue you in to what's happening."

. . . I feel the terrible weight of the Man on me . . .

But I was to wait a while. Soon as I could walk they threw me in the hole. Sometimes they call it "segregation and isolation," sometimes the "adjustment center." But any way you spell it, it's the hole. They locked me up as the troublemaker. It seems that they wanted to be sure that I'd got my mind right before they turned me out into the general population. I thought it was a real distortion of reality. Here I'd just got mad and struck out in defense at this pervert giving me a finger wave and now I was in the hole, laying on the bare concrete with no regular food and damn little water.

Three months! Three months, man, for not being a good "nigger" and taking my ass-jabbing lying down. And the hole, let me tell you, is a trip. One you probably don't want to take.

When they throw you in the hole for fighting, they usually put you in what is known as a "strip cell." There is nothing but a concrete floor and bare walls. It is dark, except for a tiny 10-watt bulb in the front corner of the cell. In one back corner is a hole that serves as the can. You sort of squat or stand over it whenever you get the urge. Sometimes you go without toilet paper for days. You don't have to worry about flushing your toilet because it flushes every two minutes, twenty-four hours a day—forever. Can you dig it? No human being deserves to live this way. The filth of last month's feces cake on the walls; the stench is overpowering. Guys have been known to go mad in the hole and never recover.

The idea behind the strip cell is to break the con's spirit. Prison officials assume that everybody who comes to the joint is a potential troublemaker. On this score you are guilty by simple-minded association —you are a convict, therefore you are guilty. I'm reminded of Jerry Brown, this young colored cat from around the Bronx that got sent up for thirty years for being involved in several big robberies. When he got to Sing Sing he really tried to play it cool. He never was really tough, but he had this reputation of being a heavy gun man. And the bulls would deliberately try to get him to foul up; they would agitate Jerry and try to trap him so they

could throw him in the hole. I guess that the bulls just didn't think it was right that a quiet, un-assuming kid like Jerry should be in the joint behind such a heavy-duty reputation. It was as if they would make Jerry into their image of the typical "raving criminal beast."

One Monday morning after Jerry came back to his cell from break-fast, there was this court "chit" on the end of his bed. Just a simple notice for him to get his stuff to-gether and have his personal belong-ings listed because he would be going to inmate court at 8:30 A.M. No reasons why; no specified charges. It was the usual hassling routine that causes a knot in the gut and a chilly feeling all through you. You rack your mind for some-thing that you might have done out of line. But nothing comes up, usually because there is nothing at all wrong with your actions.

The next time we saw Jerry was almost exactly a year later. We heard rumors of what had hap-pened. You always get pretty re-liable fragments from the prison grapevine. But we had to wait for Jerry to get out of the hole before we got the whole story. When he got down to court that morning, he had to wait in a little, bare concrete room with about forty others. The benches were hard, the overhead lights glared fiercely from above as the men fidgeted and talked to-gether in a low monotone. As usual, the captain of the guards and his junior officers took their time drinking coffee and shooting the shit before the mockery of court procedure began.

When it was Jerry's turn a sergeant beckoned to him from the other room and he went in and stood before the stern visage of Captain Jim. The captain's voice was chilly as he read the charges. "Brown, 78346, you are charged with conducting yourself in an insubordinate manner. While coming in from the yard yesterday, Officer Henley observed that you swaggered by him and Officer James with an insubordinate walk."

Jerry blew up! "What in the goddamn hell is an insubordinate walk? Where do you assholes get off with a charge like that?"

"Well, Brown, clearly you must be guilty as charged. With the kind of attitude you have now I don't doubt for a minute that you were twisting your ass in Officer Henley's face! Fifteen days on piss and punk [bread and water] will take some of that out of you. Get him out of here!"

"Not before I punch you in the goddamn mouth, you pervert," shouted Jerry. And with that he leaped across the desk and pasted the captain three or four good ones before the other officers were able to restrain him.

That behavior got Jerry Brown six months in the growler with no time off. While he was down there he got into it again with another guard, who kept putting his filthy fingers in Jerry's tray at chow time. So Jerry did another six months. What they were trying to do was to break his spirit. They just wanted him to pitch in the towel. To them, Jerry was merely an animal in a cage; anything they did to him was not only appropriate but legitimate.

When you're in the hole you feel like an animal. Sometimes your self-esteem is so low that you think its your fault that you feel like an animal. You get so down that you would like to kill yourself, and some do when they can get ahold of a piece of glass or an old razor blade. I knew a kid who got so depressed at continually receiving this kind of treatment from the guards that one night he kept bending the handle of his water pitcher back and forth, back and forth until it broke off. This gave him a ready-made probe sharp enough so's he could dig the veins out of one arm at the elbow and bleed to death. I was celled up next door in the hole when they found him; the guards just laughed. They passed it off as the kid "being weak, and not able to take his treatment like a man."

What the Man wants you to become in the joint is the routinely pliant inmate. You got to get your mind right and continually pass the obedience test. The socialization processes in many prisons are openly calculated to induce humility, to break the will of any inmate who shows the least defiance. And there is no higher motivation, no intrinsic value attached to these ceremonies. The process happens because of the institutional relationships, which insure the total power of guard over inmate in the name of security. In almost every case, these ceremonies of degradation force the inmate to adjust by surrendering his identity in cowardly capitulation or to become basically more dishonest than he was by pretending to adjust to rules overtly while manipulating and double-dealing everyone he has business with. Of course, another frequent adjustment to this systematic hassling is reflected in the actions of the boy in the hole who tore his veins out of his arm one night.

So, I stay in the growler for three months, not all of it in the strip cell. They got about three varieties of the hole in most joints. And they dish it out to you according to what you done wrong and how you react to the "court" process. First, they got the strip cell, and I spent a lot of time in there until I got my mind right and learned to evade the Man instead of come against him head-on. They got isolation, where you are by yourself in a cell with just blankets, water, and your thoughts. Also, there is segregation, where you are allowed most of the things that you have on the mainline, but where you are segregated from all other inmates. Sometimes cons who break really bad and cause lots of trouble are segregated

on "deadlock" for years, even until they die.

When I hit the yard coming out of isolation I was scared as hell. I didn't know how to conduct myself, 'cause I thought that maybe somebody would try to make a reputation by downing me. After all, I was brand-new in the joint and I had clobbered a bull. Besides, I was real young-looking and little and I thought that some big jocker might try and make an "old lady" out of me. But I lit out across the yard jig-walking like I owned the whole damn place 'cause I figured, What the fuck, I just gotta act bad. If fate says I gotta get down, there is just no way out of it.

In just a minute, Raul, my old homeboy, comes up and introduces himself. I remembered him and right away we start rapping. He clues me into everything and I am no longer a fish. I mean, in about a half an hour I begin to get wise to all the angles. Raul is in on the dope traffic, gambling, hustling food from the mess hall, and everything else that was going down. He dukes a knife on me and says, "Here, take this shank and stash it somewhere. That way if you get in a bind you'll have some artillery to break even with."

"What the hell, Raul? Why stash it? I'll just carry it on me. That way, if I need it I'll have it, right?"

But Raul says, "No, dammit!

Stash it where you can get to it easy if anything comes down. 'Cause if you carry it all the time, sooner or later the Man will pull you over for a shakedown and you'll get mucho time in the growler."

So I trusted Raul and did as he said 'cause I knew him in the streets and knew that he was a good head. I remembered that he was cool when the heat was on and had a lot of heart so that he could hold his mud when the going got tough. When he clued me in on something I'd say, "Yeah, Raul, that's the way it has to be if you say so, buddy." From that time on I was in the clique. I came from the streets into the joint, had a few problems, and then went right into the clique.

It was pretty much the same clique and the same routine as in the streets, except that joints make the operations somewhat more confining. It's weird to think back that once I got involved in joint life I didn't feel that much difference in the stuff going on around me from when I was on the outside. 'Cause in the joint we did mainly the same things as on the bricks. Outside, I stole from the Man in any way I could; inside, same thing. I'd steal from the Man and hustle from the other cons. In the joint, everyone is fair game. You better keep your guard up and your shit together if you don't want to lose your ass. Life is mostly the same inside or out—everybody tries to get the best deal possible.

I wasn't much into the racist trip that some were in at Sing Sing. I was more into the dope fiend–hustling trip. If the shit came down, I knew where it was on. That was automatic. But I wasn't one of the agitators. It really used to make us dope fiends mad when the racist trip came down and everybody would get up tight, or maybe even fight and riot. Because tensions like that just draw the heat down on the place and make it next to impossible to take care of business. When the heat's on no drugs move; there's no action and nobody can score. Oftentimes I acted like a peacemaker trying to hold down racial tensions and trying to keep the young bucks fresh in from the reformatories in line. But it wasn't out of humanitarian motives; I was just looking out for Number 1.

Lots of people have a quaint notion about life in prison. They think that there's no dope or booze or sex in there. That it's just a place where guys in striped shirts break rocks all day and lock up all night. There's all kinds of dope in prison. The walls can't keep it out. I've known cons that have had it dropped by airplane. Usually it doesn't happen that dramatically.

I remember the first time I scored a piece of dope in Sing Sing. They'd just started experimenting with the open visiting privilege. The phones and glass booths had been replaced with tables. You sat on one side, and your visitor sat on the other. No contact during the visit, but you could have some privacy of communication. My brother comes up to see me, and since I was young and they were trying to rehabilitate me they allowed us to visit the new way.

The first thing that comes out of my mouth when I see Bobby is, "Do you have any dope? Can you score?" I'm not asking "how are you?" or saying "glad to see you." I've been in there for nine months and the important question is, "Do you have any dope?"

And Bobby says, "No, I can't bring you any dope."

I tell him, "Listen, before we talk or anything, I want some dope."

But he ain't tuned in to my frequency at all. "I didn't come all the way up here to jawbone about scag. And I ain't going to bring in no dope! You're crazy."

So I say, "Now, brother, you listen. I like dope; I need dope; I ain't got no dope; I want dope. You get me an ounce of dope. I know you can score it. So you do it, pronto. Understand? When you get the job done, come and see me. I'll tell you how we can get it in."

That was the end of the visit. It lasted for no more than four minutes. I just ran it down to him and left the visiting room. I go back to my cell and when my bunkmate comes in off the yard I say, "Listen, I got this piece of dope coming in in a few days, how do I get it in?"

He doesn't know 'cause he hasn't been involved in any of that stuff. So by the time I'm done rapping to him I'm locked in for the day. First thing the next morning I go see Raul and tell him, "Listen, I got a piece of dope—my brother can bring us in a piece of dope! How do you get it inside where we can get at it?"

Raul knows exactly how. "Okay," he says, "first we have to go talk to the guys who work outside on the gardening detail. The only chance we got is to deal with Harry and Joe, a couple of good heads on the garden crew."

I said, "Hey, wait a minute! What kind of deal? I ain't about to give any of that shit away. I want us to have it. Do you realize what kind of power we can have with an ounce of dope in this joint? Besides, you and I can stay high forever, man!"

"Listen, Manny, cool it, will you, and just listen a minute. First, your brother is going to have to stash the scag outside 'cause he can't get past the bulls at the main gate. Even if he could get by, the chances of his being able to duke you the stuff in the visiting room without the Man seeing the transaction are not good at all. Then, after your visit you're going to get shook down. So, Harry and Joe will make the pickup, after your brother drops the bundle outside the wall, and they'll bring it in through the back gate hidden in their garden tool wagon and leave it in the gardener's shop. I'll arrange for somebody else to bring the stuff into the kitchen from the gardener's shop.

"And from the kitchen we get it. Dig? But make up your mind, Manny, everybody along the line is going to get a piece of the action. If your brother drops a full ounce of dope, we'll be lucky to get a quarter of the piece by the time it gets in to us."

"Listen, Raul! You must be nuts. I mean, they're robbing us. Look, man, whose dope is it in the first place? Who is getting it up here from the city? Whose going to all the trouble to bring it up? Who the hell is making the connection? Your deal is just plain outrageous."

"Yeah, I agree. But that is the only way you're going to get the dope behind these walls. Look, Manny, the dope is outside in the streets, right? It ain't in the cell-blocks, right? If you want to get it in you'll have to pay dues. That's the facts and you might as well face up to them."

Well, I don't like Raul's idea at all. I say to him, "Forget it, man. You ain't doing me any favors. Bobby brings me a piece of dope and all I get is a quarter. No way, man."

I rack my brains trying to think of ways to get the stuff in. 'Cause I know that Bobby will deliver. It's just a matter of time. So, I go and talk to this guy who used to work in the prison boiler room. He used

to go out once a week with a load of clinkers or something on a truck. And I think that maybe I can get him to pick up the scag and I'll give him a quarter of an ounce to do the gig. See, I just don't want to give up much of the dope. I ain't socialized into how it has to be in the everyday commerce of the prison.

But the boiler room dude says he won't do it. He won't have anything to do with narcotics. I put out little feelers around to other guys I have met and pretty soon I'm drawing the heat. Raul comes to me and says, "Listen, Manny, you have to be careful who you're talking to about this caper or you're going to blow it bad. Besides not getting in any dope, you're going to wind up with your ass in the hole. You can't just ask anybody and everybody in this goddamn place to do you this kind of favor. People talk, and the walls have ears, baby. I told you about a practically foolproof way to handle this operation. Now, are you going to go or not?"

I finally decide that it's going to be Raul's way or not at all. By this time I'm really getting antsy for a shot of heroin. I get in touch with my brother and have him come up the following Saturday. Again we meet in the visiting room and I don't ask him about the family or nothing, just the dope. I tell Bobby to come back on Sunday for another visit and to get there early, before a lot of traffic. I tell him how he can camouflage the dope and drop it along the trail by the wall. I want him to drop it where the first garden crew out on Monday morning can pick it up.

Bobby promises me that he'll make the drop. And sure enough when he comes back in to visit on Sunday he tells me that he got the job done and that he's sure that nobody ranked his play. So I pass the word out that the drop has been made and that Harry and Joe are to make the pickup and bring the scag in on Monday evening.

By Tuesday morning I'm expecting to hear something, but nothing happens. I go looking for Raul, but I can't find him nowhere. Now I begin to suspect that its a burn and I think, Oh, for Christ's sake! I shoulda known better; I got burned. My own homeboy burned me. That's the way you think when you're a dope fiend. And most of the time you're right. Most of the time you do get burned on capers that involve other dope fiends.

I go right to the stash place and get my shank. I'm not going to ask questions. I'm just going to start hitting. If you let these punk hustlers put one over on you, you lose. You not only lose stuff and money, but you lose rep. And I ain't about to lose my reputation. The first son-of-a-bitch I'm going to hit is Raul, then I'm going to hit anyone who was involved in the so-called deal. Makes no difference to me that the Man might catch me and put me in the growler or even charge me with assault or

murder. A con don't think about that when his rep is on the line.

I wait for Raul by the kitchen door 'cause I know he's got to come off shift soon. He comes running up to me and I pull the shank out to get ready to stick him in the gut when he says, "Hey, Manny, I'm holding the stuff on me."

But I don't really hear him 'cause I got this thing on my mind. I *know* that he's fucked over me and I'm going to get him good. I say, "Raul, I trusted you and you screwed me over, now you've had it."

He says, "I don't know what you're talking about, Manny. I got the shit; let's get up to our pad and get down."

So, it finally comes clear to me that he hasn't messed me around after all and that we have scored heroin right in the middle of Sing Sing Prison! On the way up to the cellblock we got ahold of a point man to watch while we fixed. This cost a dime bag of stuff. But now I don't give a shit about giving some of the dope away. All I can think of is that, man oh man, we're going to fix!

So we head on up to the cellblock. Along the way we pick up our various pieces of equipment where we had them stashed. All the same kind of equipment we had in the streets, we had in the joint. Sometimes we could even score better equipment in the joint because we had access to the hospital, and enough cigarettes or canteen chits will buy you anything—almost. We had synringes, pacifiers, eyedroppers, and all kinds and sizes of needles. We even had a stainless steel spoon to cook the junk up with. Tell you what! I even had a lot less chance of getting hepatitis in the slammer 'cause we sterilized our equipment in a stainless hospital bedpan using the same electric stinger we rigged up to cook coffee.

We make sure that our point man is on the ball, and we get down. In this situation there is no hassle about who is getting down first. We're in my cell; I've got the equipment; I got the dope in. So Raul just hands it over and watches me cook up. I put a little bit of stuff in the spoon and cook it up 'cause I want to see if it's been cut since my brother made the drop. I take it up in the syringe, find the vein, and put it in. Man, I really get loaded. And I know that it ain't been touched and the deal's true-blue.

But I want more right away 'cause I didn't even go into the nod. I want to really get loaded so I put a heavy load in the spoon and start cooking again. Raul is telling me, "Come on, Manny, you already went; let me get down."

"Screw you, Raul, I'm going to get loaded first." All I can think of is sucking those little white grains of necessity up into the magic wand and shooting a whole load of forgetfulness into my being. And I feel myself going out. I just pull

the outfit out of my arm and fling it into the corner of the cell. I'm really loaded for the first time in over a year. I'm down, and I just kick back! I'm not even worried that soon a guard is going to walk by my cell. I don't even know I'm in jail. Man! Nothing's happening, everything's happening!

Sometimes I scored better dope in the joint than I did on the streets.

I just kick back and I feel really mellow. And I see that the stuff is all laid out on the bunk, and Raul is cleaning the outfit. It all looks really beautiful to me. I'm feeling so good and so far out; it is hard to explain the sensation. It's like, hell, man, there ain't no bars grabbing at you; no concrete and steel to fence you in; no hard-assing guards hassling you. There is just a mellow, floating time without tomorrow feeling. No pressure, no strain, no deep-groin absence of loving pain; just Miss Heroin stroking you where it's at and the feeling of constant coming alive in a glorious spiritual orgasm, only to lapse again and again into a more glorious oblivion.

Finally I come down enough to see Raul has fixed and is passed out on the floor. The point man comes running up to the front cell and wants to get down. So he come in, takes the pinch of dope I give him, and starts to fix while I go out on the point. But I take the stuff with me. I ain't about to leave it in the cell. I just give him a ten-dollar paper, which is really a small dose. But the dope is really good. All the dope I ever scored in the joint was really first-rate. I never got burned, not once. Sometimes I scored better dope in the joint than I did on the streets.

I didn't even go to work for days. I just laid up in my bunk and enjoyed a constant high. I got the stuff in my pocket, and the outfit in my mattress. I don't sleep the whole first night. I got so much scag in me that I don't have to fix again; I'm really loaded. In the morning Raul says, "Okay, it's time to go into business."

"Business, hell," I shout at Raul. "I ain't selling any of this dope. This good shit is for me and you, and that's it, baby!"

Raul tells me that it can't be that way. "Before, we didn't have any dope and we wanted dope. There was no dope at all in the joint. But when somebody scored and got a piece of dope in and we had the money for it, we'd buy. And they'd usually always sell it to us. Now we have to do the same thing. We can't hold out, Manny. We have to give a little. It's like part of the convict code. We got dope; we got to share with the people. If we try to hog it all we'll be up against the wall with all the right people in here."

But a dope fiend is a curious son-of-a-bitch. You gotta prove to him that he'll get more dope by selling some of what he has. Otherwise nothing, not even the fear of death, will make him sell. So, I say to Raul, "Will selling some of this quarter ounce help us to score more dope?"

"It should pave the way for another score, Manny. Look, we got about seven grams, but we'll more than double that. We'll cut it with anything we can get ahold of. In the joint it's hard to score quinine or milk sugar, so we cut it with sugar, flour, or anything."

"Flour, Raul? Are you sure? I never cut it with flour before. Can't a cat get all fucked up with flour in his veins? It's not soluble is it?"

"No, it's not, but don't worry. The stuff works. Like, we aren't going to cut it that much anyway, and the freaks can suck it up through a ball of cotton."

In the joint, just the same as on the bricks, the whole idea is to make the dope look bigger than it is, but not cut it so much that you burn the cat. When you're hooked or want a fix bad, most of the time what you look at is the quantity, not the quality. If it looks big, you buy it 'cause it's big. You think you get more dope for your money. Same way in the joint. I give them a good fix, one that I know will put them down. Then I add sugar, flour, anything to fluff it up and make it look bigger. But I want to know damn well that when they fix they are going to get a jolt.

So with the dope Raul and I had, we made one hundred fixes and retailed them at ten bucks apiece. This is besides the stuff we held out to get loaded on. Remember that there was another three-quarters of an ounce around the joint at the same time, 'cause Bobby had dropped a full piece. Everybody who was in on the know was walking around loaded higher than a kite for weeks.

But, as luck would have it, my source with Bobby dried up fast. He was hooked bad himself and it was too much of a hassle for him to hustle for us too. So he just didn't come up to visit when I sent for him. He'd conveniently find an excuse. I knew and he knew I knew. But that's the way it had to be. It's harder than hell to hustle for two habits. So Raul and I wind up with a big bill and no dope to buy. We have to fall back on speed and pruno.

We used to get these inhalers like Benzedrine and Wyamine in for little or nothing at first. Even talked some screws into bringing them in for us to use as inhalers before everybody got wise to their use as dope. You cracked the plastic tube open and inside would be eight strips of blotterlike paper impregnated with the drug. You'd tear off a quarter inch of one strip, put it in your mouth, and wash it down with good hot joe (coffee). In about twenty minutes you'd follow it with another quarter and you'd be high.

Now, a bennie high falls very short of a heroin high. It's not the same thing at all. Bennie has its good points; it's not addicting and not hardly psychologically habituating. But it's not nearly as mellow either. When you're up on bennie you're just buzzing along. You can lay on your sack and kind of review past events. You're not really nodding, but most of the pain of incarceration fades away behind bennie. You don't sleep, just sort of doze in a dreaming state. You're conscious of what's going on around you, but you're kind of out of it, too. You have to drink lots of hot water to keep the buzz going and you use about a strip and a half a day if you are controlling. Thing about speed that gets to be bad is when it's out of control. Some people can control speed real well. They find a level on which they can operate and stay high, but stay in there and do their job and motate around the joint. If you are controlling you eat a little right along even if you don't feel like it. You find out what foods don't disagree with you when you're high and you become diligent about following a routine. I've seen guys nurse a speed habit along for months. They get a little skinny and strung out, and finally have to lay off for a while, but they can go right back on and stay loaded for another several months. If you can control bennie it can serve you well in the joint, because you can do your time without getting frustrated or drove up. The inhaler tubes are no good any more because the feds made them put something in the cotton that will make you sicker than a dog if you take it internally. But there are lots of bennie pills around because the drug is a common medication for certain emotional and psychological problems.

Any kind of speed is really terrible, though, if you can't handle it. And most guys get to be a pig for speed. They think that if a little speed makes you feel good, a lot will make you feel higher. And it don't work that way. I think that speed freaks are fucked up emotionally. I know that when I get on speed it really causes me problems, 'cause I have no more control over speed than I do heroin. You see, any drug is easy to abuse. Most guys can't use without abusing. A few people can control their drug use and make drugs work for them. But don't count on you being one of them. In my experience, sooner or later most guys will freak out behind the consistent use of any drug.

Pruno is a different story. Unless you're an alcoholic you can use pruno rather consistently without too much harm. I've seen old cons who've been guzzling pruno and other beverages in the joint for lots

of years, and sometimes they have liver and kidney problems, but it takes years, same as on the outside. We used to make pruno out of anything that would ferment. Cons usually call home brew pruno whether it is made out of prunes, pineapple, apricots, or whatever. Generally there are two kinds of home brew in the joint. There's potato beer and there's pruno. Potato beer is really popular because it can ferment and be ready to drink in about twenty-four hours from the time you set it. Really, all you need is half-boiled spuds, some warm water, sugar, and a chunk of yeast to get it started. You find a nice warm spot to hide the stuff and let her work. If you can't score any yeast from the bakery or commissary, you can get the brew started with fresh-baked bread heels. Only it takes about sixty hours that way. Spud beer is potent stuff and if you are not used to drinking it you may get sicker'n a dog the first time, but you'll be back. In the joint, when time is hard to do, any high makes it easier —even Jesus is a high-riser in the joint—but most cons are into a more physical high.

Pruno takes a little more time and effort to produce, but the extra hassle pays off 'cause pruno is more like wine and has a much higher alcoholic content. I never hustled much pruno in the joint. Occasionally, when there was no dope around I'd get something to drink, but I preferred any drug to booze. Pruno is a whole way of life in prison, and I can tell you about a friend of mine named Big Red the Brew-master. He was one real fine hombre.

Big Red had been around the joints in the East a long time. He was the most con-wise head I ever knew. If there was any angle going, or any way to make a buck, Big Red would be in on it from the start. But his main source of income, as well as fun, was in making and selling pruno and other consumable beverages right under the Man's nose. One time Red found a twenty-foot section of eight-inch stainless steam pipe in the boiler room that had been sectioned off and stopped up. He cut a hole in each end on the top near the ceiling and blew the pipe clean with a steam hose. Damned if he didn't fill that pipe with about forty gallons of luke-warm water mixed with melted sugar. Then, he mashed up six or eight gallons of strawberries and siphoned them into the pipe. Last of all he put several packages of dry yeast in. Now, Red knew that if he sealed the pipe up tight that it would soon begin to ferment, and when booze ferments something has to give. So he stuck a catheter hose which he had scored from the hospital down into each hole and sealed around them with wax. That way the gas from the fermenting pruno escaped out of the hoses into the top of the boiler room.

For a while, Red had an odor problem, but he figured that out, too. He drilled a little tiny hole in

an adjacent steam pipe and put liquid Pine Sol in a nearby petcock. That was the sweetest-smelling room in the whole damn joint. And the little bit of steam escaping near the ceiling served to camouflage the whole operation. In ten days or so a bunch of us snuck down to the boiler room to watch Big Red tap the pipe. That strawberry pruno came off at about 21 percent wine. I know that for a fact 'cause Big Red even had a hydrometer in his little old wine-making kit. At first, the guys were cracking wise about the rubber catheter tubes Red had got out of the hospital. Like, whether they were used or not before Red got them. But after we had a few drinks of that righteous brew we didn't care a damn about no catheters.

That reminds me of another home brew incident that happened in there. It was Big Red again. He'd set up several barrels of brew twenty feet underneath some sawdust in the big bin where it was stored to run the boilers. They were using sawdust as an auxiliary fuel when coal and oil were not available. Big Red had cased the placed and determined that months sometimes went by before anyone would move any sawdust. Also, he noticed that there was a big blind spot in the corner nearest the boiler room, where nobody could spot a couple of guys working. So he had a hole dug down twenty feet or so into the pile and a little room carved out where he could store casks and barrels. Dammed if he didn't have the neatest wine cellar within a hundred-mile radius. For over a year Red had an average of three hundred gallons of pruno going at one time.

Well, the caper might have lasted indefinitely if it had not been discovered by another con, who determined to use the room for private sex. This stud named Mike had been trying to turn out a real cute boy who'd just come in for armed robbery. The kid didn't mind giving in to Mike, only he insisted that Mike would have to find a place that was absolutely private or he wouldn't go. So, one afternoon they holed up in Big Red's wine cellar and got with it. I guess that in between sex they had to smoke. Anyway, after they had got through, about four o'clock in the afternoon, somebody noticed smoke coming from the sawdust bin and called out the fire department.

There was this big, dumb yard bull on duty called Sarge. He used to chew snoose regularly, carried his snoose can in his shirt pocket. Sarge had the habit of writing guys' numbers down on the lid of his snoose can if he was going to write someone up for a rule infraction. He couldn't hardly spell his own name, but he could write down numbers. Anyway, Sarge came running up to the fire hollering, "How did this fire start? Who was it, anybody know?"

Some smart-assed con in the crowd hollered out that it must have been spontaneous combustion that started it. Sarge said, "Give me that son-of-a-bitch's number, willya?" That's a good indication of the mental strength of the average yard bull in those days. I don't know that it's changed much.

Of course, that ended Big Red's wine cellar at that location. But he just moved on. They didn't stop Big Red for long. Funny thing, the bulls must have snapped to his operation. Why didn't they bust him more than they did? I think they kind of liked Big Red. He fit the stereotype of the old, wise convict. You could be comfortable with that stereotype. Red wasn't like the new breed of reformatory punks and dope fiends that were beginning to pollute the joint. Big Red was a guy you could understand; one of the old bunch. I think that the bulls deliberately went out of their way not to bust him. I remember that he and a few like him used to swagger in from the yard or work with maybe a two-gallon hot-water bottle full of booze under their shirt in back, with their coats thrown over it. I'll bet lots of times the bulls knew about this packing and just let Red go on about his business. After all, he wasn't hurting anyone; just kind of keeping the peace, you might say.

Another alcoholic way to get down in the joint was shellac. We used to score a brand called Shellaco from the paint shop. Now, you can't drink shellac straight out of the can; it would kill you. But it can be treated, and if there is a way there's a will inside the joint. The way you make shellac consumable is to take a pine or balsam board and whittle the corners off of it to make it like a paddle. You take the Shellaco and pour it into an empty number 10 can. And you stir and stir and stir until you get a coating formed around the board paddle kind of like a giant Sugar Daddy. By this time the Shellaco has cleared up and all the impurities are in the thick brown crust around the paddle. It is now about 120 proof pure dynamite. I only got into Shellaco once or twice up in the joint, but I still can taste the stuff. And I still can feel the headaches and the hangovers.

There's several varieties of paint and lacquer products that can be treated to be drinkable if you know your stuff. It's kind of like mushrooms. I don't mind eating good mushrooms behind a dude that really knows his business, but one batch of toadstools will take you out of the picture permanently. Same with paint products. If you know your stuff, you can do the thing, but it ain't no place for amateurs. If there's a way to do it though, a con will learn it. Sometimes the hard way, like by getting deathly sick, but he will learn the formula.

Sometimes guys will mess around with stuff that they have no business with. Like, they will try and modify wood alcohol so that it's drinkable. Usually what happens in the joint is that they will get their signals mixed up. And this can be deadly. Usually wood alcohol comes in an unmistakable off-pink color. You've seen it in clinics and hospitals. It's the stuff that thermometers are kept in to sterilize them. A little bit on your tongue won't harm you, but if you drink much of it you may soon stop breathing. I remember one time when some dudes made arrangements for five gallons of supposedly straight grain alcohol to be shipped into the hospital under the guise of wood "pink lady." Only somebody got their signals crossed up and the wrong five-gallon can got opened and consumed by mistake. This happened about five o'clock on New Year's afternoon. By ten that night there were forty-two convicts having serious breathing problems. An immediate warning went out on the prison radio that wood alcohol had been consumed by mistake, and for everyone involved to give themselves up for treatment. The deputy warden even said that no charges would be pressed against the men who gave themselves up for treatment.

As an indication of stupidity, or maybe the absence of trust, in the joint at the time, they found three guys dead in their beds the next morning. About thirty guys spent the next three days walking up and down, up and down, the hospital corridors so they would continue breathing. Two of them guys died walking. That wood alcohol is bad medicine. I'm glad that I was strung out on dexies at that time and passed up the chance to get in on that score. God, I can still remember the smell of all that alcohol that went down the drain when the cons found out it was poison.

I am reminded of the time when we did get in a tremendous supply of very potent grain alcohol and I want to tell the story as an example of how ingenious cons can be when they set up a score. One of the big wheels who worked in the furniture factory knew this ex-con who was now on the bricks and had a job in this supply company that just happened to do some business with Sing Sing. Barney, who pretty much ran things among the inmates in the furniture factory, figured out an almost foolproof method to smuggle in twenty gallons of grain alcohol.

The prison hospital regularly ordered in five gallons of wood alcohol from the supply company. It came in on the same supply truck that brought the weekly order into the furniture factory from the prison distribution warehouse. Barney had this inmate connection in the front office where the manifests were made out. This guy, we'll call him Eddie, was into Barney for a three-hundred-carton gambling debt. So Barney had a big lever under Eddie, you might say. Barney tells him

that he'll forgive half of the debt if Eddie will construct a duplicate manifest showing that the hospital had ordered twenty-five gallons of wood alcohol in. The next move that Barney makes is to contact the ex-con in the supply house where the alcohol originates and have him drop some pink food coloring into twenty-five perfectly good gallons of straight grain alcohol. You beginning to get the picture? This is kind of a little lesson in the "underlife" of the penal institution.

So the fake manifest and the good booze arrive at the warehouse outside the walls. Barney is taking no chances there, either. He has a man owing him who works at putting stuff on the trucks for shipment inside. This guy hides four of the five-gallon tins of alcohol underneath some other supplies, manipulates the manifests back so that the driver shows he has five gallons of wood alcohol for the hospital, and sends the truck into the furniture factory, where Barney is waiting. At just the right time two guys start a diversionary action over in the corner of the furniture shop. You guessed it! Barney has paid them to create a ruckus and take a fall if necessary so that the four tins of straight grain alcohol can be taken off the truck and hidden temporarily under a convenient nearby canvas.

The whole plan came off smooth as Southern Comfort. The joint stayed lit up like a Christmas tree for weeks. And Barney made a mint. I helped him sell a lot of the stuff and took my cut in booze. We took little half-pint jars and filled them about one-third full of alcohol and the rest with cold water. Each of those sold for five dollars or three cartons of butts. We didn't have any trouble doing a land office cash-and-carry business.

Although I was cut off from the outside world when I was in Sing Sing, I adjusted to my time there by getting involved in a lot of "conniving" and scoring. The object was to live as good as possible under the circumstances and to score the goodies such as dope, booze, and extra food as often as possible. In this adaptation, sometimes called "jailing," the emphasis gets placed on satisfactions for the now, and let tomorrow take care of itself. An important thing to take into account I believe is the underlife current of our activity. That is to say, it wasn't only scoring the goodies that motivated many of us into conniving, it was the sort of adventuring that this life makes possible. The constant game to outwit the Man, the elaborate schemes devised in the hustling situations themselves had lots of value for us. It is a style of adjustment, a way of doing time, wherein one is unconscious of the passing of time while caught up in the life. Some do it by playing homosexual games (we will cover this later in the chapter). Some do it by planning elaborate escape attempts. In this case, the planning is often much more important than the potential of getaway because the members of the group get caught up in the whole romantic notion of escape, more or less independently of a desire to leave.

Another very common mode of adjustment in prison is work. The keeper finds a willing slave in many convicts. Daily work, hard, dirty work is welcomed by many as a way of doing time. Some men deliberately seek the most repetitive, monotonous jobs, 'cause they can get into a rut or routine whereby the days pass one by one until they are all x'd off the calendar. I wonder how many people outside are into this style of adjustment. A similar mode of adjustment to doing time is the runner or the weightlifter. The "iron pile" has its many dedicated slaves, who live in the world of "reps" and "lifts" and "presses." Iron is a religion to them, and I've seen guys killed because they lost a race from the mess hall to the yard at noon and still wanted to lift first at a certain station. Some guys work out until they'd make Mr. Universe look like the "before" in those old Charles Atlas ads. It gets to be a real fetish with some, but most styles of adjustment in the joint are overcompensations for the pure boredom of doing nothing but time. I've known studs to play like fifty games of handball a day for years. Their hands get to be like rhino hides, and there ain't nothing that can get them off the handball court. But it's not the handball skills they're after, although they acquired plenty of that; it's time they're killing when they hammer that ball up against the wall at a rate of five million times per long weekend.

Sometimes I think that getting involved in overt racism is a mode of adjustment. I know that all racial problems in prison cannot be explained that simply. Clearly, racism in the joint is merely a reflection of racism in the larger population. But, in prison, I think that many of the "wars" between racial groups resemble the ganging phenomenon of the early fifties as covered in an earlier chapter. It is having something to do, to be involved in, that makes the time pass away. You don't think much about the fact that you might be killed or get hurt bad, you just adjust. And it is easy to hate in the joint. The seeds of hate permeate the concrete and are embedded deep into the steel womb of the walled city. So racism is kind of a natural mode of adjustment there and, in fact, where there is a wide distribution of racial identities within the prison, you would have to work actively against racism to keep it from happening.

Although I really stayed away from that sort of activity during my prison life at Sing Sing, I can come up with one incident that I was involved in that was really weird. There was rumors going around—we didn't know where the rumors were coming from—that the blacks were going to get it on with the Puerto Ricans. That sounded kind of strange to me 'cause we outnumbered every race in there five to one at least. It was mostly Puerto Rican when I was there at Sing Sing. So the rumor sounds very strange, but when you hear it you tend to pay attention. I start looking at every black I encounter and asking myself, what's this nigger up to? And I had some blacks that were talking and dealing acquaintances in the joint, and the tensions started to build between us.

And I'm telling my buddy Raul that we better stick close and have our artillery handy 'cause this whole damn place is going to go up. You could really feel it. Nobody would say anything when you walked out on the yard. It really got freaky. You begin to see more bulls when you're in the yard walking around. And I'm really becoming nervous and scared. When you get this in-gut feeling in the joint, you have nowhere to turn; the Man doesn't smell the danger until it's all over usually, and even if he did he wouldn't do anything about it. That's one thing that you free people ought to realize about life in the joint; the cons are largely on their own within the four walls of their confinement. It's a myth to believe that "social order" is maintained by the Man and his rule book. The reality is that social order is always tenuous—like a single strand of spider web is tenuous—in prison life, and, when social order is maintained it is because the cons in power, those with the moxie, got things in control.

Yeah, I'm really scared. I don't know what is going to happen next. And Raul keeps telling me, "Don't turn your back, Manny. Watch it. You might just be walking in from the yard and they could hit you just because you're Puerto Rican." And he's really building this up in my mind so that I'm beginning to get paranoid. I don't go anywhere unless I'm with a group. I don't care what the bulls tell me, I ain't about to walk around alone. I'm really spaced out, and I start carrying this shiv on me all the time.

But you gotta shower. I mean, you can go just so long without a bath and you gotta have one 'cause you can't stand yourself. Especially if you're used to taking showers almost every day. In the joint the only shower facilities commonly available are communal. When you go in to take a shower, that is a death trap. Once you're in there, they can hit you good and there is no way out. They see you go in and they got a contract out on you, you're in trouble. We used to call the shower the "death waters." It was that bad. You'll be standing in the shower and all of a sudden around your feet the water will turn red, and you realize that it's your blood that's coloring the water.

I know from personal experience, 'cause I got caught in the death trap once. This morning, I went in to take a shower with Raul. I take my shank in there with me wrapped in a towel. And the main shower room is gigantic, with all these pipes hanging down. When lots of guys are showering, the steam rises up and envelops everything and you can't see three feet in front of you.

They have this shelf above you where you put your towel and clothes. As I step in the water I put my shank up on the shelf under my towel. I'm soaping myself down when I hear Raul scream. I reach frantically for my shank and I get hit. I feel something sharp go in me and I grab onto this hot pipe to keep from going down, but I go down anyway. And I think that it's all over for me. 'Cause I'm down and vulnerable. I mean, I know inside that they can finish me off. I black out, thinking to myself, Good-by, world, I did the best I could under the circumstances.

The next thing I know, I wake up in the hospital ward. I got hit with an ice pick, they're telling me. Was I glad to hear that the wound wasn't fatal! I had lost a lot of blood, but it wasn't really a bad wound. I was real worried about Raul, so I'm asking about Raul but nobody's talking. I think that perhaps he got wasted. A couple of days later, I got out of the hospital and find out that nothing at all happened to Raul. I can't understand that, 'cause I know that he was as set up in that shower as I was. I mean, Raul didn't even take his shank into the shower with him, and here he's not hit. It don't make sense. 'Cause, if I got hit, they'd have to get past Raul to get to me. He was in the shower in front of me next to the door. And he ain't hit; I want to know why.

So I go to him and I ask what came down, what happened? And I can't get two straight words out of him. I think maybe he don't want to talk for fear of reprisals, but that don't make sense. Here his homeboy got shafted; he should be as mad as a buzzard at them spooks. I ask around my own people for what happened, and nobody's talking. Nobody knows anything at all. No wonder that I get this queasy feeling in my gut that something shitty is going on. I know I got to find out to survive, so I take the bull by the horns so to speak and get downright mad. I do the only thing left for me to do. If I can't get the straight skinny from my own people, I'll have to get it from the blacks.

They had this small black militant organization there that was mainly political. They didn't get into fighting much, but were more philosophical. This was about 1963, and black power and the politicalization of the prisoner was getting a good start in Sing Sing. Later, a lot of those guys would wind up in

Attica, and you know the results of that story. But I talked to one of those dudes that I'd known earlier on the streets. And I said to him, "You know what? I can't get no word on why some of the blacks here are down on me, and I gotta know. I want to know why me? I never had anything against you people before. The only thing I ever did was shoot some dope that I got off some black dealers by hook or crook. Man, that ain't no capital offense, especially in this here joint!"

And he said, "You know what? Maybe your own people won't tell you what came down, but I'll tell it to you straight. You weren't hit because you are a Spic. Man, you weren't stabbed because of any racial number. You got hit behind dope, baby!"

"Say, man. You're as full of shit as a Christmas turkey. I never sold any scag to any nigger in the first place." I got really hot!

Then he lays this story on me that he got from Raul. Raul had spread it around that I'd said we were not going to sell any of our dope to niggers. The thing was that this was mainly true. I did say it, but it was the kind of statement that you can't take out of context. Me and Raul were sitting around bagging up the dope and he says, "Well, Manny, we're just going to sell this dope to Puerto Rican brothers."

I say, "Yeah, and screw the niggers and the whites. Let them score their own dope." But, you see, when Raul told that out of context to some of his black friends, it sounded real bad of me to say it. And so I got hit behind that statement. That was the end of me and Raul's friendship.

I could see clearly now how Raul had tried to cover the whole thing up by running down all the week before this shit about a coming race war. He was trying to cover up his slip of the tongue. In other words, Raul had inadvertently finked on me and got me drove up tight with the blacks. And rather than hanging in tight and fessing up to his slip, he'd dug himself in deeper and deeper.

I felt really bad about the whole thing, 'cause I'd thought that we were so tight that nothing could come between us. I hadn't done nothing to Raul, and here he'd almost set me up to be killed, just to keep his image straight and his shit together. I mean, those blacks could just as well have wasted me in the shower. I got out of it by some kind of a miracle. And all my friends were telling me that I had to do something to Raul to get even, and more importantly, to show that I was not chickenshit. I mean, this is a big thing in the joint. You get hit, and you hit back. Or you get a name for being yellow.

But I just couldn't do it. I couldn't waste Raul even if he had put me in the middle. After all, he'd been good to me when I was a fish, and had clued me into the whole ball game when I'd first come in. I wasn't willing to forgive, and I wanted to stay close to the convict code, but I just couldn't bring myself to hit him. Some of my friends kind of edged away from me 'cause they thought I was soft—that I should have taken care of business. But I stayed in there and didn't go soft in other areas so the whole thing worked out in time. But I never had much to do with Raul again. I felt that we could never be tight 'cause I couldn't really trust the guy. It was more than a matter of friendship. I guess you can forgive a friend a time or two, but in the joint it isn't the same. I mean, you have to trust your friends with your life—literally. When you're tight with a guy in the joint, you're wide open, and you just can't afford to take friendship lightly. Raul had set me up, and then he'd gone ahead and complicated matters by not straightening it out with the blacks. So, after that we hardly ever talked. If I saw him in the yard, I might nod for old times' sake, but when he'd try and get close again, I'd let him know that there was no chance.

I should of known anyway. You see, Raul was a classic example of the dope fiend mentality. You can't trust a dope fiend. Man, I can't tell you that too many times. You can't trust dope fiends! Well, Raul had done me wrong, but if it wasn't for

him the cons would have downed
me when I first came to the joint. I
was young and naive and I didn't
know a damn thing. The only thing
I had going for me was a kind of
toughness. Like, I was as hard as
steel rivets and as tough as a Bronx
alley cat. I'd get down in a minute
and fight right away. But I was
small. If you hassled me, fuck you;
'cause you were going to have to
whip me in those days. But Raul
wised me up and showed me how
to get into the fun and games of
being a convict. He taught me the
ropes of conniving, of hustling. He
wised me up to the convict code,
and how to get by on a day-to-day
basis.

It's important to be
a man in the joint . . .

And I remember that I seen Raul
in the streets afterward, but I never
stopped to rap with him. I never
even confronted him with the incident. It was almost as if Raul ceased
to exist as far as I was concerned.
Or, that's the way I'd like it to be.
'Cause it always bothered me; maybe it still does after all these years.
It hurt 'cause I thought we were
really close. See, when you're a
dope fiend and you let down your
defenses even for a minute. . . . I
forgot that Raul was a dope fiend.
To me Raul was a pal and a buddy
in the joint. He saved my life when

I came in. We hustled together and
scored dope together. So I let down
my defenses and became really
human toward the guy, and I
got screwed.

When you're a dope fiend there's
no rules, no regulations, no system
of buddy-buddy or friendship that
counts. He did what he had to do at
the time, and he thought it was right.
And at the time, it was right for him
because he was a dope fiend. He
thought like a dope fiend and the
cardinal idea here is to hustle who
you have to and get by, so long as
you can keep scoring. Dope fiends
are always conning each other. And
they got this thing about "honor
among thieves" on the surface.
They'll verbalize to each other how
righteous they are. And how they'd
never fink or stand between their
buddy and a score. And I believed
this bullshit in my relationship with
Raul. I really believed that it wasn't
a con. I thought he was my tight
partner and then the play with the
blacks comes down and I go to the
hospital behind it. That scene just
proved to me what I'd really always
known—that all dope fiends are rats.
They are no fucking good. A dope
fiend is really weak morally, really
weak. When it comes to heroin, anybody's weak. Nobody can really
hold their mud when they get around
smack. If they're a little bit strong
when they're off stuff, when they
get around it again they fall apart.
And the same thing that happened
to me in the joint happens all the
time in the streets. Don't ever trust

any dope fiend; they'll turn on you every time for a five-dollar fix.

It's really important to "be a man" in the joint. There's convicts and "people" in the joint who are into doing time and get by, and then there's your square Johns, your sexual, your disorganized fuck-ups, and your rats, stoolies, and all them. Most people think that the dope fiend fits solidly among the righteous brothers who refer to themselves as "people" doing time. But in my book he don't really fit in the same category. He only makes himself "people" so long as his front holds together—so long as he has good connections that allow him to hustle bread and dope. When a dope fiend's front breaks down, it reveals him for what he is —a punk, a fink, or a fuck-up. Whatever it takes to score—he is.

It's important to be a man in the joint, to let folks know that you're really "people." I remember the time I burned a cat's cell up just to prove that very thing. That was my first experience at being a man in the joint. It was right after I'd met Raul and he'd wised me up to how to get around. I'd started in doing a little gambling as the opportunity came about. We'd gather behind one of the cellblocks or in a cell down near the end of the tier, where we could get out and around the other side if the Man started down from the front. We'd get six

or eight of us in there and play poker for cigarettes. Again, I found myself always winning. I had very good card sense, and more than that, I had the patience to wait out a bad run of cards. Lots of cats in the joint can't do this. I mean, they got to get right out front and try to make their cards come—try and make even lousy hands stand up. I just played the odds and handled the good cards right when they came my way.

One day we were in this good game and I won this guy for five boxes of butts. He says that he'll give them to me next Saturday, when he goes after his canteen draw. I don't think nothing about it 'cause you're always taking markers in the joint. You do a lot of business from week to week and month to month. After all, nobody's going anywhere, usually. Most of the time debts get settled up on canteen day. So I'm in the canteen line about to draw some supplies myself when this dude that owes me from the game comes by with his box loaded with candy and household items. I don't see my butts and I think that maybe he has them coming from someone else on the tier. But I don't want to let it go, so I get a buddy to hold my place in line and I run after him and say, "Hey, where is my five boxes of smokes?"

He says, "Screw you, bastard, I ain't paying you nothing, punk!" And I just stand there with my mouth open. Like, I wasn't expecting it at all, since I considered it a legitimate debt. I mean, in the streets if I'd won some bucks off a dude and taken a marker, when the note came up, I'd expect to be paid. Same right now. I don't know what to do. There's bulls standing around real prominent during canteen, so it don't make sense to hit the dude right here. I'm really foaming. I go back to my cell and sit on the edge of the bed really steaming, and I don't know what to do. It isn't so much the butts now, it's the way he tossed me off like I'm nothing but shit. It's clear what he's doing. Like, he's not going to pay me because he doesn't think I can do anything about it.

Raul comes and he says, "Manny, this is it! You gotta do something." He didn't even see the scene come down, and I hadn't had a chance to tell him about it, but the word had already got all around the joint. It had gone out on the grapevine that fast. I was made a punk, that's what he did to me. Raul says, "You gotta end this thing, and you gotta do it now." I'm so mad I could kill the guy and I tell Raul that I'm going to the plant for my shiv.

But Raul says, "Wise up, man. You can't get yourself in a jam. If you hit him you're so mad right now that you'd do it right out in the open, and then you've bought it. No use wasting yourself for that scum. Think of something."

And the first thing that crossed my mind was a burnout. "Lets burn the son-of-a-bitch out, Raul. I'll burn his house." That'd do it. He

was the type of dude that really took pride in his house. He had a red carpet, and one wall was painted brown with the other two white. It made the cell look longer. And he had pictures hung around. I'd thought he was a punk when I'd first met him, because he was so weird looking and he kept his house done so nice.

Once I decide to burn his house the rest is easy. I get down to the paint shop by falling into a work detail going that way. For a box of butts I buy this can of paint thinner. I walk right across the yard to the cellblock with this thinner. I thought, What the fuck, there's no other way to do it. And I got by 'cause the bulls were busy doing other things and didn't have the time or the desire to hassle me. This dude's cell was up on the third tier and I ask Raul if he's coming with me.

He says, "No, man. This is your beef. You handle it the best way possible. You have to do it. If you don't do it now, you're shit. You're all by yourself. If you don't do the job, the cons will run right over you. You may even get turned out and made a punk. You've got to stand up."

I remember thinking to myself, Some friend Raul is. He won't even stand point for me. But I pass it off and go on up to the third tier. Lucky for the dude his cell door is open. He's living in the last cell down on the end of the tier. And he's at his sink washing his face. I just stand there and put the bucket of thinner down on the tier, take out a book of paper matches, light them all, and throw them on his bunk. All this time he's just washing his face, not knowing that he's about to get it good. I pick up the thinner and throw it, not directly on him, but on his bunk. And like the whole cell erupts in flame. I have to jump back to keep from being burned. He comes running out of there screaming.

I'm standing there enjoying it all and the bull comes running from around the cellblock and throws me down on the tier. I say, "What the hell happened? His house is on fire!" Well, I go right from there to the hole. I'm in the growler forty-five days. They didn't have anything on me, 'cause nobody had seen me do anything. And the dude is afraid to rat on me 'cause he knows now that I got some power. But they keep me there for a spell 'cause they know I did it, even if they can't prove it. In the joint, they don't have to prove anything. You're guilty until you prove your innocence. And that's never, if they want to hold you. There's no way you can beat the deputy warden if he wants to keep you locked up. He just does it. And if the court process resembles a little bit the courts on the outside, that's merely coincidental. Courts in the joint are worse than in the military. You have no rights at all. No chance to

prove your noninvolvement. If they say you were involved, you were for all practical purposes involved. And the joint bulls constantly mess over you if you are a hustler, if you are "people." You may get by, you may skate for a while, but sooner or later the Man is going to get his pound of flesh. Bet on it!

All the time I was in the hole on that beef the toilet never worked once. So I spent a lot of time holding it. You don't want to take a crap or even urinate because the stench is so bad it makes you sick. What I used to do a lot was sit in front of one wall and give the walls names, girls' names. I spent so much time in the hole because I was so small and had to be rowdy to survive. I guess I got kind of dingy when I was in the growler. I used to sit and talk to each wall like they were girls I had known, or girls I'd like to get to know intimately. I would mentally caress them, argue with them, tell jokes, and sing. I would literally go berserk. When they'd let me out of the hole I'd be so spaced out that a buddy would have to take care of me for a day or so until I'd got my bearings.

When I got out of the hole this time, the dude who I'd burned out was over to my cell in less than an hour with my five cartons of cigarettes. He doesn't say a word; he just drops the butts on the end of my bed and walks away. But I'd got the job done. From that day on all the people knew that if you hurt Manny, he's going to hurt you. I could say now, looking back on it, that I became a man through that experience. I built my rep. It was kind of like a rite of passage, not deliberately set up by anyone, but the kind of initiation ceremony that naturally arises in the joint. I proved to everybody that I would stand up for what was mine. Inside myself, too, I underwent real changes during that experience. I realized that I'd have done it again if necessary, and that it didn't make a hell of a lot of difference if the door had of been on deadlock so the guy couldn't get out when I threw the matches and the thinner on his bunk. In other words, one of the criteria for passing into the ranks of "people" is knowing inside yourself that you're committed to the code. And an important, cardinal item at the head of the code is "death before dishonor." In another way of speaking, that can be interpreted: the good con is willing to "go all the way" when necessary to avoid disgrace.

In that respect as in many others, the joint didn't differ that much from the streets. When I was in the streets, the only people I'd hung out with were dope fiends and armed robbers. If you were an armed robber (a gunsel or a heist man) and a doper, we had something in common. If you were just an armed robber I wouldn't hang out with you, but if you were robbing behind dope, we shared common interests all the way. I knew some safe men, burglars and the like, casually, but I never ran with them. They had their own crowd and their shared creed. In the joint it's the same thing. You have your cliques and mine was the dope fiend world. Most of the people there who were not into drugs stayed away from our group. They knew that a dope fiend is no good, that in the final analysis when the heavy number comes down you can't trust a doper.

I really learned a lot of stuff that I could use in the streets from my life in Sing Sing. Like, how you can make people by how they look and act. I mean, when you ask a dude a question or two you can make him, you can find out where he's at. Like, cons develop this extra sense, a form of silent communication, a sense that informs you when a guy is right or wrong, especially when he is wrong. And you learn to act on that information, 'cause if you don't you get burned. And getting burned a time or two is enough. I learned how to improve my trade of armed robbery, too. We used to sit around for hours at a time and rap about capering. A kid can come into the joint green and go out knowing a lot about taking care of business.

It works both ways, though. Like, you bring a lot of knowledge into the joint about hustling and jiving, and you make that work for you, too. For example, Raul and I had the sandwich concession in several cellblocks for a long time. Our activities were highly organized and involved a network of well-understood responsibilities. One of us always worked in the kitchen, helping out on the steam tables and doing some fry cooking. We had access to a lot of food, some of which we'd steal when the man had his back turned, and some of which we'd buy off of cons in charge of commissary stores. This procuring process linked up with our gambling activities. For example, we'd always let one of the commissary people into our card game and if he got hooked bad, who cared? 'Cause we always knew that he was good for it in supplies from the commissary.

Anyway, we'd get ahold of all kinds of stuff like roast beef, ham, cheese, pork, hamburger, and the garnishes. We'd make up from fifty to two hundred sandwiches a day—in some joints they call them "lumps"—and sell them for from two to five packs of butts apiece, depending on what was in them. Business was good, especially after a bad evening meal like stew or beans, and that was usually about five times a week. Funny thing, the cons would seldom bitch at our racket, and the food was theirs to start with. We'd be getting ahold of chow that was supposed to end up on the mainline.

Sometimes it was tough getting the lumps out of the kitchen area, but we always had a way. Usually, when the heat wasn't on, Raul would just load up the bottom of a garbage can with lumps and it would be set downstairs with the rest of the trash near the vegetable room. We tipped the con in charge of picking up the cans and hauling them to a central disposal area. He dropped off our can in the trash area of the paint shop, where I worked for a long time. I'd just put them in with my stuff and head for my usual job in one of the cellblocks. They were forever painting the cells and the walls in the cell blocks. I mean, my cell area was painted six times in three years. They were always painting that place. It was all part of the game. Make the outside look nice for the visitors and the important studs up from Albany, and it don't matter a damn what the guts is like. They were always having guided tours. It was funny, because if they knew a few days in advance when some important dudes were coming through they'd have us out painting and scrubbing like hell. Sometimes they'd even issue new clothes and blankets in those areas where the tour was coming through. They'd have cons out manicuring the lawns, planting flowers, washing the streets and sidewalks. Folks would come through and exclaim, "How nice and orderly they have this place." But it was nice for us 'cause when visitors were around there was lots of roast beef and ham and stuff like that on the menu—more for us to steal.

On a good day I'd paint like hell and maybe sell fifty sandwiches. Sometimes for a steak sandwich I'd get as much as a carton of butts. I'd just tool around to my locker and drop off my cigarettes and distribute them later. You were never supposed to have over two cartons of cigarettes in your possession. But they seldom checked you out on this. At the peak of my conniving business life in Sing Sing, I had maybe fifteen hundred cartons of cigarettes. I had guys all over the joint holding on to butts for me. And I never lost a pack, either! After I burned that cat out for bum-paying me, I had a rep that wouldn't quit, and people dealt honestly with me, as I did with them.

Why didn't we get busted doing all that hustling and jiving? 'Cause, among other things, we had one or two bulls on the take. We paid them to look the other way. We paid them off in both cigarettes and cash. When I was in Sing Sing, cigarettes were going for a dollar and a half a carton, sometimes only a dollar a carton depending on the supply of money inside. The bulls that were taking from us were each getting on the average of forty-five bucks a month to mind their own business. And the thing is, when you have one bull bribed in a joint, usually you have several bribed. 'Cause when this kind of collusion exists, the bulls have their territory well marked out—although covertly. So, other bulls know that Manny and Raul are paying off and are supposed to be let alone. There's all kinds of this kind of fun and games in prison. I've even seen several transactions where some sweet little fish kid is transferred to an old-timer jock's cell for maybe a hundred bucks placed in the right officer's hand.

You see, the prison organization corrupts—bulls and cons alike. You may get this innocent, gung ho rookie guard fresh in out of junior college training. He's going to rid the world of corruption and inefficiency single-handed. But it usually don't take the fish bull any longer to wise up than it does the fish con. When they look around and see that everybody else is playing games, they soon get into it. Sometimes you start a guard on the take by working on his sympathy. We used to start them by getting them to take a letter out to a sick relative or to our "kid who's living with some other old man and who we're not allowed to communicate with." If you get them on the take once, then you usually can put the blocks on them and get them involved in more serious things. Sometimes you get a bull who just wants to make bread and will bring in dope and whiskey right off the bat.

But Raul took care of most of that stuff, I never got very involved in bribery or actual contact with the bulls. I was too young and had too much heart. I was too crazy and too new a con. I didn't want to have any truck with the bulls, even to deal with them. That wasn't my idea of doing time. I never really got into any of the brain things in the joint, but I survived, mostly on toughness and willingness to do anything. I survived in the joint much like I'd survived in the streets. I used the same tactics, there was nothing substantially different.

In the joint I knew who had the pills and the dope, just like on the bricks. All I was interested in really was drugs. And the joint really helped me sustain my drug identity. I was forever in the morning pill line. Every day I'd go in with a new complaint. I used to go to the library and study up on symptoms. I guess I'm an expert "symptomologist." I was a habitual sickie. I knew all the names and places to throw at them, and it really worked. If you wanted to stay loaded, or stay like a zombie, they gave you the pills. Like, for a long time I walked around just bouncing off the walls. I bet I took more Thorazine and Melorell in that three years than they got in the average sickbay.

They were forever sending me to see some nut doctor. When I got out of the hole the second time they sent me to the shrink and he ran all these tests on me. They were always telling me that I was too nervous, that I had to calm down. And I would say, "Yeah, well, if you were in my situation you'd be tensed up, too. You people got me living in a cage that ain't fit for a dog. I can't eat decent; I can't have sex; I'm mad. Of course I'm tensed up. If a con ain't tensed up in here, that's when you ought to be shrinking his head."

So they said, "That's all right, Manny. We'll give you something for your nerves." Hell, yes! Gimme it. I'll take it. I knew it was a narcotic. I said, okay put me on it, and they stuck me with the Thorazine trip. God! I was totally out of it for weeks! I couldn't take care of business, wasn't reliable at all. And Raul tried like hell to get me off that Thorazine, but I'd just stand around with my mouth open dripping spit and totally out of it. One thing about it! The Thorazine number makes the time go by; you don't know one day from another. I finally got off that trip, 'cause Thorazine wears on your inner man after a while and either you succumb totally to it or you kick. But going on that pill line day after day for weeks, I met a lot of guys who I could buy different kinds of stuff from. Lots of cats go on the pill line to get stuff to sell. It's easy to do. You just take it from the doctor when he sticks it under your tongue and you pretend to swallow. Sometimes a con'll want to save up enough pills to get a real high on, and he might go on the sick line for twenty or thirty days, just collecting enough stuff to really get down.

The problem with pills is that they make you stupid and real lazy, especially those reds. Like, I would end up buying ten reds off of some con who was collecting them to pay off a debt, and I'd take them all at once. I'd get really flipped out. Like, I'd stagger around running into walls and doing crazy things until usually I'd get into a fight or something.

It was in Sing Sing that my whole experience with speed started. It was during a time when heroin was impossible to score and even pruno was tight because the Man was constantly on the prowl. One day Raul came up to me in the yard and said, "Hey, Manny, you want to get loaded?"

Raul says, "Have you ever used speed?"

"Hey, Raul, you're kidding. That shit's a bummer. I don't want any more crazy trips after the Thorazine bit."

But Raul says, "It ain't like that, Manny. This is good shit. Besides, there's nothing else around; it's either bennie, baby, or not at all." So he takes an inhaler and breaks off the top and cuts the blotterlike stuff up into little pieces. It smells terrible, and you wonder if you can down the stuff.

But before long it really gets good to you. I started taking bennies and I got so damn wired I couldn't believe it. I'd take out one of my "fuck books" from under my mattress and begin to scan the pictures. Do you know that the joint turns a perfectly respectable sex drive into one form of perversion or another? You got no legitimate outlet at a time like this so you get a *Penthouse,* or even a *Sunshine and Health,* and begin to make believe. Well, on Benzedrine you got a problem. You still got lots of desire, but you can't get enough action. I mean, I get this dirty book out and I start masturbating behind this beautiful centerfold number. I almost am able to conjure up her physical presence in the cell I'm so high on speed. And my heart's going a mile a minute; so's my hand. I wasted myself all night behind the same vision, I mean all that night with this book. I had all kinds of imaginations and visual perversions running through my mind, but I couldn't get it off at all; there was never any climax. By morning my whole crotch area was sore and bleeding, and I was bone-raped; so tired! I'm supposed to go to work, but I'm all spaced out. It was like I was really tired in a way, but mentally I was superalert. And I move up to Raul in the yard and say, "Hey, old buddy, give me some more of that stuff. I really dig it."

And for a while I was committed to speed. I started to look all over for it and buy up a supply, 'cause I had plenty of money and cigarettes. I put the word out that I'd buy all the Benzedrine available, and pretty soon I was floating in the stuff 'cause it was coming into the joint a hundred tubes at a time. Soon I'm going nuts I'm downing so much speed. But that's the way a dope fiend is. When he finds a new kick he's going to go all out. Moderation is a word that's erased from a doper's dictionary. It got so bad with me and speed that I landed in the hospital all spaced out. I went three weeks once without sleep. Now, I might have dozed or been asleep walking. But not for long. I never slept in any way, shape, or form for three weeks. And I got down to skin and bones. A speed freak don't eat; he don't sleep; he just sails. Jack off and talk, jack off and talk. That's two things a speed freak does all the time.

It was outrageous. I was really wired up behind the stuff. And you know what saved me? It was that a load of heroin came in! You'll leave anything for heroin if you've once had it. And one day Raul, my savior, says, "What'ya know, old buddy, I just scored some scag!"

He pieces me off a paper and I get it into my vein and I'm off again on another wild, beautiful, soft heroin run that lasts until the supply runs dry about three months later. And I swear off speed forever, 'cause when you're privy to Miss Heroin's charms nothing else in God's whole green world is good enough to match her. Of course, I have a bout or two with speed again, but that is much later in life.

People are always asking me about sex in prison. A current myth about prison life, probably coming from our Freudian outlook, is that homosexuality is widespread and running rampant in prison—that it influences every aspect of the male prisoner's life. It is not that simple. Many cons never play any sexual games in prison. Sometimes the inmate identity is almost nonsexual by nature of the experience. Some lead a monastic life, and for them the prison becomes a monastery where they read, contemplate, and pray. But, overall, there is no standard sexual orientation to prison life. In fact, guys like us used to deliberately steer clear of sexual traps in the joint. I never had any sex life at all, extending beyond myself, that is. I was too busy with drugs and with the accompanying hustle to bother about getting into homosexuality. I had it offered up on a plate more than once—pretty little gay boys shaking their tail in my face 'cause they know that I got bread.

I don't want to lead you astray. I'm not saying that there is no sexual activity in prison; that's not so. I would guess that about 30 percent of the population in the joint is into some style of homosexual adjustment on a regular basis. Maybe another 20 percent get involved in a jock or a gay trip once or twice during their stay. But fully 50 percent, as a best guess based on several years' observation in joints east to west, stay clear of sexual activity for several reasons. Some don't like any thought of homosexuality; some believe in hell as the fruits of that kind of lustful license; most of the guys were like I was, just far too busy to get involved and to risk getting busted behind homosexual games.

Prison can be the spawning bed of homosexual behavior, however. Especially for the young, tender, first-timer. If you're young and cute and naive, you're going to get hit on for somebody, make no mistake about it. And in this sense the atmosphere of homosexuality affects every con. Although most of us never participated in homosexuality, the gay life affected us all. I mean, except for masturbation, the only sex possible in prison is homosexuality and so the fruiters and the gays and the jockers are very visible for all to see. Their behavior tends to stereotype all convict life in the eyes of guards and outsiders. Thus, in a sense, the homosexuality of the few becomes the standard that we all have to live by in one way or another.

For example, you can't even have a close friend who you really care for without rumors getting around that you're in love or that one of you are putting out body. This happened with me and Raul during our partnership in the joint. And we were only tending to business, just hustling and jiving our way

along trying to survive. But guys kind of accused us of flip-flopping and all that. It was sort of a joke, but when do you tell the difference between joking and derogation? In the joint you're going to have your manhood questioned from time to time, one way or another. You may even have to go to the wall with shivs or table legs with some dude that wants to use you sexually.

In prison you get to thinking about your masculinity . . .

You know what? In prison you get to thinking about your masculinity, whether you will still have it with broads after doing a long stretch. What's more, with all the sexual activity that does go on around you, it begins to eat at your mind. I've seen more than one sexually square dude go fruity as a bunch of grapes because, after years of trying to hold onto a heterosexual image of himself in a homo-holed prison, he loses the vision of ever making it with a sister again. A lot of anxiety in the joint is caused by the lack of good, sharp, female visual images. Most of the time when they let a female come on the interior staff of a prison, like as a guard or a teacher, she looks like a cross between Rosie Greer and a gandy dancer—or she just finished a stretch of seventeen years as matron on the Syracuse police force.

___

Although the majority of the cons in prison don't get very involved in homosexuality, those that do are very visible. There are several main styles of homosexual adjustment. The jocker-commissary punk arrangement is probably the most common. Jockers are also referred to in the joint as "daddies," "studs," the "old man," and "jockos." I seldom met one who wasn't a conceited son-of-a-bitch and a taker. Lots of times jockers are ex-punks who have got a lot of muscle lifting iron and are a little con-wise from being overlong in the joint. There's a saying in prison: "What's good for the goose is good for the gander." Or, "If you'll dive in a bush, you'll climb on a limb." It means that if you'll go one way, chances are you'll go another. Some hep cons see the jocker as being as weak as his punk. But their outward appearance is one of toughness and savvy. Jocks are the very physical homosexuals who dominate and predict sexual life in prison. The old man plays the active role in the "household" and is viewed as the aggressor in sexual relations, with the punk either the acquiescent partner or the rape victim.

The commissary punk is the most common feminine figure in the joint. Most likely he is a young,

"pretty," naive, and inexperienced inmate who is cajoled, forced, or socialized into homosexuality by an older, wiser con—who in all likelihood has taken the role of jocker before. The commissary punk "goes" for two main reasons: either for protection from other "wolves" or for material goods. The punk, or kid, will be approached and propositioned by a jocker; either he will comply immediately or refuse. If he refuses, chances are he will be severely beaten and threatened with further physical and mental punishment.

For example, when a young, good-looking fish comes into the joint everybody knows about it right away. He hasn't hardly got time to lay down on his bunk in the Admissions and Orientation Unit until one of the local daddies is working on him. Maybe the kid will come back from dinner and find a carton of butts and a case of female Hershey bars laying on the end of his bunk. Man, shit, he'll think. Who do I know in here? And his mind will wander back over all the county jail time and reformatory time he's done trying to zero in on some buddy who might be here in the prison and taking care of him.

Poor kid! In a little while he looks up and there's this stud leaning up against the bars with a shit-eating grin on his face. By this time the kid has consumed several of the candy bars and is chain-smoking the cigarettes. "Hey kid," says old jocko, "you take care of me, I take care of you! You know what I mean? Now, I'm going to send my runner up here with some more goodies that will make your fish-tank time easier to do. What about that!"

Maybe the kid snaps right away to what's coming down. And maybe he don't like any part of it. He might even tell the jock, "Go get fucked, you bastard! I'm not about to turn out. You picked on the wrong guy. I'm not pussy!"

On the whole, it's very difficult for a young, handsome inmate to never go through this trial by ordeal, and many will be seduced into compliance one way or another—by bribery or force, or both. Race, creed, or color makes no difference, and wealth is not a deciding factor either. What determines the strength and bravery of these males is their past history and present motivations. If a punk desires material goods bad enough, and has no legitimate possibilities for obtaining them, he will often give in and go along with the program. If he doesn't need goods, or doesn't want them bad enough to compromise, he might be able to stand up against the pressure and survive without undergoing sexual assault. Of course, sometimes a kid is forcibly raped or gang-shagged by three or four roving jocks, and at that time the kid is likely to be tagged as a possible sexual partner and will have to deal with future jocks who are looking for sexual fulfillment. Often a kid will just

get weary fighting off the physical and mental assaults of various jockers and be very willing to succumb to the protection of the least reprehensible one.

Queens are the feminine males, sometimes evolving from the kid role. Although queens are rarely transvestites, they are considered to be "she's," "girls," "bitches," "broads," or "ladies." They are outwardly feminine in appearance and mannerism, and to some various extent tend to have a psychological set toward femininity. They shack, up, fall in love, get married (to jockers), become wives, and exhibit jealousy. In fact, I've seen more than one killing by a jealous bitch who eagerly resorted to violence in an attempt to stop another queen from taking over "her" old man.

After you been in the joint a while, some of them boss bitches really get to resemble women. Jockers and queens are often involved in a genuine love relationship. Sometimes they get it on in a real tight one-to-one relationship and connive their way into a double cell. They then can carry on much like any happily married couple. Most joints will even allow this. I've seen them with tablecloths, curtains, bedspreads, and the whole bag. The old lady keeps house while the old man hustles the living.

In the homosexual life of the joint, the pervert or fag is considered to be at the end of the line. Sometimes guards are identified as perverts. I remember this guard who got caught "going down" on a young con in the middle of the night. Needless to say, the guard never came back inside the joint. But surprisingly enough he didn't lose his job. They just put him out on the hog ranch with a couple of convict perverts. I guess they figured that they could all go around together out there in one big daisy chain if they wanted to.

Perverts, like queens, are considered by the cons to be "natural" in their roles. Usually the faggot is an older con, completely socialized and satisfied in prison life. They are often very secretive and withdrawn. I never did trust a faggot because I've never known one who would not rat or fink under pressure. They are just weak in every dimension of their character. It takes little or no coercing to get them to "go." Often the pervert pays young kids to let them practice fellatio on him. Mother! Perk up and take notice; this is what your nice young boy is going into if the state is going to take him in hand and "rehabilitate" him. There is the possibility of living "hell" in prison, but no redemption. Redemption may come in spite of the prison experience but not because of it!

Almost all homosexuals, both jockers and punks, are the result of being made that way inside the joint. A few are that way on the bricks, especially queens, but not many. Usually the guards and administration know what's going on, but they often refrain from taking preventive measures 'cause they have some kind of stake in the inmate structure remaining essentially the same, or they just plain don't give a damn. Although all inmates have the name, many of them do not play the game. They handle their own sexual problems privately, either by masturbation or by total abstinence, 'cause it's cheaper, safer, and, the moral self-degradation can be ignored if not put out of sight.

I remember when I went to the parole board at Sing Sing. That was a laugh, or maybe on second thought, a screaming cry! It was funny standing outside the board room waiting to go in, 'cause I knew all along that they wasn't about to let me go. By law, I have to go before the board within a statutory time limit, but I knew that they were merely fulfilling the letter of the law. They should have saved the State of New York the money.

But even at that, when you get ready to go in and face the men that hold several years of your life in hand, you have a little glimmer of just maybe. . . . Yeah, like all the time I'm waiting, all the months before, I'm not getting any hopes up. I'm not talking about my board date with anybody. I tell myself over and over again, If they are going to down you, why even think about it.

But on the day of my appearance I have a little glimmer of hope. I get on my best threads, slick down my hair, shave, and all that. I think that I look like a million bucks. So I walk into the hearing room and the first thing that the chairman says to me is, "You know, Torres, you are an asshole!" I mean, that shattered me; I slumped in my chair absolutely defeated. Here I'd been playing the dozens with a bunch of ragtagged cons for the last two years and I gotta come before the official representatives of the State of New York to hear myself rectally described. I expected something from them, but not this.

And they started running their rap on me. I was in the boardroom for over a half an hour and the whole time they capped on me like I was a mangy dog. Like, telling me that I had no sense; that from the moment I'd got to the joint I'd been in constant trouble. They say that I think I'm one of them "New York gangsters." They think that I'm just an asshole, a Puerto Rican bum. They're telling me I'd fucked over my family, fucked over my friends, and screwed everyone in sight. "You're a dope fiend, and we're sorry that we can only keep you for three years! If I had any choice, Torres, I'd never let you out of this place."

He's running all this down to me like I'm a scurvy rapo dog. And I'm getting white-hot inside and sitting stiller and stiller in my chair. And he pulls out this file on me that has all the write-ups on me from since I was in the sixth grade. Every time I got a write-up, every time I went to the hole—he made me explain it. And in his mind I was absolutely guilty regardless of what my story was. I was really put down. They tried to make me eat crow right in front of them like they do everybody if they want a parole. I just got to the point where I told them, "You know what? Screw yourselves, all of you bastards. You're full of it! You crazy bastards wouldn't know the truth if you were hit with a pan of it. The most you can keep me here is for another year and a half. And I can do that in the hole standing on my head in the crapper. I was sentenced to just three years, and you people are not playing with my mind any longer. You call me an asshole? You and your like are the real assholes!" I felt like the world's first political prisoner.

The next thing I know two bulls have got me by the collar. The parole board had pushed the panic button on me and in run these two bulls and I'm on my way to the growler again. I didn't give a retail damn about the whole thing. It made me feel good inside, like a shot of Maalox on an ulcer, just to tell them what I thought of their whole lousy system. Maybe I wasn't going home now, but they couldn't do anything more to me. My top was three years and it would be up in not even a year and a half. It's like you and they live in two different worlds. There's no way you can communicate. I mean, they don't know anything about survival in your world. They're lost in the clouds of pseudo-legality and all the corrections rhetoric that ain't where it's happening at all.

While I was never in a real all-out prison riot, I was involved in a number of food strikes and minor skirmishes, especially in the hole. Rioting can be expected in prison. Convicts riot for the same reason any oppressed people riot. They riot because they want a stake in their existence. Is this a wholly unreasonable want, or need, or desire on their part? It certainly is in the prison system, as I experienced it. Prisons are not about treatment, they are about custody, prisons are not about rehabilitation, they are about repayment, they are not about reintegration, they are about punishment. Given, then, that prisons are about custody, about holding the inmate for an arbitrary term of years until payment for his crime has been exacted, about physically and mentally punishing the individual for his acts, isn't it illogical to assume that the prisoner should have some stake in his existence and self-determination while he is doing time? Most maximum-security prisons, most reformatories, most detention centers are not really concerned with correction and change. They are directed toward the administration of aversive

controls. And if the joint is doing a good job of controlling and sanctioning inmates, its officers take the necessary steps to see that they remain passive, obedient, and quiet. But passivity and obedience are always administered with the use or the constant threat of the club.

The traditional role of the guard, screw, bull, fuzz, or correctional officer—whatever you want to call him—has been one of aversive authority, and man is not so constituted that he gives up positions of authority easily. The traditional role of the convict, the inmate, the burrhead, the resident—whatever you want to call him—is seen in his necessary dedication to the "convict code," the unwritten but pervasive regulations for living in the prison environment. The rules of the con society erect an impenetrable wall between the con and his keepers, because cooperation with the officials violates its basic tenets. Traditionally, convicts have learned to survive by adhering to the convict code, which can be summarized as follows:

1. Never cooperate with the Man. Never talk to a guard except when absolutely necessary, and then make sure another con is within hearing distance.
2. Do your own time—that is, do not interfere with what any other inmate does, disruptive or damaging as it may be to the peace and welfare of the inmate body as a whole.

The process that sucks a man into the convict culture insures that propensities toward the criminal life will develop and mature. A guy doesn't stand much chance of staying out of prison if he lives by the rules of the con society, 'cause he spends a lot of his time hating the people who keep him there, resisting the discrimination that he faces, planning strategies of retaliation for his punishers; and when he gets out he keeps on hating, he keeps on stealing or whatever, and he presents himself as a natural target for apprehension.

The penal environment breeds hatred, thrives on discrimination, adds pressure to feelings of hostility and inadequacy in the case of both inmate and keeper, and finds renewed life in feelings of bigotry, racism, and all kinds of perversions. The penal environment insures that the con will emerge from prison more brutalized, more criminally secure and expert, less willing to tolerate societal norms and laws than before. The very notion that you can hide a man behind thirty-foot concrete and steel walls, cancel his identity, subject him to immeasurable amounts of peer and staff brutality, and meanwhile expect some moral regeneration and repentance is illogical and stupid.

The inmate survives by learning how to con others. Each inmate is forced into passive participation in conning by virtue of his role as a convict. Even though he may wish, as an individual, to adhere to the rules and regulations of the administration, he must at the same time live up to the convict code. The ingrained idea that "you must never snitch" has a thousand meanings.

Frequently, a new inmate will hesitate to involve himself actively in the game of conning for fear of endangering his chances for early parole or release. He soon discovers, however, that he endangers his position more by maintaining this attitude than by relaxing and joining the inmate group. So the naive first-timer soon learns how to support the conniving activities of the inmate group and still maintain a posture of conformity to the Man's book. He learns how to gamble, have sex, steal from the Man, even kill when necessary and get away with it.

The convict learns new techniques of criminal behavior in prison. Contrary to popular belief, however, the "old con" has no definite educational policy for young first-timers. This learning process comes about naturally in the prison environment. Conversations in prison are primarily with fellow convicts. As in groups anywhere, talk commonly turns to shop. Each type of con describes those varieties of technique with which he is best acquainted. The forger talks forgery; the holdup man talks robbery; the burglar refines his methodology for breaking and entering unobtrusively. And in today's prison the revolutionary gets his shit together. So, a whole lot of inmates who would like to make it in the outside society are systematically confronted with refined methodologies for doing just the opposite.

The prisoner community is a social group developed and defined by society's rejects. Not only the con can be seen as a societal reject, but his keeper, the professional guard or administrator is often an abject failure in his own right. The organization of the convict community is primarily an economic arrangement devoted to obtaining goods and services denied by the administration. The development of conniving, with its codes of deception, insures that cons have daily training in habits that make character change and reintegration difficult if not impossible. The prison community is a natural breeding ground for revolt and revolution. I am not prepared to speak to the larger issues which underlie the conversion of our Jacksons and Cleavers from members of the criminal subculture to political prisoners. My position here is that there are only two ways we can bring about meaningful change in our prisons: return to the maximum-security, Pennsylvania Dutch system of solitary confinement, complete silence, and Bible reading, or give the prison inmate a meaningful, genuine stake in his own existence.

In order to give the con a stake in what's happening to him you do away with the old prison order where he isn't allowed to speak or think. You sit down together and rewrite the rules under which inmates live, eliminating all the petty, outdated, idiotic regulations about how much hair a person sports, or how straight a line he walks on the way to the yard, or whether his shirttail is out or in, or whether he leaves any food on his plate or not. You hold secret elections whereby inmates are not only permitted but they are requested to help determine virtually all the conditions under which they live.

I believe, then, that giving the inmate a real voice in prison management, giving him a meaningful stake in his existence, is the only chance the prison administrators have to get away from complete anarchy and revolution. If this kind of a program is going to work, everybody has to pitch in and demonstrate responsibility. Both staff and residents are going to have to get rid of the old con philosophy. The emphasis is going to have to shift from keeping the count straight, from guns and bars, uniforms and keys to something much more positive. Penal philosophy has to be much wider than just locking people up, open to many more considerations than just security, custody, control, and containment.

Penal philosophy can only be as sound as the greater societal philosophy for living. This gets us to the crucial issues of who goes to prison in the first place. Do we get the real criminal in jail or are we merely puttering around with petty thieves and pot smokers? Do we merely imprison the vulnerable, the disenfranchised, the poor, the ignorant, the uninformed? I think so. American prisons develop, culture, and protect their clientele. They couldn't survive without abject poverty, injustice, rank ordering in society. They would not exist in a society without greed, avarice, conspicuous consumption, and those false needs which are superimposed upon man by particular social interests bent on their own self-aggrandizement and on his repression; that whole range of needs which perpetuate gross manual labor, aggressiveness, rabid competition, misery, injustice, and programmed failure for the socially incompetent perpetuates our prison system.

Back to the subject of riots and disturbances in prison. Lots of times they are just fights and they get called a riot. Would you be surprised if I told you that when a real riot does get going, it is often the guards that start it rather than the convicts? It is true. There is a lot of factionalism among the staff of a large, maximum-security joint. The warden has his group of loyal guards who respond to his wishes like law. But often another clique of guards will form around a captain or a deputy warden and they'll get in a political squabble with the warden. Sometimes it gets so bad that there will be the regular staff meeting held in administration just as usual, but it will be boycotted by a group of guards who'll meet somewhere else. The cons can smell out this kind of trouble almost before it gets going and turn it to their advantage. Actually, sometimes there is less solidarity among the guards than among the inmates.

And when the guards are arguing, things get lax inside the prison. Rules don't get enforced, anything goes. I've even heard guards agitate trouble on the yard by saying something like this to a known convict leader: "That chow has certainly been bad lately. I'm glad I don't have to eat that shit. In fact, I wouldn't eat it on a bet. I'd throw my tray on the ceiling first."

That is real encouragement, and music to the convict ear. When guards start agitating, life in prison can get real shaky. This plays right into the hands of the disorganized but tough state raised youths who are just waiting to start some shit and get a good riot going. I never liked it in prison, but I hated it during times of foment and disruption, 'cause you never knew where you stood, you could get shanked anytime, and business as usual was impossible.

Sometimes it seems like your prison experience is going to drag on forever. You x the days off the calendar one by one, and the shorter you get the more the time drags by.

But, like I say, they gotta let you go someday; and my day came. One day you wake up and you're gone. You don't say nothing to nobody. I mean, if you live for years in a neighborhood and you move away, you shake hands with everybody on the street. But that's not the way it is in the joint. All those friends I made in the joint, when my day came it was like they didn't exist. And I couldn't carry their hopes and futures out for them, just my own. So they didn't even say good-by. We didn't have a common cause any more. Nothing crossed my mind but that I wanted that cell door to open for the last time. The bell is tolling for you, Manny. Hot damn, the streets are out there!

And it was really weird. I walked down the tier on my way out, and for three years I'd lived and laughed with those guys but we had nothing to say to each other, no common statement any more, 'cause I was going and they were staying. I just walked downstairs, out across the yard to R and R, and sat down. I wanted to get out so bad, and yet I was scared, too, way down in the gut. What is going to happen now is the whole trip. But they open the gate. They press the button and the gate just swings. I don't think the finest fix of scag ever felt that good. The gate swings wide open and I put my foot across and who is standing right out there plain as shit but my brother Bobby. I walk right up to him, he shakes my hand, and we walk over to his car. In the glove compartment is a syringe and a deck of scag.

I'm sitting there in that prison parking lot and I can see the west wall with the guard pacing along the tower walk and I'm fixing. Everything is fine again. I coast all the way home. It's a soft nod all the way to the city.

Chapter 4

Synanon

Show and tell!

So I wasn't out of the joint five minutes and I got down. Me and my brother got home and we fixed again. I'm not hooked yet because of the infrequent use while in prison, but I look at Bobby and I see that he is really wired up behind scag. You can tell every time if you're in on the know. I think that one dope fiend can tell the depth of another dope fiend's misery every time. I could see the amount of shit he was using. I looked into his eyes and nothing happened, no reaction at all. To this day, even though I've been off dope for a while, my eyes are strange. People tell me that a lot; and another doper can tell that I've used.

I ask Bobby, "How long have you been running?"

He says, "I don't know, man, I don't know. But I do know that we gotta score some bread 'cause we're broke and we need some scag." He's laying his trip on me and involving me right away in his capers. But I know that it's part of the code. Bobby's my brother, and besides I've been freeloading on his dope supply. So I gotta go out and get on the hustle.

It ain't hard to drift back into the old routine. In fact, I'm just naturally right back into hustling and shucking and jiving and shooting. I set up a few scores here and there. It ain't long until we're dealing scag and getting our regular supply. Then, Bobby's old lady—her name was Katie—comes to me and tells me, "You know, we gotta do something for Bobby. He's hooked like a dog."

I tell her, "You know what? I can't worry about that. He isn't gonna kill himself. Every time he fixes, I fix so he won't overload."

I can't pay no mind to Katie 'cause I figure it's his life. And what the hell! I want to be hooked, too; I want to fix every day. So, Katie calls my aunt and she comes over to the house with this rap about Bobby's got to go to Synanon. She talks about Synanon like it's some magic place and all Bobby's troubles will be over if we can only get him out there. She's read some literature about this "new" community program that is supposed to be fundamentally unique in its approach to dope and crime, and she's hot to send Bobby out to California for resocialization. So she says, "We want you to talk to your brother and get him to go; you've always had a hammer over Bobby. The program costs five hundred dollars to get him in."

So I say, "Sure, I'll talk to him about it. But don't ask me for the five big ones. 'Cause I'm not about to come up with any dough."

They ask me if there is any way I could help partially with the money end. I say, "Look, there ain't any way in the world that I'm about to help. I need money to score stuff, and I'm not about to give it up to dry him up. If you got the five hundred and want to use it, then send him to Synanon, but don't bug me for it. I'm not coming up with no money!"

And they started to throw me all that shit about "Bobby's your younger brother; don't you care for him at all? What about his welfare?"

"Goddammit! Get off my back. Hell, no, I don't care for him." I cared all right. I cared because he had the bag; that was all I cared about! I told her that, and more. "Look, he's hooked and I'm gonna get hooked and all I want outa this goddamn life is some dope. You understand that! I don't want to hear anything more about Bobby's welfare. I'm gonna take care of me! Understand, dammit; me!"

So they bug off, taking Bobby with them. And I'm relieved, 'cause now all I gotta account for is me. And that's what I want; it's easier that way. They finally get the money together and Bobby asked to go to Synanon because he's had it. He's been on a really long run and he was wasted down until he was just bone-raped tired. After he goes I don't hear from him for months, and I figured that he must have really hit it good. I figured that he was scoring every day. It makes sense, doesn't it? Synanon's full of dope fiends, so there must be dope there. And if there's dope there, Bobby's getting his share.

As for Number 1, I'm back to where I'm fixing dope every day. The guy who moved in downstairs from me is dealing, so I got a source close by. I'm selling for him and piecing off the top enough to support my habit. I'm really hooked again when a panic hits New York. A lot of folks don't know what a panic is. That's when there is no dope in the streets and every doper becomes a panic man—referring to his anxiety at forced withdrawal. It is hard to imagine that in a city the size of New York there can be a situation where you can't score a three-dollar bag of scag. Sometimes you have a minor panic when dope is hard to come by because a bunch of the ounce men get busted or because a major source gets knocked off or intercepted coming into the country. However, usually there is always some dope around, even if the price goes sky-high.

But not this time. It's just before Christmas and several undercover cops get killed trying to bust up a major junk ring. The commissioner just shut the town down tight. I mean, he passed the word to all the bosses that the lid was down and they better cough up the cop killers or there would be no more rackets!

You may think that this doesn't happen, especially if you're an average square John working stiff. But don't you believe it. When the commissioner wants to put the bosses in line bad enough he can cut off their water. They came up with the cop killers too, and business as usual was restored. But that took a month. Meanwhile, you could not score one bag of dope. I must have known at that time hundreds of people who dealt in dope. There were dope fiends all over, in bunches, by the fifties and hundreds, kicking in the streets. This was Christmas of '66, I think. They were laying around in the gutters shitting in their pants and drooling at the mouth because of forced withdrawal. They were ripping into drugstores in search of meth or paregoric or morphine or anything. Like, most of the drugstores in New York have these big iron gates all across their front, and

hypes were ripping them off and throwing them into the middle of the streets, going right in after dope.

Nobody scores a lousy spoon. I'm going clear to Jersey and I can't score. It's really a bummer when you got all the money you need and can't score at all. There's some psychological principle at work here, in that if you're broke, drove up in jail, or otherwise can't get ahold of some scag it's one thing— you can live with it. But when you're right there in the streets with the bread in your hand and can't score a three-dollar bag it's deathly frustrating. And the withdrawal symptoms somehow seem twice as powerful. You are ready to take any possible chances to get dope.

Everybody in the know tells me that we ought to go to Pittsburgh. I mean, we've been stealing every day and got plenty of money but can't score any dope. I've built myself up a little bankroll, about two thousand dollars. So, I think that maybe there is something to this Pittsburgh thing, and several of us fly over there looking for scag. I don't know nothing about the traffic in Pittsburgh, but one of my friends claims to have an inside lead to a sure connection. I'm so sick that I'm not thinking at all about the possibility of a burn. I just want dope; with every twisting, churning gut inside of me I want dope. We get off the plane and go over to this so-called connection of Jack's; we give him all our money because he says that's the only way his boss will deal, and the guy is long gone. I mean, he didn't come back. All I got left is one-half of a round-trip ticket to the city. I'm sitting in that goddamn airport lobby holding this ticket, knowing that I've been had, and it's just about the end of the world.

I get on the plane and go back to New York. The only place I know where to go is over to my uncle's house—that same uncle that got me started into heroin. You know what that seducing son-of-a-bitch had to say to me when I came crying my guts out for a shot of dope?

"You're nothing but a screwed-up dog."

He says, "I ain't got nothing, no more than you have. You know what? You're nothing but a screwed-up dog. You're a filthy pig for scag. You haven't got any self-control at all. Manny, you have to kick!"

I think, Now that's something. Here, this is the bastard that almost begged me to use. He helped me out all along the way. When I didn't want to get involved, he urged me to at least snuff the shit. When I was doing that, he coached and cajoled me to go further and skin-pop for more kicks. Later he told me how much better it was when I mainlined. And then I finally went

all the way and that was like setting out on the river of no return. And here he was telling me that I was just a dog dope fiend. Motherfucker! But he was right, you know. At least he could exert some control over his usage. I couldn't.

He takes me over to my aunt's house where she lives over in the projects. He tells her, "We have to do something with Manny. He is dying." So they get a bunch of pills from some doctor and they make me kick right there. Her husband is six-four and weighs over two hundred pounds. He took off five days from his work and sat in a room with me. Every time I tried to leave, this dude would hit me. I mean, the man would knock me to the floor as hard as he could. This asshole certainly knew how to handle dope fiends. That's the only language they really respond to every time. Some counselors try to rationalize with them; some try to be their friend. Hey! That's all bull-shit; it won't work. The only sure way to get to a doper is to over-power him.

But Uncle George made me stay right there in that little bedroom and kick, cold turkey. It wasn't too long until I began to feel real good. I started to eat again; in a few days I began to put on some flesh. And then I wanted out. The house started to feel more than ever like a prison. And so I tell them, "Look, you don't have to worry. Thanks to you I've kicked the habit. I feel great, but now I have to get out of the house." Inside me, way down there where we all live, I knew sure as shit that as soon as I cut loose of this do-gooder Uncle George, I would fix. Besides, I'd heard that the panic was over and that there was mucho dope in the streets.

My aunt said, "We think that you have to go to Synanon, like your brother. Your brother went to Synanon and we haven't heard anything from him, and that must mean good news. You are going to Synanon, Manny, if I got to borrow the money and scrub floors to get you there!"

I decided, What the fuck, I'll go. I figured that if my brother hasn't come back from California, and I know he's not in jail, there must be some dope there. There has gotta be dope, else Bobby would have come back a long time ago.

So I agree to go to Synanon and they make all the arrangements. They pay them the five hundred dollars and me and my aunt take a train to Westport, Connecticut, where they got a house. We go to this Synanon house and barely get sat down in this living room when this guy named Ted Dibble says, "Torres, you're an asshole!"

I shout, "Who the fuck are you calling an asshole?" And I was going to stand up and show them who's the asshole in the crowd.

My aunt grabs me by the collar and sits me down. Ted says, "It's not that I'm personally down on you, Torres, I just wanted to show you the main technique we are going to use in Synanon. We use our own style of attack therapy in an attempt to communicate with addicts and criminals. We are going to change you, Manny. In two years or so you are going to have some human qualities and potentialities that you never knew were possible for you. What's important for you to realize is that we guarantee you that if you'll stick with the program for two and a half years, you will never use heroin again."

And I'm standing there making noises like this program is just what I want. But I've still got a typical hophead attitude. What's in it for me? If there's dope, I stay; if no dope, I'm gone. The formula's that simple. So I tell him that sounds like a good idea and that I'll go to Synanon. I've got a couple of weeks in the city before they are going to ship me to the West Coast. So I get up, pick up my suitcase, and I start to shake his hand like I'm getting ready to leave.

He says, "Well, where are you going now?"

I say, "I'm going back to the city and when you guys are ready to ship me, just tell me and I'll leave on the plane for California."

They tell me, "No, Manny, I don't think so. That isn't the way it works. You're leaving tonight. As of right now you are in Synanon."

And they shook me down right there and took my watch, ring, what little money I had off of me as if I was going to jail.

I'm just sitting in this house waiting to go to the airport. I feel almost as strange as the time I'm waiting to go up to Sing Sing. They put a tag on me that had my name and address on it, just like a little kid that you send on a plane across the country. By the time we get to the airport I'm going mad, 'cause I don't understand what is happening to me except there is this forbidding sense of being oppressed, like being smothered by a friend—but being smothered to death nevertheless. I mean, all these guys taking me to the plane are right guys in the world's sense. I think, They're almost like cops!

They put me aboard this plane bound for San Francisco. I'm instructed to just ride, not to talk unnecessarily with anybody, and not to take any alcoholic beverages. I'm told that someone will meet me at the other end. The last thing I remember Ted telling me is, "Manny, you don't understand all this right now. I know that was how I felt when I was first in Synanon. But just hang in there and it will all come out okay."

But they had to leave because the plane was preparing to taxi off. And I tore up the damn babysitting ticket they'd tied on me. "Fuck, who do these dingbats think I am?" Then I tell the stewardess to bring me a double. She says that with the kind of ticket I have I couldn't buy no drinks. This, I was to learn, is part of another special thing with Synanon. You can't take no drugs, drink anything intoxicating; in fact, you can't even take aspirin without special permission.

People on the plane were looking at me like I was some special case or something and I was getting embarrassed. And I told the stewardess, "Look, sister, I want a drink. Everybody else on this plane is drinking if they want to; I'm over twenty-one. I want a drink, now." I start to really raise hell and they can't tolerate that on the plane, so they finally give up and give me my drinks. By the time we land in Frisco I'm three sheets in the wind.

When I deplaned for the first time on the West Coast I had pictured in my mind that it would be sunny California. But it was raining and cold. I wonder what the shit is coming off! I had no money at all on me and I'm standing in the middle of this gigantic air terminal and I ain't got the least idea where I'm supposed to go or what I'm supposed to do. Just like a lost child. In looking around to get my bearings I think to myself that there ought to be a way to make some money here. I start to figure what can I snatch when all of a sudden this guy and girl come up to me and ask me if I'm Torres.

I say, "You know it. And am I

glad to see somebody who knows me."

They say, "We're from Synanon and we're supposed to take you to the house that you'll be living in." We go and find my bags and they take me to the house on 110 Lombard Street in San Francisco. It looked like a huge warehouse to me, kind of dark and forbidding. And, of course, that's what it was, a warehouse that had been converted into dormitories, living rooms, bedrooms, all kinds of rooms.

The first thing that happens to me is that some of the Synanon regulars escort me to a bathroom and make me strip. They go through all my personal stuff, even doing the prison thing of looking in my ass. They tell me that I'm on "house arrest" and can't go anywhere away from the premises. And I want out. "What the hell! You can't do this to me. You have no legal basis on which to hold me. I'm getting out of this rat trap. It'd be different if I was drove up behind some criminal beef or something. Listen! I'd expect this kind of behavior if you assholes were cops or narcs. You're supposed to be my friends and you're sticking fingers up my ass and got me on house arrest! Bullshit! Let me outa here."

I start to walk out of the place and they call a game on me—a Synanon game. It's not exactly like group therapy, but you sit in a circle of your peers and they are hollering at you, asking you all these stupid questions. We go in this room and they say, "We just want to talk to you, Manny. You know that you're just a little baby, don't you? Just a little helpless, crying, shitting baby. Don't you know that? We just want to help you grow up."

"Hey, fuck you, mothers. You're a bunch of rat fink stoolies. You're worse than that, bastards. You run around shaking people down, prying in their business. Where's your license? Who gave you a uniform?"

"Listen, Manny! Cut that tough-guy, Sing Sing Prison number. It won't get you any mileage here. We're not impressed with your command of the Bronx language. If this place was San Quentin or Dannemora, we might empathize with your number. But dig it! Nobody is any tougher than anybody else in here."

"Goddamn it! You people are trying to rip me off. You've taken everything away from me but my mouth and now you tell me I can't use that. Why, why don't you take a flying fuck at Mickey Mouse? That's where you guys are at, anyway. How long do you think you'd last in the yard at Sing Sing? Listen, I've blown better assholes than you away back home in the city."

"Hey, fellows, hey, girls! Listen to this tough New York import. Are you impressed? Maybe some of you are scared. Perhaps this sociopathic Puerto Rican is putting us all down. Anybody wilting under this barrage of purple verbiage?"

"I ain't talking no more. Just give me my shit and let me outa here. You guys said back in Connecticut that if I didn't like it I could leave. You guys brag about not keeping anyone here against his will. All right, I want to go! You got that! I want out, 'cause I want to fix, fix, fix! How's that, you bunch of lily-livered fairies? I want to use; you don't want anyone here who's using; so let me out now!"

And they start talking kind of nicer to me. "I didn't hear any fucks or shits, any goddamns or motherfuckers! Did you, Rosie? How about that? Maybe Manny can make it. Sure, you want to use now, or at least you're saying that to get out from under this haircut. But give it a week and see how you like it here. Look, Manny, Synanon is a good place for you right now. If you stay this time you may never have to put that needle in your arm again. If you go, you may die or spend the rest of your life in the bucket. Give it a chance."

. . . I was scared 'cause I had no place to go.

I really want to go for their soft story. Inside, down under all the crap and façade of toughness, I was scared 'cause I had no place to

go. It's a strange city to me; I got no artillery; I don't know a soul outside of these people at Synanon. Besides, my brother Bobby lives at Synanon, and maybe I'll get to see him right away. I'm really shook up 'cause I don't know what's going on so I decide that it's best for me to stay for the time being.

In the morning they get us all up and we go into this big living room and somebody is reading philosophy by Emerson. This is kind of a devotional-like thing that they do every morning. In fact, it was kinda like church in the joint. They read the bit from Emerson, somebody tells a joke, everybody sings a song, and they go off to their various jobs. I'm just standing around looking the place over when some guy comes up and tells me that I'm on the service team.

I say, "What the fuck you talking about?"

The guy says, "Look, friend, we try to steer clear of that kind of lousy prison and street slang around here. Most of our group members are into cleaning up their act and it starts with the language. Why do you think we get involved in reading philosophy and psychology around here? Now, about work. Everybody in Synanon works at something. We try to make the jobs constructive and interesting. Every job in here serves the needs of the organization. We're all in this together."

"Jesus! You want me to cut out the prison rap and then you lay a story like that on me. What the hell! Sounds just like the deputy warden giving a bunch of fish their indoctrination sermon."

"It's not the same trip in spirit, Manny, although you can't tell the difference now. Chuck Dederich is the Man here, but he's no warden. We want you to stay because we want you to be free of scag fever, but you're free to go if you really want to."

"Yeah, sure. Free to go out into a strange city broke, cold, with one suit of threads on my back. Some deal! Where do you want me to work?"

"We all got our start on one of the service teams. Usually that means just general housework and cleaning up. Later on you'll get a chance to function where you fit best. You might make it on maintenance or you might hustle or prepare food. You could be assigned office work; who knows? But for the present, come on over here and work with Frankie. Since you just came in you'll do the lowest jobs until you can prove you can handle some responsibility."

And I say, "That don't sound too good to me. I never worked before and I didn't come here to work my ass off either. I came here because you assholes said I could do something with my drug problem."

"Well, it's not really hard work. Why don't you just give it a try? Maybe later you can work up to the automotive crew or operations."

So they got me going around the barracks with this dude named Frankie cleaning out toilet bowls and washstands. And I'm scheming all the time about where I can get my hands on some money. There has got to be money in this house, I reason. With all these people and all this action, there has got to be dough here. I remember thinking that perhaps this was all one big fantastic front for a heroin ring. I remember having all kinds of paranoid thoughts like that.

All day long where I'm cleaning up I can't spot any money laying around so I start looking at things I could take, like radios, TVs, watches, and shavers. I had kind of a problem 'cause I didn't know anybody in San Francisco I could do business with if I did find something to hock. So that afternoon I decide to go for a walk and see if I can get next to somebody that would deal. I start going down the front stairs and a guy meets me at the door.

"Where are you going, Torres?" This dude's name is Freddie, and he looks like he used to play middle linebacker for the 49'ers.

"I'm just going out for a walk. You know, get a little air. I'll be back in about an hour."

So Freddie runs it down to me nice and easy. "You can't leave the grounds, and here that's the building. You can't go out unaccompanied until you've been here ninety days and passed some good gaming sessions."

I say, "You gotta be freaking out. This ain't a joint; I ain't committed here. I'm leaving." I was forever leaving that first week or so. I start to walk out and Freddie puts out a firm but friendly arm. He just drags me back upstairs, talking like he's my big brother. "Now, Manny, right now you gotta trust us. We know what's best for you. You gotta believe that."

Well, I didn't want to surrender my identity that I'd lived with for all those years in the streets and the joint. I wanted to be me, and it was getting increasingly harder to do. I try and just sit around and brood, but they won't even let me do that—especially, they won't let me do that. They give me the simplest job around, washing cups. And true to form, I hassle them about washing cups. They say that I have to wash cups and do whatever menial work comes along because I'm a newcomer and that's the way it is in Synanon.

They're feeding me all this psychology about how I have to learn to adjust and all this sociology about the interests of the group come first. They talk about my ego problems, displacement, transference, and stuff like that until I begin to use the terms too. I don't know from Henry what displacement means, but I can say the word. And I don't get in as much trouble with this kind of language as with my street lingo.

They keep giving me all this indoctrination and keeping me busy all the time. They order me around and arrange everything for me so I don't have time to think or scheme. They've got me running here and running there all day long. Even though we line up and get fed in a big dining room like in jail, I begin to see the difference. I began to get a handle on the sense of cohesion, a fantastic tightness that smacked of a group spirit impossible in the joint. There was little factionalism in the Synanon experience at first. I was surviving the indoctrination experience 'cause, even though I didn't exactly recognize it at the time, I was being both hassled and fulfilled by people who themselves had been in my shoes. They had been many miles in my shoes, but now they were making it. And I began to think that I wasn't involved in a caste system but more in a contractual arrangement whereby everybody was making inputs and everybody would score outcomes. But it wasn't easy. I remember my first major Synanon game.

They used to have their games on Monday, Wednesday, and Friday nights. I remember the first one very well. I'd worked all day and after chow I went upstairs thinking that it'd be great to grab a shower and hit the sack. It's not yet seven o'clock in the evening and I'm whipped. I just wasn't used to all the work and running around. After a hot shower I jump into bed, thinking I'm going to cop some Z's.

No luck! This guy comes and wakes me up shouting something about it being game time. The game is a main form of social control in the Synanon organization. At game time the behavior of every member can be adjusted, tuned up, confronted, and regulated. I get outa bed and I go and sit in this big living room with most of the people in the house. Somebody's calling off names and they tell you to listen for your name and go with the group with which it is called.

So, I go into this room with about ten or twelve other people and they run the rules of the game down to me since I'm the newcomer. One guys says, "It's just a game, so don't be scared. There's a few rules you have to know in front; they are just the same for all Synanon games. One, everybody is alike in these games; it don't make any difference if Dederich or you is the center of attention. Like, anyone who has a 'haircut' coming, gets it. Two, there is no violence or threat of violence here. We operate on the assumption that there are better ways of problem solving. Hitting and lashing out with your fists is unforgivable. Don't forget it! You can say anything you want to, but don't threaten violence or do a violent physical act. If you do, you get thrown out of Synanon."

"Great," I say. "Just what I want." But deep down where I live I'm beginning to think like maybe I'll stick around and see what these crazy bastards are up to. So I just sit there and take it in. I hear them start in with the questions. Like, they were trying to dig into this new guy who'd come in just before me and they were asking him about his "ego involvement" in an argument he'd had with some broad the night before.

I thought they were really dumb questions. So I jump into the conversation and say to the big shot who was on this kid, "You're a pig. You got it made because you been around this fruity hole a few days." And this guy just sits there and takes that shit. I get madder yet, and I turn to the group and I say, "Hey, isn't he a fucking pig? Where does he get off rapping to that kid as if he were a lousy inmate in court?"

All of a sudden they all start staring at me as if I was an outsider. One of the broads tells me, "You're a pretty big mouth, aren't you? I've been listening to you come off the wall for three days now, and you haven't said anything yet."

And I'm not at all used to having a broad talk to me like that, and I jump up hollering at her and shaking my fist in her dumb face. Freddie and some other dude sit me down and proceed to inform me that I don't understand the mechanism here. "You got to get into the Synanon game. Why don't you just sit back and relax? Sticks and stones may break your bones, but names will never hurt you. Especially if they speak the truth. So, dig it for a while."

So I cool it for a minute or so, but I've already seen that this is just a bunch of bullshit and I ain't that easily convinced. Synanon goes against the grain of a street person. It's really hard to sit still under the put-down, the game haircut, especially when you perceive that those putting you down are weaker than you are—as you have always measured strength and weakness. Life in the goldfish bowl of a game session is merely a reflection of the total atmosphere of Synanon. In the joint there were always the good guys and the bad guys. You played it cool, hustled, and stayed clear of the cops, squares, snitches, and administrators. But streetwise and jointwise definitions of reality don't make sense in Synanon. The guys giving the orders are not cops, guards, principals, or even squares, they are people just like yourself.

I found that the Synanon group sucked me in little by little. In Synanon there is almost total suppression of preexisting statuses, which is achieved by the assimilating function of the group. They won't let you stay outside. The new member has low status and limited privileges only because he is new and lacks orientation to the goals and means of the group. You are restricted to the warehouse for six weeks, not because you're in a different class or hierarchy, but only for purposes of indoctrination

and socialization. Although I and many others that I knew in Synanon resisted this fusion process that ultimately incorporated us into the common cultural life, anybody that stayed got assimilated.

I was at Synanon for two months before I met its founder, Chuck Dederich. It was my luck to come head-on against him in a game situation, where more than ever in Synanon everybody is supposed to be equal. They had a saying that nobody wears a hat in the game. If you're president of Synanon and you walk into a game, well, you're supposed to be a sitting duck just like anyone else in there. So, I'm in this game and I'm in the middle of telling this broad that she is a snake. I tell her, "You know what? I don't care what you do here or what you're rep is here, you're just a snake like me. You're a dope fiend and you're a broad. In my mind that means that you'll go any route at all for dope, you'll take it in the ear or anywhere for scag. And you're going to sit there and tell me that you'll never use again because you're going to stay with the group and not get the resources to use. Shit! You're sitting on your resources and you'll use them."

To me, she is just another dope fiend trying her best to snow a room full of dope fiends. And I'm in the middle of my number when Dederich walks into the game. Right there is a violation of the rules 'cause nobody is supposed to come in and sit down and participate in the middle of a game. 'Cause the newcomer never knows what has gone down before and can come to some unwarranted conclusions. But Dederich says to the broad, "Tell him to shut up."

I holler at him, "I'm not talking to you, asshole, I'm giving this bitch a haircut and it ain't none of your business." And I have another go at trying to pin the broad down. He tries to interrupt our conversation again and I shine him on. "Hey, Chuckie, can't the big man let the plebe have his day?" Dederich turns to the group and calls off the game.

"Wait a minute! What do you mean, the game is over?" I'm mad now. Before I was loud and sassy, trying to make what I belived to be a valid point. Now I'm mad! "According to the rules the game is not over until I'm through, and I'm not done with it." You see, as long as someone is confronting in the game it is not considered over.

And he says, "I say the game is over and I have the final say around here. I'm Chuck Dederich."

Hey, I didn't care about that. "I don't give a fuck who you are. I'm not through with this issue. When I get through talking to her then you can do whatever you like." Then he tells everybody to leave the room, but he doesn't say a word to me. He just kind of leaves me hanging there feeling foolish as everybody drifts out of the room.

Finally he comes over and tells me to pack my gear and leave the house. And I say, "Screw you,

dictator. I came all the way from the East Coast to get this treatment; I paid my dues in more than one way around here. This is supposed to be an attack therapy session and I was just asking that the broad face reality. How can you kick me out for that?"

I was really kind of funny. Here I'd been around this "military" organization for a couple of months, trying every way I could think of to leave. Now that I had an ultimatum to leave, I wasn't about to go. It becomes a big conflict. Jack Hearst and another wheel come in and they're trying to tell me that he's the founder of Synanon and he can do anything he wants.

And now I really get up on the air. "For two months you've been beating into my head that nobody wore no hats in the Synanon game; that the only two rules of the game were that everybody is alike and that there were no threats or physical violence. According to your own rules I should be able to tell this fat fucker anything I want in a game."

They get very hot, because in truth I have them in a philosophical bind. They can't justify throwing me out of Synanon because now they figure that I am finally venting all this anger that has built up in my system for years. And they are right. I was a very hostile dude. Besides, I had the morals of a dope fiend. Part of what I was gaming that broad for was for kicks, excitement, fun; mainly just to roust her.

The point is, my honest motives were dope fiend oriented, but out front I was playing their game. And they knew that.

Anyway, they call me down into another room and have kind of a court session. They put me on pot detail. I washed all the kitchen pots and pans for over a month. I certainly found out who Chuck Dederich was through that experience and I paid him all due respect after that. The important thing is that something was beginning to happen to me at Synanon. Because I stayed through that experience I started to change. It was a subtle process at first, and I hardly noticed. For weeks now I wasn't using! But that wasn't the most important thing. My whole mentality, all my thought processes were changing. I was beginning to see in Synanon all the possibilities of life. I was beginning to break away from an ideological system that had held me captive since adolescence. Although I had left the addict subculture behind months before, I was still bound by its many justifications. I had played all the roles far too often: addict-pusher, criminal-addict-victim, sniveling addict-victim, criminal-addict-fence. I was locked into a character set with one dominant imperative—score! Besides all this there were overlayed characterological traits from prison. I had lived for some years by the inmate code, at least as much as a doper can live by that code. In prison I

was a right guy. I believed that a fink or a squealer was the lowest form of life, and it was hard to accept that in Synanon there are no secrets—that everybody is a "fink" for the good of the all. In prison as well as out I *believed in stealing.* It was an ideology, not a pastime. I had no guilt feelings at all. It was a way of survival, the prime method of scoring, and that made it right by definition.

In my "old" ideology there were solid lines of demarcation between good guys and bad guys. We were the good guys and cops, guards, stoolies, squares, and punks were the bad buys. Maybe it was an inverse psychology or ideology, but the point is that it was the only one I had, and it worked for me on the streets and in the joint.

But the new experience of Synanon was breaking down this old ideology. It was really frustrating at first to find that everybody was a good guy by definition in Synanon. Anytime you tried to stereotype a member as being an outsider in any way, somebody would come against you. Sometimes they would laugh at you or use an ironic comeback. Sometimes they would just tell you that you were dumb; that you were not in the joint any longer and "please quit playing those stupid prison games around here."

I don't want to convey the notion

that Synanon people were robots or that they had no individual differences. But there was a sense of *unity* there that sucked you in if you stayed. You became of like mind with the others through a process of closed, common cultural identification. For every member, Synanon becomes a unity of experience, a common orientation from which develops an iron-bound sense of community purpose and action which might be said something like this: "Together we will prevail over drugs, prison records, or any other hassle. We will lift each other up at all times, and in the Synanon society every member may find a means of expressing his best human qualities and finest potential."

Synanon opened up my thinking and learning processes.

For me, it happened by the interaction of two processes, one which worked on my mental state, and the other constraining the physical. Synanon opened up my thinking and learning processes. All the time I had been in New York I didn't know anything about philosophy, psychology, sociology, or even literature. I couldn't tell you what philosophy was if you'd have asked me. Psychology and sociology were strange words to me and I knew little or nothing about art or litera-

ture. Can you believe it when I tell you that I had never before read a book! But here in Synanon I was in daily contact with a group of intellectuals. Most of the people at Synanon during my years there were beatniks. They had gradually dropped out of society and got into heroin. As we came into contact there I couldn't help but get interested in philosophy because that was their whole life.

So I began to read the philosophers. At first, I was reading them and not understanding anything. But I would sit there and listen to people talk about Hesse and Camus like everybody else did. As I start to get seriously involved in reading the books I find that I can understand. Jesus! I find out that I ain't naturally stupid like I had thought all these years. With my behavioral problems in school, I had been labeled a dummy, and I had just more or less accepted that, not thinking that it took brains and cunning to survive in the world of drugs and crime.

And my language began to change, too. I found that I didn't have to keep using four-letter words over and over again in order to express myself. I was picking up words daily from conversations around me and from my readings. Soon I found myself using a kind of semi-intellectual language that I didn't always understand, but that I was learning to understand. Like, sometimes I would drop a heavy word like "existential" in a conversation.

I would be afraid that the next time I dropped it I would have to define its meaning. So I would sneak off to a dictionary and try to memorize the meaning. But it wasn't all a phony process meant to impress others. It got to be a very meaningful exercise for me. I knew that if I was going to use the same language as the others I would have to be able to back it up. Why I even wanted to comunicate this way with my peers probably speaks to the second reason for change that I mentioned above, the physical process of assimilation in the Synanon group.

I guess I've already talked about the suppression of your previous identity including the systematic destruction of any status you might have had in the "underworld." This is easily accomplished among the people who stay in Synanon because of its almost total institutional character. New members are totally isolated from the world of their former selves. They are not allowed to venture forth "outside" again until they have demonstrated stability—until they have been indoctrinated. The new person in Synanon does the shit work. He is assigned low status and soon learns that he has to work for anything he gets. Synanon is the ultimate adjustment center.

The control system is operated through a form of class hierarchy.

The "upperclassmen" are the people who have been there for years and are totally assimilated. They live, move, and have their being in Synanon; they are Synanon. Everybody else is learning and therefore, by definition, is something less, at least in respect to responsibility.

It is certainly true that Synanon effects harmony between its members. You kind of blend in with everybody else in sort of an intimate way. The Synanon community blots out the outside. No longer is the control of consciousness affected from Washington or Sacramento, downtown, or somewhere far removed and impersonal. But the control is a sort of benign dictatorship of the poor proletariat, with Chuck's presence ever felt as the ultimate authority.

And another thing that I always had trouble with in Synanon is the fanatical philosophy that everyone and everything outside its boundaries is sick and stupid. Members are socialized into renouncing the world at large by providing them with an atmosphere of physical, mental, and moral sufficiency within the community. Not only is the member's past behavior on the outside condemned, but his whole present and future are perpetually redefined for him as Synanon-oriented. Public relations with the outside are maintained in a pragmatic and utilitarian manner, but it is clear that the upperclassmen in Synanon consider their "way" to be morally superior.

In Synanon stigma is attached to the new member as a method of breaking down his dysfunctional character in an attempt to build a new identity. Confession, constant self-evaluation, and frequent group criticism of the individual are all part of the game of "sweat" therapy, which is called "the stew." Although Synanon shuns medicine for its members unless absolutely necessary, its therapeutic methods are strongly oriented to a medical model of social reality that sees the patient as both sick and bad. Freedom and dignity of individual character are perpetually offered up in sacrifice to the group ideal. I was brainwashed and my thought was controlled by group pressure. The norms of the group at Synanon were institutionalized with a force and style similar to the hazing techniques in the armed services during wartime.

Hazing in Synanon is highly organized. Generally, hazing is not allowed in informal circumstances or situations and is confined to the game session. Authoritarian punishment and verbal aggression are administered for the "common good." It is this internalized knowledge of common interests and a shared destiny that binds the people of Synanon together. This always gets expressed by identifying the interests of each individual with the interests of Synanon. A person's rank or position within the group is always an indication of his maturity

in the Synanon philosophy. You must "get your mind right" in order to prosper in Synanon. There is an assumption in Synanon that the social skills learned there will be highly useful in the larger society. But I have a problem with that because I believe that Synanon makes one a social cripple—outside Synanon. I believe that the highly selective nature of socially constructive attributes cripples one for operating in the society at large, when the truth is he can't survive on philosophy, can't live off of group cohesion and community purpose on the outside, and may have to hustle to get along. To my notion, Synanon is fine for its incarcerated members, but ex-Synanon status is often as problematic as ex-convict status.

Well, anyway, I was getting a broader perspective about what life was all about, and I wasn't using drugs of any kind. And I was beginning to show them a sense of responsibility. So they transferred me to Tomales Bay House in Marin County. They had just acquired some new property there; it was later to become known as "the academy." We go out to this house as its first members. It was in real bad condition, all beat up and nobody had lived there for a long time. They just moved us out there with little advance planning. There's no heat, no running water;

we have nothing, it's a dump. It's like they say, "Okay, this will be your new home, fix it up." So we either got to live in mud or fix it up. It was then that I got my first indication of the "Mafia" in Synanon.

When we first went to Tomales Bay it was kind of a joke because there were so many Italian dudes from New York in our group. Most of the people that were in Synanon at that time were from New York. I figured that out of the fifty of us that were sent to Tomales, thirty or more were from New York. Many of these were Italians who used to hang out together in a clique. Since I had grown up around Italians in the city and knew them well, I just naturally hung out with them. One or two of these dudes had some prior connection with the Mafia and so we decide that we are going to take over Synanon. We are going to use this house as a base of operations from which to unseat Dederich. Most of us have been in the organization for about six months and we figure we know it all. We'll take over Synanon and get some of those assholes at the top fired.

Our gripe centered around the fact that they'd sent us out to this hole and expected us to do it all ourselves without any help from the parent organization. At least, that's the way we saw it. One of the leaders at the new house was an old man who had a lot of building and maintenance experience. He knew a lot about renovating old buildings and we figured he was too into the system and so we should try and get him fired. So we began trying to screw up all the work details. When he'd tell us to do a job, we'd do it backward, like install plumbing and electric stuff wrong deliberately. That didn't get him fired. Then we decide we are going to bury him alive. We'd had a big mud slide that had taken out a bunch of our water and drainage pipes. So we got to go down and excavate the pipes and fix them. Hank has to go down into the hole and fix the pipes after we got them uncovered. He's way down in the bottom trying to get two pipes linked together and the bunch of us rebels are around the top of the hole.

We're standing there and Jerry tells us, "Now's the time. Let's bury the bastard." And it sounded like a good idea so we start shoveling like hell. We shovel so much mud down on him that he can't get out of the hole. And if Chuck's wife, Betty, hadn't come along, we would have killed him. Our plan was to bury him and say that the excavation slid in on him by accident. She comes running over and we're throwing mud—it's already up above Hank's chest. But then she came and the jig was up. We couldn't bury her too, 'cause it wasn't plausible that she'd be down in the hole with Hank.

So, we're nailed to the cross, and Chuck Dederich comes over to adjudicate the situation. They have a general meeting for us, sort of like a general court-martial. They put us all on the stage and shave our heads. They make us put on dresses and hang signs on us telling everybody what fuck-ups we are. Then they're going to toss us out of Synanon. First the example for everybody, then out! That's what most of the members wanted to do to us. But then Chuck takes over. "Look, you assholes, I can't just throw you out because I have too much respect for society. If I throw you out now, you'd end up killing, stealing, lying, and fucking up. I'm using your own language on you because that's what you understand. We thought by now that you'd got another message, but I guess you weren't ready to be on your own at Tomales Bay."

He couldn't do it. He couldn't have it on his conscience that he'd been responsible for letting us loose on society. He was going to keep us in Synanon. I had mixed emotions. I'd got sucked into the same old line of reasoning and acting for a while. But I think I recognized some good in Synanon. To this day I don't know what it's all about for sure, but deep down I knew then that I wanted to stay. Of course, Dederich hadn't even considered letting us go. That was the last thing on his mind. That is his usual story in a like kind of situation because they figure if they put you through a lot of changes they make you a stronger person. And

just to put you through a lot of changes you gotta listen to Chuck's line of shit.

I am wearing a sign on me that says, I AM A GENERAL FUCK-OFF. On Saturday night we used to have general meetings where guests would come in, people from the streets. And I'm walking around with a bald head and this crazy sign on me and I gotta serve these people. I serve them coffee, little cakes, and doughnuts. Don't ask me why I did it or how I could stand to denigrate myself that way. All I had to do was leave. This was the first time in my life when I wasn't using dope when I wasn't locked up in jail.

That was the one fact that really fascinated me. I, Manny Torres, wasn't using dope. I guess that was the only living thing that kept me there. All this time I had been trying to get in touch with my brother Bobby. He was in the house in Santa Monica. Their strategy is to keep us apart, but nobody comes out and tells me that. You see, Synanon is supposed to be 100 percent on the up and up with you, but they can be terribly smothering and paternalistic. Just like any other organization—anything is justified if it is for the good of the client. I keep asking to see my brother and Jack Hearst says no, not at the present time. Jack was like the general director. I tell him

I want to see Bobby and he would say, "Well, we don't think that you're ready."

"When the hell am I going to be ready, then? We haven't seen each other for a long time. You can't naturally keep brothers apart." And he'd say something like that on the next trip down south I could go, but that trip would never come up. The whole two and a half years I was at Synanon, I didn't see Bobby once.

By this time I'm beginning to like Synanon. I think it was 'cause of everything they did for me. Many things were fun, like we'd get tickets to movies, plays, and the good restaurants 'cause Synanon was still at that time a tax-free foundation. They bought every member who smoked a carton of cigarettes each week. Every week I would get three dollars spending money. That doesn't sound like much, I know, but you gotta remember that we didn't really need mcney. The three bucks was sometimes hard to spend. Everything we needed was right there. They housed us, fed us three squares a day, we got good clothing —what could we possibly want? Come to think of it, that pretty well describes conditions in a minimum-security correctional facility. Synanon is not fundamentally different than corrections as far as I can determine. Only the more harsh external restraints, the almost unnecessary steel and concrete garbage thrown up to keep the public out, were absent from the Synanon approach. Synanon is a private minimum-security correctional facility, and Chuck Dederich is a benevolent warden.

I was beginning to get really comfortable with the routine of Synanon. Most major decisions were made for me; I was subject to an authority that was not too corrosive, an authority structure that I could understand and even dig occasionally. There was an esprit de corps that was tighter than the Marine Corps at times. I was even getting into work. For quite a while I managed two service stations for Synanon. I couldn't drive a car because every time I got a license I'd foul it up. I never could learn when to stop the car. By this time I'd been at Synanon for two years and I had my own apartment, for which the organization was footing the bill.

I was working pretty hard, and long hours. The service stations were doing real good and I kept looking around and noticing that Chuck and the board of directors of the organization were making a lot of money. They were living high on the hog, driving new cars, wearing good threads, having the best of everything. So, I ask myself the inevitable question: What the hell is going on?

It seems like I'm working my ass off for them. They are getting all the benefits, all the cream, and they keep telling me, "Well, you're getting the ultimate benefit, Manny.

You're not using scag, and you can't beat that benefit. Aren't we entitled to a living?"

And I keep saying that that's good work if they can get it. In fact, I point out to them that it's slave labor. "You're not paying me; you're keeping me like I was your two-bit whore! I'm running two service stations, working eleven-twelve hours a day. If you ask me, I'm getting creased without grease."

Every week I gotta go sit in a game where people keep telling me: "Manny, it's good for you, you're getting more mature every day, you're learning how to cope. Just hang in there and settle down."

Pretty soon, one dominant question keeps running through my mind: What is their game? What are they up to? You know, to this day I don't have the answer. I don't know what Synanon is all about. I just know that a process of assimilation, a binding together into an almost total institutional community is at work there. Sure, it keeps guys off of dope—so long as they stay forever. They might as well of told me: "Manny, you can stay forever."

"Now, thanks my friends. Thanks, but no thanks. There's a great big orange juice world out there, and I want to get me some. You guys told me that if I stayed here for two and a half years that I would never use again. Well, I accept that and I believe it. Now it's time to try it out. So, Jack Hearst, I'm leaving."

They spent a day trying to argue me down, but I had them where their logical hair was short. I was willing to take them at their word. As I walked out of that place, I was confident that I would never shoot dope again, ever. I was to find out that it was impossible for me to transfer the inside experience outside. Even as I walked away from the organization and headed for Market Street, a clock started ticking deep in my guts, winding toward the hour when the alarm would go off. "The bell tolls for you, Manny. Once you've tuned in on her wavelength, Miss Heroin will ring your chimes every time." I didn't know it then, but I would tunnel back to my white-hot love once more.

Chapter 5

After "Sesame Street"

Through the looking glass again.

I left Big Brother and went looking for little brother. Bobby had got out of Synanon two months before I had. And I go down to Venice to where he is living. First thing he does when I find his house is open up a bottle of wine and pour me a glass. And I tell him, "Hey, Bobby, what are you doing? I don't drink! Didn't you learn better habits than that in Synanon?"

I came out of that place really brainwashed. I tolerated no drinking; I insisted on it! No drugs, no stimulants, no nothing. I even start to give my brother a Synanon haircut in his own house. I said, "What are you doing drinking? If you drink this kind of shit, next thing you know it'll be whiskey and then in no time at all you'll be mainlining scag." I really strap it on him. The whole trip that I been subject to for the last two and a half years starts pouring out of me.

Bobby says, "Shut the fuck up! I don't want to hear that propaganda. If you want to drink, there it is. Take it freely. If not, shut up and go to bed. Anyway, leave me alone."

So I sack out, feeling kind of bad because I can see that Bobby is slipping right back into the old life. Next day I go out and look for a job. I can remember thinking, I'm cured! Hell, I've got freedom and I'm not stealing. I'm not locked up. Even at Synanon I was sort of like locked up; at least I was locked into a way of life that I couldn't hardly get away from. Now I'm out! Whammo!

But instead of seriously looking for a job, I find myself walking on the beach. I just make my way up and down the boardwalk there in Venice. It's a very warm, sunny day and I'm taking it all in. Looking at all the freaks with the long hair, and the girls so sleek and tight in their little sunsuits. I thought of the longhairs as Jesus freaks. Boy, was I conservative, coming out of Synanon. I had short hair so I thought everybody else should be just like me. My conservatism was not the thoughtful variety at all, just kind of a simple like-mindedness. It was the classical response to authoritarianism.

Instead of being totally free, I felt almost totally bound.

But I don't seriously look for a job. I don't know where to begin. It's like everything has been decided for me for so long that I'm completely alienated from my working self. My dependency was a function of my lack of experience, and a very limited knowledge of the ground rules used by society for organizing and explaining work experience. The authority figures in prison and in Synanon had been so concerned with controlling my behavior that they had given little or no thought as to how their closed-ended notions of reality would ever allow me to broaden my range of imaginations and interpretations in an open society. You see, neither the warden of Sing Sing nor Chuck Dederich were really into helping me grow into

maturity. Neither of them understood the relationship between my consciousness and freedom, and how socialization within the "total" institutional setting restricts the inmate's consciousness. (I realize that Synanon is not a total institution; I only believe that a comparison between prison and Synanon is quite valid and worthwhile.)

When I say I was experiencing alienation it was like I wasn't able at all to use my freedom in an autonomous and constructive manner. I was not able to relate realistically to the world around me. Instead of being totally free, I felt almost totally bound. I mean, I couldn't even bring myself to hit on one of those cute chicks along the boardwalk for some body. I'd been so used to going without in the joint, and scoring occasionally in Synanon by using traditionally articulated methods of "courtship," that I couldn't even score a piece of ass!

As for choosing alternatives and priorities in other areas of my life, a sense of meaninglessness and apathy cut me off completely from even visualizing the possible choices. As I see it now, I was drifting aimlessly, unable to imagine any possibilities for me, *my will* to act in my behalf completely eroded. So, I don't look for a job seriously at all. I just kind of drift around for a few days. One afternoon I go back to our pad early. My brother is away working; I see the wine on the table and I think, Oh, what the hell! One drink isn't going to cut it. I remember feeling really ambivalent inside. It was as if I knew that if I took that drink I would soon go all the way again. But you know what? Who the hell cared anyway?

I get about half high and I go down to the beach and flirt with the bare-assed girls. I don't really want to score without Bobby along, 'cause I'm unsure of myself. But it does me good inside to be able to sock it to them broads verbally. My brother comes home from work and he wants to go out. He says, "Manny, it's about time we pulled the covers off this town. You've been around here for days now and we haven't done a damn thing. Don't give me any of that Synanon shit about drinking, either. You've just about got that outa your system by now."

I'm more than willing to go by this time. He takes me out to the Cheeta, a real far-out night club in Venice. When we walk in Big Brother and the Holding Company were rocking and socking. Janis Joplin was appearing with them at the time. The place was absolutely packed out. All these strobe lights were flashing their myraid colors along the walls and the sounds of the Holding Company were piercing. I begin to get really freaked out, kind of superdisoriented, and I ask Bobby, "What kind of a place is this, anyway?"

He just says, "Shut up and open your mouth." He puts something in my mouth and I ask him what it is. He replies, "Acid, Manny. Just wait a few minutes." I had never experienced acid before. I'm in the middle of all these strobe lights and piercing music and all of a sudden this acid kicks me. It was a riot. Everything began to waver and jump out of proportion. Unreal images of a thousand weird forms invaded my mind, ever changing and fantastic in their coloration. Joplin's sounds were translated into visual images in some mystical way. It was as if my personality split in two. On one level I remained calm and almost detached from it all, sort of standing outside of myself and taking into account the whole crazy scene. But on a more important dimension the sights, sounds, and even smells of my forever were all paved into a freeway on which I was making no headway. It was as if I were running a million miles an hour through liquid music dripping from surrealistic landscapes—running into eternity with lead feet. It was alternately a very bewildering and exceedingly fulfilling experience, like nothing ever experienced in a thousand lifetimes.

I'm on such a kick that I think I'm going crazy. I grab Bobby, wanting to know what's going on. He tells me to relax and don't panic. "If you don't panic you'll have a beautiful trip."

I'm standing in the middle of a

million people, it seems like, and everybody is dancing around me. Janis Joplin is hollering at the top of her lungs, and I remember thinking that this is weirder than the furthest-out Esther Williams movie I ever saw in the joint. I close my eyes and the weirdness of it all cuts at my consciousness like a knife and I begin to fall away from reality. I keep hearing about ten layers of my brother's voice somehow set to colored music. "Don't panic, Manny. It's so fine. Just keep cool, everything will be ultimately together."

I can't take any more. I yell at Bobby and run out of the place. I run along the boardwalk all the way to the house. I run inside and get into bed, clothes and all. I sink deep down under the covers, wanting a smoke with all my life, but I remember thinking that I dare not light up or I'll burn to death. Death, Death, DEATH. I thought I was starting to die. I look out from under the covers and spot the butcher knife on the kitchen table. But I can't bear to see it because every time I look I feel like stabbing myself. What am I going through? Am I looking at my last moments? I want to get out of bed to save my life but I'm scared. It's the knife again. So I put the covers over my head and start to ease off the bed. My brother walks in and I don't recognize him. I throw the covers off my face and I don't think it is him. He's trying to convince me that its all right, but I think he's

come for me. I go for the knife and there's this big hassle and my brother tries to wrestle the knife away from me. He don't want to hurt me, but he knows that I didn't handle the acid trip right and he's beginning to get scared for me.

The landlord comes up to see what the big commotion is and he sees my brother holding onto me for dear life. Now I have the shakes. I'm deep down in the guts scared. I begin to cry like a baby. I start to get a little quieter, though, and my brother and the landlord whisper about something and then the landlord goes downstairs after some reds. Later, my brother gave the redlins to me and I chased them with a beer. I just kept hanging onto him as if he was the only thing solid around me. I remember crying like a baby, and I got so petrified that I passed out. I woke up the next day and I swore that I would never again take any more acid. Never again!

My brother wasn't shook at all. "You just freaked out; happens a lot the first time you get loaded on acid. You have to know how to handle it."

"Listen, Bobby, I don't want to handle that stuff." But, like the dope fiend I was—the only drug around was acid. That night he comes home with a bag of white tabs and he pops two right away.

"You want to try it again?"

I say, "Not a chance! You got any weed or any wine in the house." It was a terrifying thought to me to see my brother getting off and me just sitting there hurting. "Well, give me some of that acid again." I took it, but this time it was different 'cause this time I knew what to expect. I was prepared for the sights and sounds of weirdsville.

So, I was right in the middle of the drug lifestyle again. Being out from under the boiler room pressures of the Synanon stew, I felt free in one sense but I became captive to dope again. And I went back to that place I knew best, 'cause once I started using again I had to be in a place where I could score easily. So I beat it back to New York and the street life that I could handle and an environment I could understand.

But it was cold in New York and somehow it wasn't the same. I found out that I could never really go home again. Some of the same old stands were there and I could still score at many of the familiar places, but the New York charisma that I'd always experienced, even in my most miserable days of being hooked bad, was gone. Maybe it was just the very cold, windy weather. Anyway, I was using quite a bit of stuff; I'm not hooked at this point, but I was using every day. I decide to go to Florida and get out of the cold.

I firmed up a connection in Florida that I could score from and I started hitchhiking down there. I had never been that far south before. All these years I had heard people discussing going south for the winter, so I figure it's about time to try it. A little ways out of New York I got a ride that took me all the way to Tampa, Florida. I had about a hundred dollars on me and the first thing I do is to hunt up the connection. I find that dope is easy to score in Tampa. There was a big Cuban community there at that time and a lot of cheap but good heroin. So I think that I better stay down there and I start looking around for a hustle so that I can survive and sustain my growing habit.

There were a lot of check-cashing places around. I never had seen a town with so many check-cashing stores. And I think to myself, You know what? This is going to be a good town for robbery—it has gotta be simple to hit these places. Just one person in there, it will just require a slight caper that'd be simple compared to some I'd been involved in in the city. So, I'm not worried about money 'cause I see that this is my kind of town. Once a dope fiend sees that there's plenty of marks around, plenty of places where he can get money, he doesn't worry about it. He just goes and gets it when necessary. A real doper has no conscience. He can't be scared off easily 'cause he knows that he has to have money to score scag. He doesn't get scared easily, either. A doper is not usually scared off by threats. If he needs, he gets, and nothing much will deter him short of death in the streets.

I check into a hotel room and I meet the guy that works at the desk. I made him for a dope fiend, you can spot a brother doper every time. You just take one look into their eyes and you know. And the silent conversation that passes between strangers when they meet soon makes them the best of acquaintances in the scag world. I said acquaintances; a dope fiend doesn't have friends 'cause he will burn anyone he has to behind drugs. You burn acquaintances if necessary but you should never burn friends.

The clerk gives me a room and I go upstairs and stash my belongings. This takes just a minute because a dope fiend travels light. I come back downstairs and I ask him if he knows where I can come by an outfit. I only got one, and I really need two in case one clogs up. He tells me that outfits bring two bucks. So I duke him the two dollars and he goes in the back room and gets me a syringe and needle. He asks me if I want to score. "If you got twenty-five dollars you can buy a quarter, not a quarter of an ounce but just a quarter, which is three spoons."

I tell him, "Sure I need to score soon, but all I got is about twenty-five dollars and I can't spend it all on scag. Anyway, I don't really need that much at a time because I'm not hooked."

He says, "Don't worry about it. If you're looking to make money I gotta good thing for you. Are you particular about how you earn your daily bread?"

"Hell, no," I tell him. "Sure, I'll have a go at anything to make money." And I'm thinking to myself, well, here we go again! He's the connection and he's got some way I can make money. Far out! I give him my last twenty-five bucks for dope to get down, and I share it with him. It is rare that I would share my dope with anybody, but I figure that this dude is going to do something for me so I'm going to give him a tad bit. I'm not doing it 'cause I like the guy or because I got a big heart all of a sudden, but 'cause I know damn well that there's something in it for me. So, we fix and get down. Now we are as tight as dope fiends can get; we've scored together and we've shared.

And he asks me, "Do you have any solid connections in New York?"

I tell him, "Sure, I got lots of places to score in the city. I've lived in the streets there all my life, except for a couple of years out in California."

"Manny, I'm more interested in fences, not ordinary dope connections."

"I know several ounce men who'll take pretty much anything of value, and can handle any amount, too. I think that I could sell anything that you got."

He says, "How about truckloads? If I gave you a semi full of name-brand cigarettes could you move them?"

"Wow! Let me get on the horn and find out." I was going to tell him anything to stall him 'cause I really didn't know.

So I get on the phone to my uncle and I tell him, "I got a guy down here who tells me he can score semi truckloads of cigarettes at a time. Can you get rid of them?" He tells me that he'll have to call me back. I know that my uncle will have to go upstairs in the Organization.

In a few hours he calls me back. "We'll take all the butts you can score. Our price will be five thousand for a regular-sized semi load of quality cigarettes."

So I tell my dude that my connection in the city will take all the cigarettes that we can produce, but I don't quote him the price. "We got somebody that will buy them, now how are we going to come up with the product?"

Then he starts telling me this story of a hijacking scheme. I don't have the slightest idea how to drive a semi, and I tell him I don't want to have anything to do with hijacking. "That's not my game and I've had no experience at it. All I know about hijacking is that a lot of people get hurt sometimes." Besides, I was still just chippying around on dope and not really strung out, so I was capable of thinking bad thoughts about going to jail and getting caught.

He tells me that he and his two brothers have this hijacking scam and that it's a cinch. He runs the whole game down to me and I can see that they have a good thing going. And I decide that I'm going to get in on it. That's a typical dope fiend reaction. So we go to a truck stop in a car, just the four of us. One reason that cigarette hijacking is so profitable is that there is no tax on butts in Louisiana, and in New York you have the highest tax in the nation. Guys have even made a fair amount of bread by buying cigarettes South and selling them illegally North. A lot of tobacco comes out of Louisiana that way, especially Chesterfields in those days. Here was the way we used to operate.

We went to a popular truck stop and sat around drinking coffee, waiting for them to come in. We would dress like truckers and it didn't take us long to learn the lingo. We would sit in the café and see every kind of truck come off the road with all kinds of cargo, going everywhere. We'd just wait until our truck came along. When we identify our mark, we watch the guy until he has his coffee or his meal and we establish whether or not he has a helper. When he hits the road, we follow him. Sometimes we had to follow for two hundred miles or more, till he hit another truck stop. Almost always they would not lock their cab. When he went in to eat, one of us would get up in the cab and crawl back into the sleeper. When it was my turn to be the heist man, I would get up in there and wait patiently for the trucker to come back. I would just sit there with my pistol ready. When there were two guys on the truck it was a tad bit tricky; it is always harder to watch two than one. That was the worst time for me—the waiting. 'Cause you're sitting there and all these things go through your mind. You wonder if you set the job up right, if you have all the information. Maybe the truck is bugged and the trucker is onto your game. Is this fool going to have a gun, or will he go crazy when I throw down on him? I would really get nervous and work up a sweat. Sometimes I would wait there for an hour and a half because the cat would be eating his main meal.

But as soon as I would hear his footsteps and the door open, all my fear would go away because I knew that it was time to get down. If two guys came back at one time, I would get a little shook. Usually I'd be hiding behind a curtain, and one time a guy pulled the curtain the first thing when he got in the cab—and his eyes balled out like two big saucers. I didn't point the gun at him, but I had the gun in my lap. He saw me and he just froze and did what he was supposed to do. Most of the time they'd get in and start the truck, not knowing that they'd soon have it. When they'd get out of town a little ways

I'd pull the curtain over and show them my piece. Most of the time a trucker won't do or say anything. They understand perfectly what's happening and they're not about to be a dead hero for the insurance company. It's not their cigarettes and they know that if they cooperate the chances are good that they won't get hurt. And I'd tell them, "All we want you to do is to drive the truck like I tell you. I'm not alone, there are others following us. All we want is the cigarettes. No hassle. All you have to do is drive up the line a piece and nobody will get hurt."

When you tell it like it is to a sucker and you mean it and you got the pistol in your hand, it kind of shakes them up and prepares them to cooperate. Like, all the time I was involved in that hijacking scheme I never had one hassle with a truck driver. They never said a word usually; they just drove. We've already planned the caper out real well and we want to get the cigarettes as close as possible to the drop. 'Cause we are going to take the whole semi. We won't unload the cigarettes, we'll sell the whole thing. The truck, trailer, and cargo all gets sold. So we would drive out to where it was hilly or woody and we would park at a prearranged spot and let the drivers out and handcuff them to a tree where it was real secluded. Then we would drive the truck to the drop and leave it there to be picked up. We'd go right to a phone and call the highway patrol and tell them where the driver was. We didn't want a murder beef on our heads. If they weren't found they could die out there. Hijacking cigarettes is one thing, but murder is another. If a trucker dies behind a caper they'll hunt you down like a dog, but just a heist—they have 'em every day.

We didn't want a murder beef on our heads.

The next day the money would arrive. Like, I never knew who actually picked up the truck. I didn't need to know. All I knew was that the money would arrive from my uncle. And the drop was always somewheres different. We only did this a few times; you can hold a lot of cigarettes in a semi truck. And I wasn't giving them all the take, either. A doper don't work that way. I gave them three thousand dollars and we were splitting it three ways. So two thousand off the top was mine. According to the ethics of the street world this wasn't bad. I quoted them a price of three thousand and they went for it. If they'd have said they had to have four thousand then I'd have only

grifted a bill. But they had asked me to help them get rid of the merchandise and I'd set up the connection so I was entitled to my cut off the top.

Well, that scam lasted for a while, but like all good things it had to end. When you're shooting dope and all strung out—like I've said before, it demands a daily income in three figures to support your habit. We had a good thing there, but like every other set up it don't last. Somebody else jumped on the bandwagon and pretty soon trucks were getting heisted all over Florida. It got so hot that the FBI men started swarming around and I knew it was time to leave.

I was on my way out to California again when I decided to go up and see Bonnie, my sister-in-law, who was living in, of all places, Lake Elmo, Minnesota. That country is swarming with middle- and upper-class white Protestant Anglos. It was exactly what I'd always pictured it to be, with the woods, light snow falling most of the time, kids and grown-ups skiing and sledding around. When I went out there to visit I took along plenty of scag 'cause I just knew that there wouldn't be any dope around that place. I'd been there a week or so, walking around loaded and enjoying myself. When I found myself running low on heroin I told Bonnie that it was time to go south for California. "I can't stay longer 'cause I'm running short of dope."

She surprised the hell out of me. "Don't worry, Manny, there is a connection here."

"A heroin dealer in Lake Elmo, Minnesota?" Damned if there wasn't. In fact, there were two dope fiends in Lake Elmo; I made the third. Three dope fiends and one connection. I've been using dope a long time so it was no problem at all to build a quick relationship with the connection. I play the big-city-slicker dope fiend with the dude and I scheme that when I leave, I'm going to burn his ass. One day I just take all his dope and move on out. Not because I didn't like the guy or anything, it was just the thing to do. If I meet somebody and I let him take all my dope away, well, I deserve that. He was a dope fiend himself. He knew the game as well as I did. You cover your back all the time. He didn't cover and I just took his dope and left. One more lesson for him! Next time he'll learn to never trust a doper. The thing that really freaked me out about Lake Elmo was that there were two dope fiends, and a single righteous dealer! How about that? If you find it in Lake Elmo— the land of the square John blond German-Swede backbuster—you'll find it anywhere.

I went back to Venice and fell into the same old rut. For several years I was constantly in and out of Venice, California. Anything for a kick, an escape from the freedom of an eight-to-five life. I got back into smoking pot, dropping acid, shooting speed, and, when I could get it, mainlining stuff, which is always the best go. My behavior was very freaky and I was doing all sorts of flunky capers, taking very large risks to get money for drugs. I wasn't about to deprive myself of anything. I became a real garbage head. I would take any drug, it made no difference at all what it was. If it would make me feel different, I'd take it.

I got this genuine job, working in a sheet metal place. I worked there about three weeks; I don't see how they put up with me. When I left I managed to cop a couple of extra checks that were made out to salaried officials of the company. I got them cashed and so had a pretty good bankroll. I decide to clean up my act and use nothing but smack. It isn't long before I'm getting around to the end of the cycle again. The little bit of money I'd accumulated is blown away because I'm using a lot of stuff. For a while I try to just chippy around, not using every day and deliberately staying away from my stash. But I get to where I'm hooked bad again. You can always tell when you've reached that stage 'cause you keep yawning and your nose won't stop dripping, and you have to get the yen off your back right after you've just fixed.

Now I'm where I got to have more dope. I'm thinking that I need to make some more money, but then the only thing that I knew how to do is rob. I sure ain't got no front to hustle behind. And the first thing I'd noticed about LA was the amount of police all over the place. It was unreal. I never seen so many cop cars all the time—especially around Venice. They have a board-walk in Venice and there's a cop car always on it going back and fourth, twenty-four hours a day.

I decide against resuming my career of robbery. I didn't have no car, so how am I going to go out and rob successfully? Dressed like a hippie; hair kind of long; all the clothes I got to my name is a pair of overalls. Except for when I was first on dope, it's the only time I'm really a bum. I'd always been used to dressing pretty nice—except when I'm hooked like a dog. Here I am in Venice, California, again acting like a hippie. Hell! Only a few months ago I'd been cussing out hippies and now I was one. The longhairs see me walking every day back and forth on the boardwalk and they must of figured I had a route. One day one of them comes up and asks me if I know where they can score some weed. It just happened that I knew someone who was usually holding and I said, "Sure, I can score some for you."

I went over to this cat's place and scored for them and they pieced a little of it off on me.

So I thought to myself, That's far out. I'll just hang around here and act like I'm a dealer and people will do business with me. I'll get them the weed but charge them twelve for a ten-dollar pack of pins and make two for myself. So, for a week or two that's how I made enough money to eat on. But I wanted to get a supply of weed for myself so's I could get ahead. I asked the connection if he could front me a kilo. He didn't want to do that, but he said he'd get me all I wanted if I could come up with the bread. Of course, I didn't have any money. I went over to Bobby's pad and he was broker'n shit too. But he was hooked again.

We decide to pull a burglary, any burglary, we didn't care. And since we didn't have any wheels we knew that it'd have to be right there in the neighborhood. That night we were out walking around just looking for opportunities. Coming back to the house for a cup of coffee we notice that our next-door neighbor's car isn't parked in the garage where he usually has it. So I go up and knock on the door, no answer! We go on in the house and take a color TV, a chain saw, and two jars full of change. In counting up the change it comes to more than seventy dollars. We take the stuff upstairs to our apartment and leave it. Then we go over to a bar a couple of streets away on the boardwalk. There's a guy that hangs out in there and buys hot goods. I tell him, "Listen, I got a good color TV and some kind of chain saw. The stuff is hotter'n hell and I want to get rid of it with someone who'll take it clear out of the neighborhood. Come up and look at it and I'll make you a good deal."

He came right up and bought the stuff from us for two hundred dollars. Funny thing. In the old days back in New York two hundred dollars was just "lunch money." Now, it was my stake. I beat it over to the grass connection and tell him that the bread is down. He leaves for about twenty minutes and when he comes back he's got our weed. So Bobby and I start making lids up, and since I am always on the beach and everybody knows me, we start moving lids like crazy. I would go down to the beach and sit in the sand with about fifteen or twenty lids on me. People would come over and buy one or two at a time. It's surprising how fast you get known in an area as a dealer. Business really got good. I was moving over a hundred lids of maryjane a week. That's a thousand dollars.

We begin to get fat and right away we decide to move up from selling lids to getting right into the kilo business. But we don't know anybody to score big amounts from. The only contact we have is this guy who sells us the kilos. Bobby and I figure that the best place to get the weed in profitable amounts

is in Mexico. We want to go to Mexico and score, but neither of us knows a damn thing about that country. But we both speak Spanish and we figure that we can find our own connection.

We rent a large panel truck from this friend of Bobby's and we drive down to TJ. We get a cheap room and start looking around. We're walking through all the bars asking the bartenders, cabdrivers, and anyone else who looks like they're in on the know. They are suspicious of us and think that we're undercover agents of some kind so they just shine us on. After a while this kid comes over to us in a bar and says that he overheard us talking about weed. He says he can help us get to the connection that can supply us with a barn full of good stuff if that's what we want.

We all get into the truck and drive out—I don't know where—it must have been about fifteen miles southeast of TJ. We drive up to this place with a house and a couple of barns on it and are met by this kid's grandfather. He takes us over to one of the barns, after looking us over real good, and I never seen so much grass in my life! We load up our truck with weed at fifteen dollars a kilo and we head right away for the border. We just drive right up to the border, not even thinking about guards or anything. We get up to the gate, roll down our window, and they ask us if we are American citizens.

I say, "Yes. We're over here in

TJ looking around."

"Have a good day." That's all they said, I swear it's the truth. And we were in business. We made runs like that for nine months, one a month at least. Never shook us down once. It was a good score until some fools killed two border guards. Remember the ones they kidnaped and took up in the woods and shot to death? What the deal was is that they were only shaking down a few cars each day. The whole time we were going across, we never seen anyone stopped. Not once! We must have crossed nine or ten times. Not only were we not stopped, but we were drunk several times. Plastered with tequila. It was good stuff. We'd be drunk, singing, joking, and carrying on, come to the border and they'd just wave us on. We were doing real good in the weed business, but we got back into the groove on scag and were using a whole lot.

We were dealing in weed and using stuff. 'Cause weed dealing is kind of penny ante. Weed is bulky, though. There's a lot of bread to be made in weed, but it's too bulky to be carrying around. Lots of people use weed and you got a ready market, but the risk is in transportation. Lots of guys get busted on the road, like for faulty taillights, or they get a flat tire and have to pull over. When you're stopped alongside the highway, you are very vulnerable. The patrol is always checking those kind of situations out. If you use the road a lot and you're into some kind of shady transport, you need to keep up your wheels real good, lights, brakes, and all. That's how most people get busted. The cops stumble into it by accident.

We decided that since we were using stuff, we'd get back into dealing stuff. So we bought some stuff in LA and we're dealing in Venice. But the thing is that we were into dealing to weed people. Weed heads are not criminals. People who buy lots of weed are usually not dope fiends. Now we're back dealing with heroin users again and the long trip we'd had with weed had kind of mellowed us out. Dope fiends were playing their games on us and we found ourselves getting took. They would come on us with a big sob story about needing to be fronted for a few days and we would fall for it. Sometimes they would come in saying they only had fourteen dollars and they needed twenty-five worth of stuff to get down. "Give me a break" was about all we were hearing. We started giving too many breaks and we got ripped off for lots of bread.

You see, not only is the dope fiend less trustworthy and more sneaky than the squarer weed head, but the West Coast user is even less "cool" than the Atlantic Coast variety. This is a subjective opinion, but it's based on observation over some time and I really believe it's true. Anyway, one day we really got ripped off good. Three dudes came to the door and I asked who it was. They said they'd come for some dope so I opened the door. They threw their arms around me and took all our heroin. Shit! Now I'd been had.

These guys were nervous as hell. All they took was the dope. There was a lot of money in the house, up in my room, but they didn't even try for it. I gave them the dope without a struggle, though, 'cause they had good artillery. You can always come up with more dope, but you can't get your life back. My brother came in and I said, "Bobby, guess what. We've just been had. Three black dudes just came in and stuck us up."

"We're going to have to move, Manny. Or they'll just get us again. Them or their friends."

"The hell we'll move! Not a chance. You know what? We'll just have to get us some artillery. Those cats are crazy, so maybe we'll have to be a little nuts ourselves. We wouldn't have been on the short end of the stick back in the city."

"You're right, Manny. We'll get us some guns." Bobby was ready to quit nit-picking around, too.

I found that the easiest thing in the world to score was a gun. I contacted a guy in Venice that used to buy hot stuff off of us and asked him if he could get us some guns. "No problem," he says, "what kind do you want?"

I order us a .45 and a .38 police special. And he says, "Okay, I'll deliver them tomorrow for forty-five bucks each." I couldn't believe it. I was so anxious that I gave him the money right there. The next day we go back and he's got 'em for us. Now we feel safe. Next day we go down to San Diego and we score a couple of pieces of stuff. Now that we got guns on us we start thinking like cowboys. Anybody that fucks with us is going to get blown away. We're strung out real bad by this time.

Each time we go south we come home with two—maybe three—ounces of dope. When you got three pieces to cut you've got a lot of work on your hands. You have to shave it and fluff it up. Then you cut it into short pieces. But you don't cut it so as to screw the user too bad. It's an art to learn how to keep your customer happy and still come out on the long end. It takes a long time to break pebbles or blocks of heroin down and make the shit up into dime bags.

We learned to do it with a plain, ordinary kitchen blender. The first time we tried a blender we forgot to wipe the moisture out of the glass top. And we put the shit in there and turned it on. What the hell! It all dissolved on us, right before our eyes. We lost a hell of a lot of stuff, 'cause the customer is used to getting his little white powder in bags. We used most of it ourselves, though. We learned to take the blender glass and dry it in the oven. You don't let it get real hot, you just dry all the moisture on it. Then you take these little heroin "rocks" and you stick them in the blender and it powders out real fine.

The raw heroin looks like little rocks, but we used to call it "cheeva." There's a million names for it, "shit," "scag," "smack," "garbage," "stuff." Out here we called it "cheeve" or "cheeva." And the stuff out here is usually brown. Back East it is white. Sometimes they call it "morta," although "morta" is a slang expression for weed, too. Anyway, we got all this stuff and I run out of milk sugar— they use milk sugar out here to cut heroin, back East you usually use quinine. So I leave the house and go to the store and I buy ten pound boxes of white powdered sugar. Somebody must have been watching me. If you are in on the know and you see a cat buy ten pounds of powdered sugar you know he's either got to be making a lot of frosting for a cake or he's cutting dope.

I get back to the house and I fix right away. Any time you leave the house you fix, and when you get back you fix. I was really nodding good, slobbering all over the dope on the table. I'm just going to it, really feeling good. Bobby tells me, "Man, you know what? Why don't you go to bed? You're not any help here."

"Sure, why not?" There's nothing I like better to do than to kick back. I'm going in and out of the nod. Faintly, I hear this knock at the door. I hear Bobby say something and some dudes come into the house but I don't snap to anything until I hear somebody say, "And where the hell is the money?"

When I hear that I come out of the nod. I jump out of bed looking for my gun. I get this big .45 out of my coat—man, it was big—I never had one like it before or since. I could hardly hold it, but I liked it 'cause you felt like you were in command of the situation. I walked right over to the bedroom door, where I could see into the living room at an angle. I could see Bobby in there with his hands in the air, sitting on the floor. There is one John with a pistol pointed at Bobby's head and this other dude is going through the dresser drawers. I fire at the guy with the gun. If you never heard a .45 go off, it explodes like a cannon and sounds like you're being attacked from all sides. A shot goes off from inside the room. I fire again, but I'm not firing at anyone in particular. I'm just shooting into the living room. I run into the room blazing away and this dude with the gun catches a slug and falls into the kitchen. It was a wild shot, but it got him good. The other guy went out the front door in a hurry.

The dude that I hit is lying on the kitchen floor bleeding all over the place. Bobby is sitting on the floor like nothing has happened, just staring at me with his mouth open, and I'm beginning to realize what happened. I'd really gone berserk and flipped out for a moment. First thing out of my mouth is, "Did they take the dope?"

Bobby says, "Hell, no, they didn't get no dope. They'd just went into their act when you came outa the nod and broke bad. Man, you must have fired off a whole clip in here. But we still got all the dope and money."

We go into the kitchen and this guy has got a hole the size of my fist in his upper leg. He's out and bleeding like a stuck pig. I think he's going to die on me, and I ask Bobby, "What if they guy kicks off?"

"Well, if he dies we'll just get rid of him in the ocean. We'll just sink him or do something with him."

The guy comes to and is yelling, "For Christ sake, take me to the hospital."

Bobby goes over and sits right on the guy's chest and sticks a .38 special in his mouth and tells him, "Now, we are going to take you to the hospital 'cause we don't want to see you die. But if anything, anything at all comes down from this, me, my brother, or our friends will get to you. You got it? We don't want you to kick off so we're going to take the gamble, but you better keep your fucking mouth shut! Understand?"

I know we're taking a gamble, 'cause if he dies we're in trouble. We drag the guy outside, must have dragged him about a block, all the

way to the beach on the board-walk. We prop him up against a garbage can in an alley and run back to the house and put in a quickie call to the cops. We tell them there was a shooting on the boardwalk and if they hurry over there they might save this guy's life. And we hang up real fast.

Then we scrubbed the house from front to back. By now we're not excited at all; it had happened so fast that there was no time to think. We had no aftereffects from the shooting. I didn't care that I'd shot a guy. He was after my dope and nobody is going to take my dope and get away with it so long as I can stand up. They can take anything else I got, but not my dope. We never had any hassle from the cops over it. Lots of people in the neighborhood knew what'd come down, but if the cops heard, they didn't move on us. Word got out, though, that you don't take those people's dope. They're crazy and will kill you behind a dime bag. So, again, the reputation comes and you live up to it. And we did quite a good business for a while.

But good times come and go for the small grifters like we were. It was only a matter of weeks till they busted our connection in San Diego and we didn't have anybody we could score large amounts of dope from. But we're hooked good and we have to keep buying stuff. We had a lot of money and there's nothing so frustrating as to have enough bread for the ounce man and not be able to find one to do business with. We were reduced to buying no more than an ounce, and very often we could not even score that good. As long as we'd been able to buy in large quantities we could use all we wanted and still make money. But buying in small quantities, we would wind up using all of it. And the money started to go fast. We get down to our last couple of hundred dollars—enough to fix for two days—and I get panic fever. I decide to write a check to get more money.

A few days before, a dope fiend had given us a string of credit cards and a checkbook in exchange for a few bags of dope. So, I decide, What the fuck, a lot of my friends in the streets have had success with personal checks, nothing else is happening, so why can't I handle it? I go over to the Bank of America in Santa Monica with this guy's checkbook and identification. I even had his picture on a piece of ID and he don't look nothing like me; in fact, he was a brown-haired Anglo. I write out a check for one hundred dollars and shove it at the girl in the teller's cage. She looks at it and at the ID that I present, stamps the back of the check and hands me the hundred in twenties. I came home and told Bobby, "Hey, look at this shit! How easy." So, I would go out every day and get a hundred. It was so simple I didn't

know when to quit, and my new scheme lasted about five days. On the fifth day I walk into a branch of B of A and they are waiting for me. I didn't snap to it; the clerk just took a little longer with the routine, not that much longer. When she handed me the hundred and I start to walk out of the bank, there's two LAPDs waiting for me.

I know what you're asking. How could somebody who claims to have been around as long as you have run that silly check game into the ground? Well, I knew from in front that you can't do that too long, and that it's really risky to keep cashing fake checks off the same account. I knew the risk, you see, but I was a dope fiend and I was hooked bad. Every morning when I'd wake up I say to myself, You know, I need a fix—bad. How am I going to get it? I got money yesterday by writing a check. Yes, but if you do it again you're going to get caught one of these times. But screw it! I can make one more run for one more time for one more fix.

It's always that one more fix. You don't think about consequences. The most important consequence is what happens if you don't fix. Nothing else is of much importance besides that. It happens just like it always happens; sooner or later you're right back in the clink. The Los Angeles County slammer was a pigsty, a black, un-believably murky hole where you never really see daylight. A tomb for the barely alive. I'm stuck, can't make bail, got no money. I'm hooked like a dog and now I have to kick. Bobby ain't no help at all 'cause he's having to scrape the bottom of the streets to keep his habit alive.

You don't think about consequences.

So, I kick. I get lucky and get into a cell with three other dope fiends who've already kicked. They give me lots of rubdowns, sympathy, and understanding. But I was sick. The worse thing is the muscle spasms in my arms and legs. By this time in my life I'd kicked enough times that I could pretty well handle the psychological problems. I couldn't kick without being drove up in jail, but once the Man had me locked up, I didn't go nuts and space out like so many who kick for the first or second time. But there's no getting used to the physical symptoms of withdrawal. They come and you just gotta work through them. So it was good that I had some help.

After being locked up for a few weeks and seeing that I couldn't

get ahold of any dope, I start to get into the old con routine of con-niving and gambling. I spend most of my time in the day room playing cards. Really not worrying much about the case against me. I figure, what the hell, they only got me on one check; what can they do to me for that? I start to make a little money 'cause I always can win a little at poker. I just start with a few pennies and build it up. Also, you can lend money and cigarettes in the can—two packs now for three back in a few days. In ninety days, while waiting for trial, I ac-cumulated over five hundred dollars in that jail. There are lots of suckers in jail, one comes in every day.

I thought as the day grew closer for my trial that they would surely offer me a deal. After all, I was a small fish. They wouldn't waste valuable court time with me. And I was ready to cop out for a short hitch in the can. The DA calls me down just before my date and says, "No deal. We've got you cold. What'ya going to do?"

I figured, What the hell, no deal— then I would hold out for a jury trial. If they were going to hassle me, I'd hassle them. Then they really poured the cobs to me. First, they had me on the one count on which I'd been caught. When I asked for a jury trial, they pressed all five counts against me. My public defender was no help at all. He didn't raise one objection to the proceedings. And when I got on the witness stand, not only did the DA rake me over the coals, but I got tore up by my own lawyer. Man, that whole court thing was a laugh.

Bobby comes up to see me and I say, "You know what just happened? Those fools found me guilty of all five counts. They could send me to the joint for one to fourteen years on each count. The DA wanted to line them up like boxcars. That's the word I got from upstairs. I'll never get out of these damn jails again." I'm all mad and I have Bobby send up another lawyer.

This real cool lawyer comes up to see me and lays on the salve. "You ain't got nothing to worry about, Manny. You are probably going to wind up with probation. They will give you a prison sentence and then suspend it for a year or so probation."

Man, he really cooled me out. Before I was worried and tore up inside. Now this guy told me not to get hassled. But deep inside I knew that I was in for it. I go before the judge and he says one to fourteen on all five counts. And I stood there waiting for him to suspend it and he didn't. Instead of stringing the counts together consecutively like the DA wanted, though, the judge ran them concurrently. I just stood there, not getting mad or anything, but kind of in a trance. They had to walk me back to the holding tank.

Once you're sentenced, that's it. As soon as the initial shock wore off I started to prepare myself for going to the joint. I'd gone through it before and I knew what I would have to do. I started hustling in earnest. While waiting for the transportation people to move me to Chino, I made money any way I could, gambling, hustling food. A couple of weeks later I'm on the Gray Goose headed for Chino, but I don't go in broke 'cause wrapped in cellophane, stuck up my ass, is four one-hundred-dollar bills.

Chapter 6

The Turnaround

Sometimes the medicine was worse than the malady.

Chino, the Reception and Guidance Center for Southern California, might look different from other prisons to the casual observer. It has wire fences instead of stone walls; it is considered to be a medium-security prison as opposed to maximum-security like Quentin or Folsom. But to me it was like any other joint. It was a lot cleaner than Sing Sing, and somewhat more modern. But the same attitudes, same numbers, and same faces. Nothing much changes when it comes to the prison experience. You can talk about your "wide variety of vocational training and industrial programs offered in a diverse, modern correctional complex," but, basically, the way things come down in the inmate body are similar—one lockup to another.

Funny thing, you always encounter the old, familiar faces, empty of recognition. They all look the same. You can look at somebody and swear that you've done time with him only to find out that personally he's a stranger. But he's not really a stranger. Convicts who are *people* are in a sense brothers, sharing a common social experience over and over again, which is why the recognition. Another thing, when they strip your outside threads off and put the prison gray, blue, or brown on you, something very tangible happens to your sense of identity—no more real individuality. A convict is a convict, and they all look the same.

Chino has the same intake as other joints. The difference was that they stuck me in what I thought was minimum-security quarters. The place was surrounded with a double barbed-wire fence, but it was only a fence, not a high wall. All the time I'd ever done before was behind high granite walls where you don't see anything but stone. The first thought that enters my mind is that if I want out, I got an easy way to go. They don't put me in a single cell, I go into a dormitory. And immediately I got to begin socializing with a lot of other convicts. So, Chino is not physically like some prisons, but mentally and emotionally it's like any other jail.

I go into the dorm, find my assigned bed, put away my gear, and I see right away that I'm going to get tested. The old cons are going to try me to see what kind of stuff I'm made of. Cons seldom accept outside appearances, they want to look in the heart. Anyway, I'm small of build, and sometimes cats think they can fuck me over. One reason that I didn't get tried much was that I rarely smiled. I'd look like I was mad, and not associate randomly with a lot of guys. I'd pick my shots and hang around with only those few who could do me some good. You know, cue me in to what was coming down, where the dope and the food could be ripped off, who had the real power in the inmate body. Those were the important questions. That way, I soon began to acquire things and work my way up in the inmate system. For me, in prison, everything settled around one idea: take good care of yourself by learning how best to con and connive. Any time is bad time, so slide by as comfortable as you can.

For the first few days I'm just walking around in the yard, not saying much, but keeping my eyes and ears open. I don't know anybody there and I'm looking for some Spics, because bloods can generally be trusted to give good, solid information. Soon, I run into a Puerto Rican dude who works in the kitchen. I start rapping to him in Spanish, telling him that I'm from New York but my family is from Puerto Rico, and so I made a contact. Somebody I could talk to and be around, because in the joint you really need somebody. You can't do time completely alone. You need somebody to cover your back. So, I start hanging around with Jimmy and I notice right off that he's a dope fiend. All you have to do is look at his arm; he's got a line of tracks running from his wrist to his shoulder. I hit on his ass right away. I tell him, "You know what? I got some money, I want some dope."

He says simply, "I'll see what I can do." A few days later Jimmy comes up with some good dope and we get down together. Now I start doing time again—the same way I've done time everywhere else I've been. I use my money wisely, investing it in various conniving schemes around the prison. Dope was hard to come by 'cause there was no steady packing connection. I could have lined up several scores in the streets, but getting a screw or a freeman to pack it through the gate was another problem.

Jimmy had a job in the kitchen, but he wasn't very con-wise and he hadn't turned his job for profit. I clued him in to how we could make plenty of money by turning out booze and selling sandwiches. Before long I was living as well at Chino as I had at Sing Sing. I was shooting up as much dope as I could find, 'cause there was always money for it.

We were on the hustle constantly, every day. I never got into any trouble with the officials. The whole time in Chino I was considered to be a model prisoner. I even took some continuation classes at night, not because I wanted to learn anything, I just didn't like being cooped up in the dorm with all those people. If I'm going to do time, put me in a cell by myself. I didn't like the constant crowds in the dorm, getting on your bed when you want to read or sleep, shucking and jiving about all their big capers and righteous women. They get pretty loud sometimes.

I went to the parole board in nine months, expecting nothing. I figured the minimum was going to be two or three years. They might give me a date sometime in the future, I thought. I didn't even bother to go into the board room "bonnyrood," in pressed and tailored clothes. I had on clean threads and my hair was slicked down, but I didn't go through any of the mental or physical hassles that I'd been on before at board

time. The board members complimented me on my school performance. They were real pleased 'cause I had taken five classes and got good grades. I didn't say anything; I just let the record stand for itself. Then, another board member said, "I see that you did three years for possession of a gun."

I replied that I had a gun in the house. But I didn't in no way admit to having used it. One thing you learn right off in prison, or before while you're on the streets, is never cop to anything. Never admit any more guilt than you have to. It's not a matter of integrity. If it were, the system would honor integrity, honesty, coming clean. But they don't. If they got the goods on you, let them prove it. Bargain if you can, but admit nothing without getting something for it. I would have been a fool to tell the parole board everything, things not even brought up in court. Too much integrity will get you in trouble every time.

Another parole board member asked me how I felt about having written all the checks. At the time, I really did feel sorry for it 'cause I had been caught and put in jail. I told them that I was sorry, but that I was hooked on dope. That was all they had to say except, "Thank you and good-by, Mr. Torres," and I left the room.

Everybody in the dorm was asking me, "How does it look? What kind of questions did they ask? Are they hostile or open? What's their mood?"

I replied, "It's really hard to tell. I can't measure their mood and I sure don't know if I made a parole." Cons are very sensitive to the mood of the parole board. They assume, rightly I believe, that parole board members are influenced significantly by the public pulse. That they are trying to read the generalized public wish constantly, and regulate the outgoing parole pipeline accordingly. To the extent that this is true, the parole function is political rather than professional. And this is one significant aspect of the political nature of prison life.

A few weeks later I got my "slip" telling me that I'd made it—I am going home in ninety days. I thought that I would be overjoyed at the prospect of getting out, hitting the streets. I was happy that they were letting me go, but that didn't change my life at all. I continued my same routine, thinking nothing about it. I suppose that I was reaching the point where prison was part of my life. Jail? Good! I'll be out in ninety days, but deep down inside I knew that I'd be back. 'Cause nothing had changed. I was intaken, processed like on an assembly line, and I would be discharged. Big deal! I didn't know what I would do when I got out. I had no sure place to go; no secure plans regarding work. I *knew* that I would get right back into the life. What other options did I have? You

ask a cat to straighten up and fly right, but you keep cutting his wings. If you want the cat to fly, build wings, don't continually cut 'em!

When I got out of Chino it didn't feel the same as when I got released from Sing Sing. I took a bus and went back to Venice, looking for my brother Bobby. The whole time I was in the joint my brother hadn't come to see me. I didn't expect it 'cause I thought he was still hooked like a dog. It don't take me long to find Bobby, even though he'd moved, and I just carried my stuff in his house like we was going to live together again. Everybody knows me. Only one thing, now Bobby has a wife and kid. When I'd bogied, Bobby had no family. I walk in the door, Bobby hugs me, and I say, "Nice to see you, let's fix."

He says, "Manny, I got married. Bonnie and I are back together again." And I say, "Fine." I sit down, sensing that something is very different here. "Are you using?"

"No."

I tell him, "I don't care what you're doing, I want to fix."

Bobby says, "I won't fix, but I can get it for you."

Bonnie comes into the room and lights into me. "You never were any good for your brother. You shouldn't make him go out and score for you now that he's trying to stay clean."

Bobby told her, "Now, Manny's my brother and he's just got out of the joint. He deserves a fix."

I gave him fifteen dollars and he came in a few minutes with a spoon. I get down; really get loaded. It was the best dope I'd had in a long time—so good that I don't need it all so I pass it over to Bobby. He starts to tie off and draw it up in the needle, and Bonnie comes running. That was the first time I ever seen my brother hit a broad. She grabbed Bobby's arm, where he had the outfit, and he knocked her flat. We both got down; we're sitting there nodding out, and Bonnie runs out of the room crying.

I just thought that this was the way I was supposed to live.

She was working in the Green Stamp redemption center and Bobby had a job doing something. I couldn't find work, but to be honest, I didn't try hard at all. I would just lay in the house and not do anything. Bonnie hates me to this day. I wouldn't do anything. I'm in the way. I went out walking for a few hours at night, but I wouldn't even steal. If I wanted dope, I'd fix if somebody would turn me on. Being an ex-con and known around the neighborhood, I got lots of free fixes. So, I'm getting down whenever I can and Bobby's fixing quite a bit, too.

Here I go again, I thought one morning, I'm on my way to being a real doper pig. I decide that it's time to split from Bobby's place 'cause I can see that problems are beginning to develop with his marriage. I feel uncomfortable and that my problems are causing it all. I guess that is about as close as I've come in a long time to having guilty feelings about the way I acted.

I move in with three other dope fiends and we start fixing both heroin and speed. I wasn't stealing much, I was just fixing. That went on for over three months; hardly eating, but not really strung out either. You get all these holes in your arm fixing shorts all the time that don't really do much for you. I don't remember even being disgusted. Nothing much moved me at all. I just thought that this was the way I was supposed to live.

One day in early summer, 1970, I met a guy from New York named Frank Mendino, an Italian dude. I'm walking on the boardwalk and I spot this guy sitting on the benches. He's dressed sharp and something just flashed across my mind, New York. He looked like he'd just got off the plane from the city. We strike up a conversation and find out that we got things in common. He came from the same kind of neighborhood as me, only from a different part of the city. He tells me that he's a dope fiend and just got into town. He had to split from New York for some reason; he'd drawn a lot of heat. He didn't say, and I didn't ask. He asked me did I want a fix, and I told him, "Well, of course."

So I took him up to the room where the other dopers were, and he had a bundle of three-dollar bags of righteous New York stuff with him. That white dope was really good; we all got loaded. Frank had money, but he'd just got kicked out of his hotel room for not paying the rent. He didn't want to blow his green without making sure of a dope supply. We have him move his stuff in with us. Apparently Frank has a lot of money 'cause we're buying dope every day and he doesn't worry at all that he's coming up with the bread. Neither do we. Do you know how when you go out to eat with friends, you want to pick up part or all of the check? And you feel funny down inside if you're sponging? Not a dope fiend. He don't give a damn. Any doper I ever knew would take a free ride whenever he could. No conscience about things like that. Of course, I feel like I'm doing my part 'cause it's me that's scoring. And you can bet that I duck in somewhere and squeeze out an extra fix or two just for myself before I deliver the bag.

A couple of days after he moved in we're just sitting around and Frank says, "We've got to go out and make some money."

I'd just seen him peel off a couple of twenties from a large roll and I wonder to myself, Why do we have to go out and score bread when he's holding.

Frank leaves for a while and when he comes back he says, "Let's go, we've got work to do!" Out at the curb stands this fine-looking Pontiac four-door.

"Where did you get this set of wheels, Frank?"

"Where the hell do you think, Manny? I stole it."

Right then I knew what we were going to do. I get in the car and settle back on the cushions feeling anxious inside and a little glad that life was taking on some direction. Frank hands me a .38 special. I just take it, not saying a word. One look at each other and we both knew it was cool. I stick the gun in my belt and pull my shirt down, not worried at all. We cruise around that way for over a half an hour.

Finally, I tell him, "Frank, let's find a place to hit. I'm getting tired of doing nothing and I want to fix." I know that Frank's got dope on him and that we ain't about to fix until we make the hit, so I'm getting anxious. I'm also beginning to feel artificial withdrawal pains because of the situation. We get to a stoplight and I spot this clean-looking dry cleaning establishment. I tell Frank, "Park here and keep the car running." He parked.

Without saying another word I

get out of the car, walk straight into the shop, pull my gun, and tell the two people in there to lay on the floor. I open the register, take all the big money, look around the stand and nearby shelves for a cashbox, and tell them, "I'm going to leave now so give me a few minutes. If I see or hear anything before I'm gone outa here, I'll start shooting."

I jump in the car and we drive leisurely off down the street. That's how Frank and I became crime partners. We did a lot of them. They weren't big jobs. A hundred, two hundred, maybe four bills. Anytime we needed the money we'd just go out and get a car. In the city you can find a car in maybe three or four minutes, keys and all. I know how to hot-wire most cars, but seldom have had to do it. I've found keys in cars in the middle of the night. Sometimes in parking lots that are attended during the day, they'll leave the keys in some dumb place after hours. Like over the visor, under the seat in front, or underneath a tire. I've even looked for those magnetic lock boxes with the extra key stuck in around the motor. We pulled jobs every day sometimes. Small jobs draw a certain amount of heat because they are the ones that you have to do more often. But they also take a lot less planning. We'd just jump in the car and ride around until we saw a place that might have money. And we'd hit it. Sometimes we only got twenty or thirty dollars, and we'd

taken the same risk of having to injure or kill the clerks as if we'd got a million. We thought nothing of it, though. Just get in the car and find another place. After a while I got hooked on dry cleaners, they were so easy. Of course, I knew from past experience that you don't set a pattern, but we set one right away. The cops were onto us and they even came out in the papers to the effect that a couple of nuts were hitting dry cleaning establishments and it was only a matter of time until they'd get caught or killed. We didn't care, we just continued to stick our necks out. We must of taken turns hitting about twenty places without ever casing out a single one. But taking chances and laying down patterns is the dope fiend's style of robbery. Even going against your better judgment consciously is a dope fiend trait.

You know if you walk into a place and don't have a mask on or your features disguised, people are going to make you. You know that if you don't check a place out there might not be enough money there to bother with. You know that a stickup man never goes in blind 'cause he's afraid that the owner might be one of those nuts that won't give you the money. You don't even check to see how the neighborhood is patrolled or if someone is staying in the back room. All that information is necessary if you want to stay alive. I wonder sometimes if the doper isn't just trying to commit a good-looking suicide. Actually, you are always looking for one thing—enough money to fix. You can't be hassled with all that planning. You ain't after the big sting; all you want to do is get the money and go to the connection.

***

Word soon gets out that Frank and I are doing these stings and I decide that I should go back East for my health. But Frank doesn't want to travel, probably 'cause he's hotter in New York than in California. I'm hooked and getting scared in the gut 'cause we're hitting places every day. I just want to leave, so one day I go to the airport and fly, without saying a word. I get to the city and turn into a speed freak.

When I got to New York, this was in the spring of 1971, I was real worried about my junk habit. I couldn't seem to hustle like I had before and I wanted to kick for a while. So I got into speed. Real weird things happened to me when I was on speed. I'd shoot speed for three or four days in a row, then one day I'd fix dope, then back to speed.

I'd been going this route for a long time in New York, I don't really know how long. Just hustling any way I could for enough to survive, when I had this real strange experience. I hole up in this apartment for days thinking the feds are after me. I'm peeking out the window and barricading the door. I get it in my mind that the whole FBI is about to storm in on me so I decide that I got to make a run for it. I get my brown windbreaker jacket and roll it up in a tight ball and stick it under my arm. I run over to a friend's house, his name was Kevin, and tell him I got five pounds of speed under my arm and the feds are right on my tail. "Kevin, for God's sake, you've got to hide me!"

And at the moment I really believed that. It was as real to me as I'm sitting here now. That's what speed does to your mind.

Kevin's roommate, Kelly, says, "He can't stay here. We can't afford no hassle with the police."

But Kevin argues, "No. We've got to hide him. We can't just let Manny get busted." So they stick me in this little dark closet.

But I scream and yell and pound on the door until they let me out. "I don't want to hide in there, I want to get in the shower." All they have is an old fashioned bathtub with a shower curtain, and so I get in there still clutching my coat so hard my fingers are turning blue. I believe that I got five pounds of speed. I believe it so well that all the others are believers, too. Kevin comes in and tells me that he doesn't see anybody suspicious in the neighborhood, but I tell him to keep standing point 'cause they may have sneaked in.

Somebody leaves the house, slamming the door on their way out. I come running out of the bathroom and holler at Kevin, "The feds are coming in the bathroom window!" Now, Kevin lives on the sixth floor, so he knows that something is up. I run out of the house; all I got on is a pair of pants. No shoes or shirt, just a pair of brown pants. I run down the main street with all these vehicles coming at me from every different way. I run clear out to the pier in Coney Island and I hide under the dock. I actually see men coming after me with guns. And I'm saying, "This is it. I'm dead." I get behind this big log and I'm trying to dig and claw my way under it. My fingernails are torn off and bleeding; I have a long cut on my face. It's like I'm in a war. I remember peeking over this log, seeing all the people, and holding onto my coat for dear life. That's the last thing I know, 'cause I crash. I just passed out cold. I'd been up for over sixty days without any real sleep, and I just fell out. I must have laid there for two or three days. I lost some time. I mean, the only thing I remember was the feds coming after me. When Kevin sees me a week later he asks me about the five pounds of speed.

"Kevin, you won't believe it. I don't have five pounds of speed, and I don't think I ever did have. I was on one of my speed trips."

But Kevin believed, to this day he still thinks I had five pounds of speed and didn't want to share.

Speed makes you very weird. You lose control. Heroin is different. You never lose control when you're using stuff. Heroin keeps you in control all of the time, except in the moments of deep nod right after you fix. You're programmed on stuff to get the money 'cause heroin is so expensive and so *necessary* that you're in constant bondage.

The trip behind speed and heroin is completely different. When you steal on speed, your body doesn't really require speed. After a month or so of really abusing speed, you get so spaced out that you can't steal the change out of your own pocket. Besides, speed doesn't require a lot of money, it's not expensive, and it's available in a lot of places—you can get prescriptions for it or even use certain weight-reducing medication directly off the druggists' shelves. The regular speed freak is not often a criminal. A person who has been up for five or six days without sleep can't eat, he can't even write his own name—let alone go out and steal something.

But with dope, once you begin to use heroin you become a hustler—regardless of what you were before. That is automatic. Stealing comes with heroin. It is really strange to look back on all those years, and all that money that I've shot in my arm. I've had some really good scores from capers. I could have settled down three or four times with that kind of bread. I could've had something better out of life.

But no. A doper don't think of that. He uses money, anybody's money, all the time.

Well, I hung around New York for a long time. But it was never the same. I found out that you can never go back. I wasn't stealing a lot, just enough to survive. I felt lonely inside and sort of estranged, like I was always looking for some-place to hide. I guess that, mostly, I was just physically worn out. Lots of times I went to visit friends and fixed dope; but it seemed like I could never get into the swing. For some reason, the city life seemed too fast, like it was constantly passing me by. The dopers I hung out around were moving too fast for me; they were continually on the go—constantly. When I was strung out on dope, I hustled and frantically scurried around, too, but not like that. I tried to get back into the swing of New York life as I'd known it before, but after a while, I gues it was in the spring of 1973, I got the itch for California. So, I got together the bread and flew back.

I don't know why after all those months I just naturally expected things to be the same. And they were, nothing had changed. I get into LA International and call Frank. Sure enough, he's still alive and well. I think that he must have quit his frantic capering. He comes out to the airport to pick me up

and I'm a mess. I've been on what you call a Pepsi-Cola habit for a long time. You are not really severely hooked physiologically, but you want it so bad mentally that you continue to use until the monkey really crawls inside your guts and you've physically had it. I was somewhere near that state at the time.

> I felt lonely inside . . . like I was always looking for someplace to hide.

Frank picks me up at the airport. My nose is running and I'm crying—telling him how hard I'd had it in New York. We're cruising along somewhere between the airport and Venice when Frank gets tired of my sniveling. "All right, shut up," he says, and stops the car. He goes into this place and must have made a hit right there. I think it was a supermarket; I don't know 'cause I was so out of it. Frank comes out; we drive into Venice and score some dope. And we're right back to using and scoring same as when I left almost two years back. Nothing has changed, nothing at all. I was right back into the "I don't give a shit for nothing" life of hustling constantly to keep the monkey off my back. I guess, as I look back on it, there was no ambition at all in me at that time. I'd lost all the polish and most of the nerve I'd ever had. Frank and I were hitting places nearly every day again, and again it was a desperate, unstructured, and impulsive way to go. Frank liked me 'cause I would go for anything. Part of what we were doing by frantically robbing was trying to escape from the absolute boredom of our lives. I can't tell you how mundane and dull the doper's days are. Any kid that thinks there's something romantic in heroin addiction needs to wise up. What a strain, what pressure. You gotta constantly stroll your beat, try and stay on the ball, hustle your buns off for the next fix. And for what? It's shit, man, that's a good and proper name for it. 'Cause when that shit gets into your system, into every fiber of your being, you're nothing but a goddamn sewer. If you're reading this, some kid out there whose bigshot uncle or friend has showed you some smack behind their big come-on smile, tell them to fuck off. By all means tell them to split and never come back. The best advice I can give anybody who's exposed to the dope scene is, "Turn down your first gig forever, man!"

Well, Frank and I went wild around the area again. Word gets out that Frank's been made and that cops are kicking down doors around town looking for him. We go to the connection's house one day for our supply and he says, "You guys better cool it 'cause

you're about to blow. The cops were here looking for you, Frank! You are hotter than a firecracker. Go! Get out while you still can."

For days Frank keeps saying that he's going to go up north for a while. But the whole time we're still doing our thing. And we're still fixing even though we had to go to another connection 'cause we'd put heat on Jack and he wouldn't touch us any longer. Frank puts off going too long. One day we're coming out of a parking lot in front of our house and they swoop on us. It was like a world war. They came outa nowhere with shotguns and rifles, and they rammed Frank's car, pushing it off the street onto some citizen's front lawn.

I just froze in the car, man, 'cause I knew this was for real. They tear open the driver's side and drag Frank out on the ground. They are kicking and punching him as they drag him out. A cop comes around to my side with a gun. And real slow, I don't want one of those dudes killing me, I get out of the car. They force me on the ground with my head in the grass. I can see them going through the car, ripping out the upholstery, throwing the mats in the streets, just tearing hell out of things. The only thing they found in the whole search was a plastic toy pistol.

They throw the cuffs on Frank, stand him up against the car arresting him. They go through their entire routine, doing what cops usually do, being assholes. But they surprise the hell outa me. They stand me up and tell me to beat it; they tell me to go! I can't believe it, 'cause it just ain't like cops usually operate. I should be up for investigation. But I don't argue at all. I don't walk, I run like hell soon as I get around the corner. I know they've made a mistake, but I'm going to take advantage of it.

I go over to our new connection's house, a broad named Helen, who kinda liked Frank. "Hey, Helen, they just busted Frank, but I got away." She gives me a fix and I sit around her house a couple of hours waiting until I can call the station and find out about Frank. I call and they tell me that he's been booked on about a jillion counts of armed robbery.

I just hang up. I hang up on Frank. There's nothing I can do for him, nothing at all. I ain't got no big money; he's busted; and that's the way it goes. He was a fine crime partner while it lasted, but now he is wasted and I gotta look out for me lest I become his fall partner. I know inside that I better split town. They just made a simple-minded mistake by cutting me loose and sooner or later they'll snap to it.

I tell Helen that I'm going to split tonight. I want to go out and make some getaway money, then I'll come back, pick up my stuff, and leave.

Helen tells me, "I've got some money here and a little extra dope. If you go out and try to hustle this town as hot as it is for you, you'll get nailed for sure."

"Sure, Helen, I'll take it and you can be sure I'll get it back to you someway." I always promised that when somebody'd go out of their way to stake me, but my promises never held water, 'cause a doper never refuses nothing, and never returns nothing, either! I wait for the sun to go down 'cause I'm going to split at night. Helen offers to take me to a bus station over in the next county. She takes her dog out around six or seven o'clock and comes running back in hollering that the house is surrounded, they're all over the neighborhood—nothing but a sea of blue out there.

I run to the closet where my artillery is stashed and hand Helen one of my guns to hold. Making sure my gun is loaded I run into the bathroom. I open this little tiny bathroom window—I have no idea how I'm going to get through it—and the next thing I know this shotgun is poked in my nose. "Drop your gun." I freeze right on the spot. He holds the gun on me until several cops have run into the house. They check our arms and see the obvious signs that we've just fixed. They read us our rights and tell us they're holding us for being under the influence and internal possession of a dangerous drug.

I think they are going to take Helen in—and that is a bummer. I don't feel too bad about being busted because I'm still high, but I hate to see a good connection like Helen get wasted. We are sitting in the living room with the cops questioning us. Helen says that the gun they took off of me belonged to her. She was really a far-out chick. One of the cops tells her that he doesn't care about the gun. He is a narcotics detective and he's busting us for drugs. He asks her if she's got any dope in the house. She tells him no, and he ain't about to find her stash, either.

Convinced now that this is a pure and simple bust for using, I tell the cops that I'll go in and cop to that if they won't bug Helen. They go for it and as I'm getting my gear together Helen whispers to me that she'll bail me out within an hour. The bond is only two hundred dollars for being under the influence.

I'm just kicking back in the cell waiting for Helen to bail me out. Nobody calls right away so I just nod. A few hours later this bull comes in and says, "Come on, Torres, get out here." I think I'm going home so I get out of the bunk, put on my jacket, and walk out with him. They take me outside to the interrogation room, stand me against this long white wall, and this guy is taking pictures of me.

"What the hell is this for?" I ask.

He replies, "Don't ask me. They just want a series of full-length shots

of you." They take two series of four, back, sides, and front. Right then I go back to the cell and it's no kicking back this time. I'm really worried. After a while I nod out. By morning I'm sicker than a dog and I know something is wrong, 'cause if it wasn't I'd be sprung long ago. They call me back outside again and they bring me into the interrogation room. A mean-looking detective from West LA has a folder in his hand that says Robbery Division. And I think, Oh, shit, I've had it.

He sits me down and says, "Is your true name Manuel Julio Torres?"

"Of course it is. You know that."

"I want you to know that the influence charge is being dropped. We're picking you up on one count of armed robbery."

I say, "You guys have got the wrong man. I never robbed anybody in my life, leastwise with a gun. Besides, I don't know what you're talking about. I was loaded out of my mind last night. I'm a dope fiend, but I ain't done no robbery."

He doesn't say another word. Just throws the cuffs on me and takes me to West Los Angeles. By now I'm starting to get really sick. They got me in an upstairs detective's room handcuffed to a chair. Nobody is saying anything to me. And for several hours I just sit there and stare at the walls. I'm really getting sick and I start complaining, "I want to go see a doctor. I'm going to die right here in this chair if you guys don't do something." I'm running down the whole dope fiend game just to see if they'll go for it and give me something. But my dope fiend tricks don't get me anywhere.

The detective "heavy" comes back in the room and asks, "Do you have anything to say?"

"Just that I want a doctor. You bastards gotta give me some medical attention."

"Never mind that shit," he says, "I'm going to read you the rights. Now listen real careful." The other detective comes in and they are reading me my rights and I don't really care a damn! All I want now is a fix. He gets done reading and asks, "Do you have any statement to make?"

I say, "Not one fucking thing!"

They take me back to my cell and I just lay there for about two or three days, I don't rightly know because I'm sick all over. Sick and alone. Junk sickness is bad anytime, but when you're alone it's deathly.

Sometime or other the detective comes back and says, "Listen, we know that you're from Venice, and we know a lot of robbers are living there. I think that there's some help that you could give us. You know, help runs both ways. You scratch my back, and I'll scratch yours."

I didn't say a thing. I just stared stone-cold straight at him, being a cool con. I might as well. 'Cause if they got me, they got me. And I might as well get into practice for the joint.

He asks the question again and tells me, "Manny, if you're really sick and can help us, then maybe we can help you by taking you to the hospital and they could give you something."

He is playing "Mr. Good Guy" now, but I'm onto his act. They are just assholes, and are as dishonest as those they deal with. And they expect you to play into their hands. I tell him, "Man, save your time and just take me back to my cell."

Later, he comes back upstairs and says that he is filing another count of armed robbery on me. "We are going to bury you in the joint so you can't rip society off again for a long time."

"I don't know what you're talking about. File all the charges you want. But you can't make 'em stick, 'cause I'm innocent. I never pulled no robbery."

He says, "Yeah, sure. But you've been arrested before."

"So cottenpickin' what?" This cop doesn't like my attitude and he lets me know it. I decide that I won't say nothing from here on out.

He takes ahold of my arm, and I got a finger missing. He says, "Two years ago, some guy over in Venice was robbed by a Latin with a finger missing on his left hand."

I say, "Any more you want to give me? Now, I ain't rapping to you no more. Do what you have to do." I figured that if they had the goods on me, I was gone. If they didn't, I'd better shut up before I got mad and said something that'd get me in a world of trouble.

The next day I was arraigned and had bail set at $10,000. They filed two counts of armed robbery, one count of possession of an illegal firearm, and two counts of ex-convict in possession of a firearm. The law in California freaks me out. I couldn't believe it. I started adding up the time and came up with something like thirty years to life. Knowing now that I was in real trouble, I sent for a public defender.

That guy was zero help. With friends like him, who needs enemies? First thing out of his mouth when he sees me is, "You're in big trouble. We'll make a deal and get ten to life for you."

I said, "What are you talking about?" He just said that like it was nothing. Some deal! Ten years to forever in the joint. No, ma'am! I figured on going to the joint but not for that kind of time. I thought that I might cop to one count of something for five to life. I'm thinking that way because they're talking all this outrageous time.

On top of all this, I get assigned to the worst judge in Santa Monica. Anybody like me who goes before him is gone for the joint. He is known around there as the "hanging judge." And he had a history of being especially hard on armed robbers. But right about then I got the biggest break of my life. One of the local jailhouse cons told me that this judge had a real soft spot in his heart for dope fiends.

As we go through the trial process I can see that the judge is watching me, and he's constantly going through my jacket from one end to the other. Every five minutes the district attorney threw in something bad about me. Sometimes true, but sometimes an absolute distortion. He made me look like another John Dillinger.

After all the evidence had been presented—it took my attorney about five minutes to present my case—the judge said, "Mr. Torres, how long have you been a user of heroin?"

I told him, "All my life, as far back as I can remember. Certainly since I was sixteen."

"Have you ever had any help? I mean, have you ever been committed to a formal program for addicts?"

I wavered about telling him of my time in Synanon. But I decided that it doesn't fall under the label of "formal commitment." Anyway, if the judge wants to find out about that part of my life, he can easily enough.

The judge decides to postpone the trial for two weeks so he can go over my case. I wait two weeks, anxiously, because I know that decisions are being made that will affect my life in a serious way. This kind of jailhouse waiting is murder. You pace back and forth. You don't use dope, 'cause you want to clean up and look good. You think that maybe you'll make the clean life a permanent style if you get a break. On top of all this, I was still in the final stages of withdrawal. I'd kicked physically, but the mental withdrawal is longer and harder to handle.

The judge calls me back into court. I remember the day well. The sun was bright and it was a hot scorcher. As I walked up the corridor toward his courtroom a door opened and a cool breeze hit me. I wondered if that was an omen. I've never been superstitious particularly, but I hoped that I was going to get a cool one in court. When I get up front of the bench, His Honor tells me that he will give me the choice of commitment under the civil code to the state hospital for drug abusers or continuing the trial under the penal statutes. The DA is mad as hell. I can see that he doesn't like it at all 'cause he thought that I was a bad hombre and needed to be put away. Besides, he didn't need to bargain, in his opinion. He thought he had the goods on me.

However, the judge had consulted with my lawyer and they both thought that all of my robberies, if I were guilty of any, were committed under the influence of drugs. My lawyer did point out that many entries in my jacket with respect to violence were questionable.

The judge instructed me to admit to simple robbery. Then I had to sign myself into the California Rehabilitation Center. He called it a hospital.

I say, "Yes, Your Honor. I'll do that." So, I cop to two second-degree robberies and they drop everything else. I'm really happy. I'm going to a hospital! Maybe I'll get some help. For the first time in a long time, I saw some daylight. I wanted help. Not a lot, but at least I felt like quitting dope.

I get back to the tank and I'm really happy. I start spreading the word around about my big break. Everybody tells me, "If you go there you'll wind up getting screwed! You have violence on your jacket, and judge or no judge, they'll exclude you and send you back for sentence. You're going to go to the joint anyway. Face it, Manny! This is just a postponement."

"Shit!" Oh well, it's a postponement. Maybe I'll have a chance. I've got nothing to lose at this point. I ask about CRC and find out that the guys live in dorms, they got schools, a ball field, track, lots of recreation.

"Man, that's a country club!" So, I thought I was headed for something like Lompoc is now, where they keep all the Watergate offenders. One morning they call us out and put us in chains, and I thought that this was strange; why chains if I'm going to a hospital?

Our first stop was at Frontera, 'cause we had some girls with us in the Gray Goose. Then we go to Chino and on to CRC. Driving up to the gate, right away I can see double fences and gun towers. Barbed wire and gun guards. This is a funny hospital, I think. No hospital at all. It is a prison out in the middle of nowhere. CRC is really a strange place. It is all a farce, a big organizational front. But it is good for dope fiends. When they get strung out, or too weird, they just send them out to CRC to go through the program. Some have been through the program five times already.

Most guys wind up going back to CRC five or six times. The recidivism rate there is about 94 percent, or so I've heard, and I believe it. They make you sign a civil commitment for seven years. If you do three years in the streets clean—not using any kind of drugs—they cut you loose. But it seldom happens, and if you slip once the whole seven-year trip begins again 'cause they make you sign a new commitment. Of course, remember that they got a big club over your head. If you won't sign for civil treatment at CRC they'll take you back to court on the criminal charges still pending. What a vise grip they got you in! It's a neat trick the state of California thought up. Gotcha either criminally or civilly, take your choice. Most guys wind up taking both, 'cause after a few years of

failure they get excluded from CRC and get sent up to the joint on the original charges.

It's ironic in a way. Here they're trying to teach you how to be an honest, upright citizen, having wholesome, legally correct attitudes, and they don't think nothing about pulling double jeopardy on you quasi-legally. Can you dig it? First you do several years as a "volunteer" civil committee, then whenever they classify you as a failure, zappo! On the very same charges, up the river with your ass! Teach you? Hell yes, that kind of phony "legal" manipulation will teach you one thing: disdain for the system.

There are dudes that I know who've been on the CRC program from the beginning. They keep going back for testing dirty, and they do another year or so. If they catch another beef they get a new number. CRC is just a place to store dope fiends, if they're not too violent, if they're mostly into boosting and pilfering. The kind of record I had made me really an exception there. Most robbers never get sent to the Rehab Center.

After I was classified, they put me in the educational dorm 'cause I told them I wanted to get into school. But they made me wait around for a while to see if I was really motivated for education. I lay around on the yard for a few weeks looking at the double fences and gun towers. Some things are no different here than in prison. I know that if I make a break for it they're going to shoot me. Do they shoot you if you decide to take off from a hospital? CRC is referred to as a hospital under the California Health and Safety Code, but they've blasted people off the wires trying to get outa there and in my books it's a fucking prison.

But it's kind of like a big country club in other ways. It's a dorm living situation, no cells. Also, there wasn't the hassle or tension that you always find in the maximum-security prisons, where guys are doing big time. The most time you would do at CRC is about a year to fourteen months. So you know that you're getting short for the streets when you go in.

They have group counseling sessions every morning. That place is built on diagnosis, therapy, and treatment. You ain't necessarily bad, you're just "sick." You go to these meetings and just sit around lying and bullshitting the Man and each other. Hell, nobody but a fool would let his front down there. Besides, I had a lot of training in group therapy from my Synanon days. I could really snow 'em. You would sit in comfortable chairs in this room, about ten men and a counselor, and discuss problems. That is, some guys would discuss problems. I never did. Either I would just sit there for the forty-minute session or I would some-times manipulate the meeting with rhetoric and bullshit.

I spent a lot of time reading philosophy. A lot of that stuff I didn't really understand. But I read it anyway 'cause I was kind of interested. This bull would get me into the games in the morning group discussions and I wouldn't answer. I don't want to hear his shit! Then a counselor tells me that if I want to get out of CRC, and if I want to get cured, I better start cooperating and give them a little something to make them feel good about me—or themselves as professionals.

It's the same technique that psychiatrists use. How I used to play the nut doctor games. That's the same thing we used to pull with the bulls and the counselor at CRC. Do you know what any psychiatrist wants to hear? I know! I've had lots of experience with them on the streets and in the joint. When they send you to see a psychiatrist it means that they've labeled you as crazy. Not that they think you might be crazy, but that you are crazy.

The public looks at the dope fiend and sees that he is crazy. He must be crazy 'cause he acts and thinks strangely, not like normal folks. There must be something wrong with him and the first thing that you can come up with is, he's out of his mind! Nobody ever looks beyond the dope fiend, especially the psychiatrist who sees him professionally.

So you go to the shrink, who thinks you're nuts, and you know in front that you'll play a game with him. You are going to prove to him that he is right. You're going to show the psychiatrist how smart he is and that he really knows his literature. So, you go in there and you act crazy. When they ask you questions, you babble incoherently or you throw things around. Maybe you throw a fit on the floor, kicking up your feet and frothing at the mouth a little. It feels good and may even give you some release from your tensions—but at fifty dollars an hour cost to the state?

The shrink looks at you and he thinks, "This guy is a nut." He's got a dictionary full of terms to classify you. Well, you gotta be a little bit cool when you go into your number or they'll wise up. He asks you a question and you whistle, or maybe you holler at him and stare sort of vacant-eyed. I used to be able to cross my eyes and that really got them.

The whole game is that when you first are referred to the shrink, don't cooperate. Present a good case for him to get his teeth into. Then he'll be happy. I would see this shrink at CRC once a week, and every time I would do something else that he would write down. He used to sit there pulling at his beard (is a beard standard equipment for a psychiatrist?) and stare

at me out of the corner of his eyes. I really had him hooked, 'cause he thought that I was crazy, but he couldn't specify just exactly how I was nuts. But he would talk to me, kind of soothing, using a special technique to draw me out.

After a while you start acting a little saner each time you see him. This makes him feel good. You have to show him that everything he has picked up in school and in his practice is working for him. After five or six months you can con a psychiatrist into believing that you have really improved. Now when you have your interview you're not screaming, you seldom throw things, and you never froth at the mouth. On his chart, this is progress. You want them to see improvement, any kind of improvement.

It seems that in the world of corrections the rule is that if something is written down, then it is true. If a licensed psychiatrist says I have improved, then I am well. I would always ask to go see the psychiatrist 'cause I knew that I would need his help for the board. Especially since they thought that I was violent. It is all a game. If your jacket shows a lot of violence or strange stuff, parole board members always want reports from the shrink. So I learned how to use a psychiatrist. Cons learn how to orchestrate their whole folder if they're smart.

I don't know if the psychiatrists really believe that they can do something with the dope fiend. Every doper that I've ever known to have contact with the shrink has done the same routine on him. We've sat down lots of times and discussed new techniques to use on psychiatrists. We discuss various methods of setting them up. All dope fiends do that. If you want drugs in the joint, go and see the shrink. The same way with the counselor. I knew that to get out I would have to get a report from him. I was really doing good and this cop would ask me questions, and I would really run my mouth to get a good report.

The way I looked at life in relation to myself all started to change during the last six months I was at CRC. I do not think it was the program at the center that began to effect these changes so much as it was the effort extended by one correctional officer, Mr. Champian.

One day I'm sitting on my bunk reading and this correctional officer came over and sits down besides me. Now, this is bad news for a con. And my face gets kind of red 'cause I don't want any of my friends to think that I know this guy. But he's really friendly; he wants to know what it is that I'm reading.

I look up and tell him that it's *Homage to an Exile* by Albert Camus, but I'm not willing to discuss it with him. He gets up and

leaves. The next day, I'm laying on my bunk and Mr. Champian comes over again and says, "Did you finish Camus?"

"Yes, I'm looking around for *The Stranger* now."

"Did you enjoy *Homage*? Do you agree with his position on paternalistic tyranny?"

I say that I did on both counts, but I don't volunteer any additional information. He stares at me for a minute and then leaves.

I'm beginning to get upset with this officer, he's being too friendly. I didn't see any reason to be friendly to him; anyway, it doesn't look or feel right for a convict to be on friendly terms with the jailers.

This doesn't stop my correction officer (that's what I started calling Mr. Champian, My Correction Officer). Every day that he was on duty, he would try and get a conversation going with me. I would try my hardest to shine him on, but that was almost impossible since he was the jailer and he could stop me and talk anytime. So I had no choice but to listen to him, and he began to talk a lot about self-improvement. Particularly, he wanted me to get more serious in the school at CRC and then try and go on to college.

The school there was run in a very strange manner. They had classes, but many of them were supposed to be job-oriented, offering different kinds of trades you could learn—like draftsmanship. The problem is that most of what they offered had little relevance with what you could do in the real world. You could get a whole wall of certificates in drafting, but when you get out you find that nobody needs draftsmen. It happened to a lot of guys I knew. You could go to baking school or small engine repair, you could work in the kitchen on vocational training, and there were a few other choices, like printing. The academic school was a very strange place. You would go in and they would give you a book and tell you to read some chapters and answer some questions. When they tested you they'd leave you alone in the classroom. Most of the people gave themselves A's and B's. It amounted to that 'cause you could just look up the answers until you got the right one. If you made a B it was 'cause you didn't attend class regularly. It was the Job Corps method of instruction, I think. I know that they assumed that we were all stupid and that this give-away program was the only way we could learn anything at all.

I guess that I'd of never tolerated that school if my correction officer hadn't encouraged me. He kept saying that I shouldn't get discouraged, but try and get as much out of the experience as possible. It helped, and I started talking to him a little more. In fact, now I'm doing pretty good. When I go before the classification committee they recommend that I stay in the program and not be excluded to criminal court. It's 'cause I'm

showing improvement and trying to do something in education. I try to look really passive and like a nice guy before the committee. They say that all they can do is recommend; it will be up to the superintendent. They say, "You're doing really good, keep it up."

However, the detective that busted me writes a scathing letter to the superintendent saying that if the judge hadn't intervened they would have had me cold and could have put me away for life. He said that I didn't belong in CRC and that the only reason I even was there at all was to keep out of the joint. He said that I was dangerous, and that if the superintendent was smart that he would exclude me immediately.

The superintendent called me into the office and read the letter to me personally. He also took out my jacket and read all the institutional reports. He said, "I think you belong in this program and no detective from downtown LA is about to tell me how to run my institution. As long as you keep your nose clean you can stay at CRC. What's more, Manuel, Mr. Champian tells me that you have good, sound educational potential. Get the most out of school as you can. It may be your ticket out of here and back to society."

So, not only did my correctional officer help me a lot, but the big honcho detective also did me a favor. Now I'm on the program permanently, so long as I don't screw up. Now I realize that I've caught a break. What am I going to do with it? I begin to take my classes more seriously. I actually do all the readings for my courses.

Mr. Champian continued to work on me to get interested in college. He said that if I began to make plans to attend school that it would make a hit with the parole board. I began to see that the board might react the same as psychiatrists do. If they saw a lot of improvement in my character, if they saw that I was genuinely trying to better myself, and, most importantly, if they had hard data like excellent school grades, they might think that I'd improved enough to get out. So, partly because I was interested, and partly just to get my correction officer off my back, I told him to get me the college entrance papers and I would fill them out.

One thing that I knew was that I needed to have a sound parole plan. I had already been told that I couldn't go back to the Los Angeles area, and San Francisco was out too because they didn't want me in an urban area.

I had no idea where to go. But I kept hearing about a halfway house up in Eureka called Redwood Manor. I also heard that everyone who presented plans to go to Eureka had been passed by the board. So, I decided that I would go to Eureka—I would go anywhere to get out. I asked my correction officer for papers from Humboldt State University. He brought all the necessary forms to me the next day. And he bugged me for two weeks until I had them filled out. A month later I was accepted. I didn't know where Arcata or Eureka was, I knew it was way up in the timber of northern California somewhere, but that was all.

Now I really have a vision!

Now I was approved by the school, but it takes money to go there. My correction officer gets all the necessary papers for financial aid and sits down with me to fill them out. A few weeks later I hear from the Educational Opportunity people. They write me that all my school and many of my living expenses will be taken care of. Wow! Now I really have a vision!

When I left CRC, I left with seventy-five dollars in my pocket. If you stay at the program more than six months, you receive two hundred dollars when you get released. You usually get twenty-five at the gate, and the rest is mailed to your parole agent, who gives it to you when he receives it. Which may take from a week to a month.

I received seventy-five dollars at the gate 'cause I had to fly from Corona to Eureka. I first had to fly to San Francisco and then to Eureka, with a six-hour layover in San Francisco. The cost of the tickets was seventy-one dollars, and I had to save three dollars for the bus from the airport to Eureka.

I arrived in Eureka July 23, 1974, around 10 P.M. I knew that I was to stay at a halfway house called Redwood Manor on G and Ninth. After walking around for a while looking for the house, I found it. When I arrived at the halfway house nobody there knew anything about me staying there. They told me that they didn't have any bed space. I told them that I just got out, didn't have any money, and needed a place to sleep. They told me I could sleep on the couch. In the morning I went to see my parole agent. He took care of everything at the halfway house. I asked him if my money had arrived, he told me no. (I needed money real bad.) A week later my money arrives; I spend most of it on clothes. Since I had two months to wait until school started, and I didn't want to hang around the house broke, I started job hunting.

My parole agent gave me some job leads, but they didn't pan out. I was getting bored hanging out at the halfway house. The house itself was fine. It wasn't the house that

was boring or making me up tight, it was the feeling of despair running through the house. Most of the dudes in the house were just like me; no job, no money, lonely and bored. All we used to do was drink cheap wine and talk joint talk. I was thinking of going to LA but I knew what would happen if I went. Nothing but drugs and jails, so I stay up here hoping something would happen.

Something did happen. I met Eric, I made a friend. We didn't have much in common, but that wasn't important. What was important is that we became friends. He would take me dancing, drinking, hiking, or just for a ride to get me out of the halfway house. Eric made life a little more livable. I still had no money or job but I was enjoying myself. But the most important thing Eric did for me was to introduce me to Buddhism (nichiren Shoshu), where we chant NAM MYOHO RENGE KYO. From the day I met Eric and started chanting, my luck started changing. The first thing that happened was that I got a job. It didn't pay much, but it was a job. I was looking for a house close by the school in Arcata. Eric ends up buying two houses right behind the school and asks me to share one house with him. We moved into the house a few days after school started.

I am ending my third quarter at Humboldt. It isn't easy, but it isn't as hard as stealing or using drugs.

Chapter 7

From the Horse's Mouth

Although the proliferation of national and local prison reform organizations in the past decade has done much to provide ex-offenders with a more credible platform to air their grievances about the criminal justice system, as well as to voice their opinions about the social circumstances and conditions that promote crime, there remains a reluctance by many to listen to "inside views." For one thing, self-reports of criminal careers are often suspect because they tend to glorify and sentimentalize the criminal role. Bold capers that demonstrate bravado, "close calls," where the criminal narrowly escapes the arms of the law, or incidents where police or correctional officers are outsmarted can be interpreted as a means of ego enhancement. Similarly, if we assume, as many do, that inmates and ex-offenders alike have a vested interest in reducing the harshness of the prison experience, as well as the penalties for law violations, then their sometimes radical indictments of the criminal justice system raise suspicions of questionable motives. Moreover, the hostility that is generated in those who have undergone long years of incarceration adds an emotional dimension to self-reports of criminal and prison careers that often damages credibility as well as objectivity.

Although careful attention has been given to presenting a straightforward and accurate report of Manny's experiences—yet still providing a narrative that reflects the personal meaning that Manny attached to these events—the fact that this account is told in the first person will no doubt raise these very suspicions among many readers. It seems worthwhile, however, to remind ourselves once again that rarely in one's lifetime is one asked to verify that one's perceptions and interpretations of one's experiences are as one claims.

Despite differing evaluations of how well Manny has succeeded in reporting his life objectively and in going beyond official "con stories," in this chapter Manny takes a more academic approach in discussing his experiences and particularly his observations of the prison system. These dialogues, focusing on different elements of Manny's criminal, addiction, and prison career, offer a more in-depth perspective of some of the issues raised in earlier chapters. It should be pointed out that these commentaries were made at a very different stage in Manny's life. He has experienced two years of college; he has proven a successful parolee for over two years; and he is some distance removed in time from his career as a heroin addict.

In Dialogue 1, "At the Office," Manny reflects on his early life experiences in a discussion with his instructor at Humboldt State University, who himself has served nearly fifteen years in maximum-security prisons. The themes that surface in this dialogue are probably not atypical of the men and times of Manny's background. For example, he demonstrates hostility and resentment over the events following his father's death that left the family in deprived circumstances. This in turn seems to generate attitudes that justify "taking what you can get," or in Manny's words: "When you get shafted, you at least goose 'em in return . . . screw over the other guy before he could do it to me."

Of particular importance in this dialogue is the issue of causation: What causes the "Mannys" in American society? Who or what is to blame? For Manny, the principal causes are seen as external to the individual: "Society created the situation where you have to have dope fiends . . . everybody in control of this system contributes to criminality, drug addiction. . . ." Although this explanation for many readers may appear to be an unjustified effort to shift the causes of criminality from the individual to the society at large, Manny's ideas in this regard are neither atypical of prison populations nor of many sociologists, who see crime as an inevitable outcome in a society in which the political and economic interests of ruling and power elites are served at the expense of the working and lower classes.

In Dialogue 2, which was recorded during class sessions with students in a criminology seminar at Humboldt State, Manny and Rettig engage in an exchange highlighting the problematic nature of typologizing criminal conduct. Manny's experiences and comments emphasize numerous underlying assumptions that must be questioned by the researcher with respect to assigning labels such as "professional heavy." Manny's observation with respect to ethnocentrism as an undermining condition of prison reform is a rather new concept that the student will want to examine. Manny goes on to elaborate further on the prison sex code, the importance of homosexuality for understanding prison social organization, and the ways in which incarceration imposes a deprivation of sexual needs that makes homosexuality in both adult and juvenile institutions an expected outcome of the prisonization process. Further attention is also given to what Irwin (1970) has called "state raised youth," discussed earlier in Chapter 3. The discussion here places in high relief the fact that graduation from the juvenile to the adult institution is a very natural transition for the "state raised youth." His self-identity largely derives from his institutional experiences, in which he has learned survival patterns that emphasize toughness, craftiness, and physical force.

In an exchange of ideas between Manny and Rettig, various dimensions of the prison community are brought into focus: the prison/prisoner community, a discussion of the custody/treatment dichotomy and the problematic aspects of this fracture. The inherent conflict in interests between inmates and correctional officials is constantly placed in high relief. The ways in which this conflict promotes solidarity within the inmate subculture is discussed, along with prison social roles and their function in maintaining social stability in the prison and prisoner community. Additionally, Manny alerts us to the importance of understanding the public's conception of those in prison. Views that promote an image of the prison community as comprised of "dangerous criminals who are a menace to society" not only strengthen support for maintaining custody-oriented institutions, he asserts, but also divert efforts at providing inmates with essential services that might help them out of their predicaments. Similarly, this dialogue critically examines "treatment" in correctional settings, the assumptions on which it is based, and the implications of using a treatment approach based on a "medical model." For Manny, "Calling a cat sick just adds another label to his jacket," which raises the question as to whether the "treatment approach" serves the ends of rehabilitation or whether it is, as Manny implies, just another label that complicates reentry into the community.

Finally, there emerges from the latter part of the dialogue certain suggestions and inferences with respect to "redemptive processes" that tend to take issue with the more classical models of penology based on punitive or even rehabilitative perspectives. In sum, this chapter should serve to promote considerable discussion about basic issues and dilemmas in the criminal justice system.

Dialogue 1

At the Office

Manny: Well, that about wraps it up, I suppose. There are a lot more war stories, especially in the early New York days. But I have to be careful of How much I tell. Some of those guys are still alive and well. The racket setups are basically the same now as then.

Rettig: Manny, you've certainly had a lot of experience. It seems almost incredible that one man could touch so many bases in the criminal world.

Manny: I didn't do anything unusual. It's just everyday stuff for the man in the streets. The square John doesn't realize. What he reads in the papers and sees on television about both organized and disorganized criminal life is just the tip of the volcano.

Rettig: Who do you blame? You know, for all that happened? For your life?

Manny: If the machine goes berserk and starts wiping people out, I can't blame the machine. Was Frankenstein the problem or the man who built the monster? It's not the machine's fault. Blame, for what it's worth, should be attached to the builder. Society created the situation where you have to have dope fiends. Dope fiends exist, not because they are pathological inferior humans, but because people make millions off the poppy, the pharmaceuticals—and booze, for that matter.

Rettig: Somebody pulls the strings, then?

Manny: Not just somebody. Everybody in control of this system contributes to criminality, drug addiction, and the bone-raped, insular poverty of our ghettos. Somehow, some way, in our modern industrial society we have created numerous situations and conditions where people are unhappy, alienated, disgusted. Especially poor folks and disenfranchised minorities. The pressures of making it on the square get too difficult. Life gets too harsh too early, and you turn to drugs, or wine, or just robbing and killing.

Rettig: So, it's all a social problem, then?

Manny: You're damn right it is, in my opinion. This produce-and-consume society, whose god is their belly, they manufactured the problem right along with their fancy goods and services. It stands to reason: if you got upper crusts, you gotta have sewer rats. If you got super successes, you gotta have dismal failures. The American dream, competitive kind of success don't make sense without *failure* to measure it against.

Rettig: I think that Emile Durkheim [1958] said something related to that several decades ago. Criminality serves the useful social function of educating the rest of us—so we know where the boundaries are.

Manny: That's just fine if you're on the right side of the tracks. But what if you are locked into the streets and locked out of the jobs because of your background or your dope habit? Hell, man, its simple for me to see, because I've been there. The social order created the drug problem and anything that comes out of heroin addiction is their fault. Personal breakdowns are an aspect of societal breakdowns.

And you know what? Corrections people will tell you, "You're right, the problem lies in society. It's our fault, but we're going to lock you up." The lockup is for punishment. There is no rehabilitation. Who the hell wants to be rehabilitated, anyway? Rehabilitation means to bring someone back to where they were before. Shit! I don't want to go back to my former state. I've done that too many times already. I don't need rehabilitation; I need redemption. To be lifted out is what I need, not to be oppressed. Joints exist for two reasons, to punish and to warehouse. And that's really one and the same thing. Of course, joints are big business. Lots of people work in prisons, halfway houses, jails, and camps. What the hell if they had a jail and nobody came? Do you know that as of June 1973, the eleven California Department of Corrections prisons employed almost six thousand persons and had an annual payroll of over $80 million. You tell me that prison isn't a big industry!

You know, when I was sent up to Chino, they told me they was sending me up there to learn a trade. This was supposed to make me a better man. They assigned me to the laundry and I learned how to shake shit outa dirty sheets and how to fold them coming off the mangle. I was supposed to be a laundry worker when I got out? Who the hell wants to wash and fold clothes all their life?

Rettig: Somebody has to wash clothes.

Manny: You're right! Society—the military-industrial complex—needs niggers, and they'll take 'em where they find 'em, regardless of color. But I'm not going to do it! You know what I mean? I'm not going to stay down, one way or another I'm going to have me some sunlight too!

Rettig: Why can't you live in a cold-water flat in Puerto Rican Harlem, carry a lunch bucket, and be satisfied?

Manny: I'm not going to be satisfied because that's not what I want. Nobody deserves that prison. Living in the muck and filth and stench of the ghetto. Where you get up in the morning and it's been a good night if you didn't get chewed up by rats or carried off by the roaches. And it's a good day if you don't get raped or knifed in the back. I got out of that concrete shithouse and I mean to stay out. I can do better than that.

I've proved that I can do better than that. If I could survive in the animalistic dope fiend world, I can make it in your world. Maybe I can do something to change your world. God! What boundless energy I had when I was on the hustle! If I could turn all that energy around. You know, I had to be pretty daring, and just a little bit slick. I had to con a lot of people a lot of times to come up with hundreds of dollars a day for dope. Sometimes that life back in New York seems like a dream. And I wonder how did I get away with all the boosting and robberies? But I did! What energy.

Rettig: You don't think that you had a choice back in the early fifties? When you lost your father and you and your mother got ripped off.

Manny: Well, I know that I was eleven years old at the time, and I got really mad when it happened. I couldn't fully understand the details of the court case. But I got frantic and up tight when Mom wouldn't quit crying. You gotta realize that our sudden poverty caused a dramatic shift in our way of life, and in my world view. One day I was a store owner's kid who thought like a child and moved around my world like a child. I wasn't hip at eleven or running the streets!

Yes, I think that when my father died I got ripped off. We end up with nothing. My brother Bobby is nine. I see my mother crying. She's telling us that we have to move from our nice house into this rat-infested, crummy tenement and I don't understand it. I'm really mad. Pissed off at the whole damn world!

Rettig: When a boy can be mad at the world, at the system, maybe he has suddenly grown up.

Manny: Right! Then and there I learned something. When you get shafted, you at least goose 'em in return. I remember that when I hit the bricks the first week in my new neighborhood, I looked at things differently. When I sized up people, friend or foe, I'd be thinking, "What can I get outa this dude?" My whole attitude changed overnight. I learned to always, no matter what it takes, screw over the other guy before he could do it to me.

Rettig: This was about the time that you joined the Young Stars. Could you have done something else with your time besides joining the gang?

Manny: No, and besides, I would of joined the Stars in any event. You had to join a gang if you wanted to be out in the streets. In that part of the Bronx every kid who stuck his nose outside better join the gang if he wanted to survive in one piece. But I wanted to join the Young Stars, and I wanted to be the best goddamn gang fighter on my block.

Rettig: Did you feel like you belonged in the gang?

Manny: Yes, really I did. Because I became good at it, and I felt that I was useful. I became skilled and competent, getting elected to office. I took pride in my sense of toughness. Although I was small, I could stand up to the trial by ordeal in the streets. I knew how to get prestige. To stay on top you gotta be good at whatever you're doing. So I became one of the good gang fighters. I knew what I was talking about, and I had a sense of personal power. When I said, "We're going to down this dude," I knew how to get the job done.

Rettig: Perhaps Cohen [1955] or Miller [1958] would say that you found a sense of legitimate identity in your gang membership and ganging activities. What do you think?

Manny: You bet. I felt right about myself when I was in the gang. And when I'd be roaming the streets with two or three of our members—with our red sweaters for all to see—I'd feel good way down inside. I can recall that feeling clearly. And I had a strong sense of confidence. When I walked into the clubhouse, when I talked to my people, they'd listen to me and that made me feel real good. I used to say to myself constantly, Win or die; win or die!

Rettig: Everybody is a mark, then? You're either a mark or a mark taker?

Manny: That's exactly how I thought. Everytime I met somebody, I was thinking, What can I get out of this guy? I'd be friendly toward them, and I might even like them, but if I got the chance and things fell out right, I'd hit 'em. Get something from everybody was the way I thought. I think I developed that attitude immediately after my father died. I learned right away what to do to survive, and how to do it most effectively. I started playing the tough gang-boy role, and I believed in this role. The best way to tell a lie is to believe it.

Rettig: Are you saying that you were conscious of living a lie in terms of your gang identity?

Manny: No, I didn't mean that exactly. I think my willingness to get into the gang came at least in part from my rejection of the legitimate world— whatever I thought that was. No. The automatic lie was a survival mechanism. Lots of kids in my neighborhood lied like troopers. But I was especially good at it. I could lie about anything. Like, I used to be playing blackjack and I'd be cheating them blind, trying to cop a few pennies, and I'd get caught. Somebody would say, "Manny, you cheated! I saw you switch cards."

I would get real loud and threatening, denying everything. Soon, the guy who saw me cheat wouldn't be sure about it any more. That's what I mean ' y *real* lying. I even convinced myself, me inside, that I couldn't have cheated when I knew damn well I did, had, and would.

Rettig: You say that you rejected the "legitimate world." Or, did they reject you?

Manny: Hell, yes! It was mutual. What comes first, the chicken or the egg? All I know is that when I'd go over to the old neighborhood to play, after we had to move, mothers would lock their doors on me. They didn't want their little kids playing with "poor Manny." Sure, I felt rejected. When I had to move I faced a problem of adjustment and was in the market for any reasonable solution.

Rettig: You said something about your mother being sick at this time. Wasn't she able to influence you at all?

Manny: No. She was a very small woman, and it was all she could do to keep a little food on the table. But my mom isn't to blame for what happened. You know, I'm ready to accept a good deal of the blame. I guess I could have been a good nigger and not fell into all that trouble.

Another thing. School changed for me when I moved. People there related to me different after my father died. I remember one time when he was still alive and I'd got into some little scrape at the schoolhouse, I think it was a fight with another kid. They tried to screw over me and they called my pop over thinking he would take their side automatically. And he would have too, except they were wrong. And they were trying to come down too hard for the offense. My father really gave them hell. He let them know that he was somebody in the community. After he died, Bobby and I were fucked in that school. It was hell for us. We got so we just wouldn't go. There was no way we could succeed there, and besides that I got very bored with school. I was learning a lot of things on the streets—was growing up overnight—and the school people wanted to keep us children. "Come in, children. Sit down, children. Do you know the answer, boy? Listen, we were making it in the streets. We were kings in a way. We were street people. How could they ask us to take the funny-farm school seriously?

Rettig: Can you tell us a little more about the transition between the gang and Leo's operation? It seemed like you jumped right from the gang to being an important part of the Organization.

Manny: Well, it *didn't* happen overnight. When those cops were downed by some crazy kids it put a lot of heat on the gangs. But actually, I was ready to get out of the Young Stars by that time. Remember, not many older adolescents stayed in the gangs around New York at that time. Gangs were mostly kids from eleven to about fifteen. In the Bronx, at fifteen, most kids had become men. Leo needed someone to start running numbers, and I was available. I was kind of like a mascot of Leo's, like a water boy who gets good enough to make the team.

Rettig: When you were getting involved with Leo did you have any feelings of guilt about what you were learning and doing?

Manny: Nothing. Not a thing! Because, you see, numbers, gambling, prostitution, and the protection rackets might have all been illegal, but they were normal, daily activities in my neighborhood. It wasn't deviance at all to us. There was sort of a built-in collective justification for our conduct. Some people survived and prospered one way, some another. There was no guilt felt by most of us, of that I'm absolutely sure.

Rettig: You weren't going against the norms, then, as you felt them? And what about the cops? You knew they were against your behavior; how did you deal with that?

Manny: Look, the neighborhood supported the gangs without much opposition. When somebody got ripped off, or their storefront caved in, they'd get mad, naturally. But gangs were not viewed, in my neighborhood at least, as abnormal. And when a kid grew up, he just naturally got into some kind of shady business—or he became a dope fiend right off—or he died. I know of damn few kids in my group that made it. Can think of one or two. But lots of them got fucked up. I don't know that the rackets were considered criminal by most folks in my neighborhood. I doubt it. There was a lot of social support for the rackets. Everybody's uncle or brother or nephew was working in the rackets. And almost everybody was a customer. Even the little old grandmothers would pinch a dollar from their tithe money to buy a number. The dope pusher was just another guy on the street. Legitimate opportunities to make a buck were closed to lots of us, so we made the rackets legitimate by our definition. And that is what was important. After all, we lived there.

The cops? Who gives a shit. You know what I mean? Like, the cops could be from Mars for all we cared or for all they influenced us. And we were from Mars as far as they were concerned. There was no interaction of values. No interaction at all, except mutal hatred and war. We felt that we were legitimate because we made ourselves legitimate. When I graduated to white-on-white shirts, pinstripe suits, and alligator shoes, like Leo, I knew I'd arrived. Nobody, especially a cop, was about to tell me different.

Rettig: If you'd arrived, why the heroin?

Manny: That's the good one. I don't know. I had a lot of money; I was a successful gambler. But I couldn't spend it all. Remember, I was still in the middle of my teens. I was lonely, I guess, and felt a lot of pain inside. I had pain inside like a knot of churning, molten iron since I was a little kid.

I think I know the reason, though, like the real action behind why I went to drugs. My uncle fascinated me; he was a *guapo,* a good head. And even if I had seen guys wasted on scag before, my bad-assed uncle made it look good. So, I tried it. Soon I could care less about my job with Leo.

Rettig: After you decided to try heroin, it was just a matter of time until you were a mainline addict?

Manny: That's about it. Even though I resisted at each point, it wasn't hard to go from sniffing to popping to mainlining. I could never get enough once I started.

Rettig: Becker [1964, pp. 1-6] talks about the formation of a deviant career. He says that when a decision to act is made, the techniques of action are learned step by step. At each step there is a contingency awareness. Are there contingencies at each step for the dope addict that might lead him to stop along the way or even reverse himself to preaddict status?

Manny: Not at all, with heroin. With speed or maryjane, sure. But the only contingency to heroin, once you've tried it is, where's it at and how can I get my hands on it? I don't believe in maintenance heroin habits. They may exist, but not to my knowledge. Once you're hooked, you will do anything for a fix!

Rettig: All right. Let's look at it objectively. Not Manuel Torres whose life is at stake—but let's look at the problem out front. You look back on your past life and you can see the addict mentality. When you were hooked, by your own admission you'd rip off your own brother or put your own sister on the line for dope. You'll do anything in the world for drugs. How does that balance out in your mind with society's motivation to hold a dope fiend? Do you have any feeling, for example, against California for the indeterminate sentence; for trying to hang onto the guy who will rip them off or kill them or whatever to maintain his dope habit?

Manny: Is society in the right for locking me up because I steal from them? Is that what you're asking? Am I supposed to like it?

Rettig: Can you respond to that?

Manny: Yeah. I'm mad! I don't care what anybody says, people have taken away my life. Yeah, I'm mad. I took from them and I'll take again if I'm put in that position. Why did I turn out to be a dope fiend? It was that most of the people in my neighborhood turned out to be dope fiends. Was I without balls? Hell, no! I wanted to be a standup cat too, you know, a *guapo,* the man with the heavy balls.

Why, man, why? I wasn't born wanting to be a dope fiend. But I grew into it. And I didn't live in a cocoon, either. Sure, society is to blame. What do you need? Six or seven more Watergates? Couple of Vietnams? A hundred more ghettos? Who are the real criminals? Most of the people in my generation in the Bronx turned out so-called bad. They either became crooks, dopers, or they dropped out. One way or another they were wasted. Now, where's the problem—individual pathology or social disorganization and chaos?

I don't know exactly how I blame society, or what for. All I know is that I never had the opportunities someone else had to grow up on the hill in suburbia, and I'm mad. Are they right for locking me up? No! Because I didn't steal to support me. I stole to support a habit. They created the habit, and they're still creating habits for sixteen-year-old kids. Society creates the rat, roach, rapo conditions that led me to pick up the habit. And I want to do something to change that. I'm so glad that I'm at Humboldt State. If this college program had not come up, I would most likely still be in trouble. Now I have a chance to get a degree and go beyond. Besides, I don't have to have my front up any more. It's easier to be your own man here and have a sense of personal worth or integrity. I may make it now. I've got a good chance!

Rettig: Manny, what about the indeterminate sentencing procedure specifically? Are you against it?

Manny: You bet I am! It causes the inmate to lose hope and die inside. When you have no release date, why care? You might be there forever. It's so easy to get busted in prison for some little rule infraction, for not "having your mind right." Sometimes you can get busted behind just feeling bad. You know, get up on the wrong side of the bed and say something out of line to a guard. And this write-up might cost you a year, two years' setback.

So, an inmate will often turn into a con—he'll get so shifty and careful he'll not get caught at all. He may get out, but you haven't touched his character, except to make it worse.

Rettig: You've articulated a double principle here. First, a built-in antagonism toward what is in effect a life sentence often instigates trouble in that inmates have no way of knowing where they stand with respect to making it out. Second, a reaction formation may often set in whereby the inmate learns to be con-wise, thus institutionalizing the very behavior the prison is raised up to deal with.

Manny: Exactly! I wish I could tell people that so they wouldn't think it was just a snow job.

Rettig: I think you have, Manny. Another assumption that stands as a driving force behind the indeterminate sentence philosophy is that we are technically equipped to "treat" offenders so they will become "well."

Manny: If there is any single message in this book I meant to get across it is that treating the convict as if *he* is sick is absolutely the wrong approach. It's not so much that we don't have the psychiatric "tools"— although we don't—it's that we persist in treating mere symptoms of a far deeper pathology. Our social life and its organizational forms are sick. In my opinion, a lot of crime happens because people are knocking on the door of opportunity, and in this frustrating, highly stratified society the "losers" tear down the first likely door they find.

Dialogue 2

Criminology Class Session

Rettig: In this session, Manny and I want to answer questions and develop things further along the lines of Manny's earlier presentation. I asked you at that time to write down questions about things that interested you or areas that required clarification.

Student: Manny, I'd like to know if and when you considered yourself to be a professional criminal. This is a little confusing to me because in most of the typifications of criminal careers we have studied for this class your status would appear to be unclear.

Manny: Yeah! I've sometimes wondered about that myself. I guess that when I was involved in that long streak of armed robbery with Izzy and the boys I identified with it as a work or a way of life. I used to like to think of myself as a "stickup artist," a cool cat who lived by a real righteous combination of wits and guts. I guess you could call it a vocation. I certainly wanted a payday, and money was a primary reason for me being out there.

Student: But you were out there pulling robberies first because of dope, right? I thought you stressed that a lot in your presentation.

Manny: Sure. I think I kind of got "hooked" behind the excitement and feeling of power—the symbol of the gun in the guts of society—there for a while. But you gotta remember that robbery wasn't my sole interest at all. I don't ever remember pulling a job except that I needed the bread for dope. A dope fiend is always looking for more dope.

Rettig: The line between vocational and other types of theft and robbery in various typologies is not always clear. On the one hand, Manny can be seen as a "addiction-supporting predator" [Glaser, 1972, p. 37] because he maintains that he committed property crimes "primarily to procure funds for the purchase of some mood-altering drug . . ." On the other hand, Manny can be seen as a "vocational predator" [Glaser, 1972, p. 44] because he supported himself for many years by taking money and property from others. For me, his addiction largely predicted all subsequent behavior. As Irwin [1970] has said, everything else is filtered through the drug effect.

Student: You said many times that you liked to think of yourself as "able to take it," "able to dish it out." Would you say that you were a professional heavy?

Manny: Oh, you know, I got just as much pride as the next guy. I'd like to say I was a "professional heavy," but not really. We capered a lot to survive and get drugs, but a lot of our jobs were not very well planned. And we picked on cleaning shops, candy shops, and the like lots of times. There wouldn't be much cash there; we'd just go on to the next one. Another thing, my attitude wasn't often what you'd call professional. I didn't like work. Remember that good thing I had going with the checks? And cops! I never did like cops from when I was a kid in the Young Stars. The professional views the police as an occupational hazard; he doesn't waste time or effort in hating them.

Rettig: Manny's reporting squares with the Gibbons and Garrity article we read for this course. In "Definitions and Analysis of Certain Criminal Types" [1962, pp. 28–35] they point out the differences between the "professional thief" and "professional heavy" on the one hand, and the "nonprofessional property offender" on the other. Manny fits pretty well into this latter category, especially with his self-definition as a criminal coupled with his self-view as a victim of society, which is fairly common among drug addicts. Even here though we see contradictions. Anybody notice one?

Student: Probably you mean having to do with skill, technological expertise. The nonprofessional is characterized as lacking in crime skills, working for meager profit, and not planning the crime well.

Manny: Yeah. I was involved in lots of things where the caper was well planned. Like the cigarette heists, and some of the robbery. And what about the dock-boosting and check-cashing outfits?

Rettig: We can't divide criminals into clear-cut species. Manny's reporting highlights the major difficulty of all classifications of this nature: people just do not fit neatly and naturally into categories. Rather than think of dichotomous variables differentiating criminal types, we should probably try to organize their behaviors and attitudes on some sort of a continuum arrangement. The range of ways in which Manny and his friends can be classified, even on the basis of this meager evidence, allows for a great deal of variation.

Student: You brought out something the other day that I've never seen discussed in the literature on corrections. You mentioned the "old con" and the "old guard" mentality as being at the heart of our prison problem. Will you elaborate on that?

Manny: In a class where we're studying racism, I've been turned on to the term "ethnocentrism." That notion is useful here. I believe that there is a very strong, perverted sense of ethos in the prison community and it affects the cons and guards alike. Prejudicial attitudes are real strong in prison. There is a violent, underlying sense of hatred and destructiveness in the joint. Both cons and guards like to think of themselves as "having it all together." They want to appear stable and together like everybody else, but actually most cons and guards are incapable of genuine identification with others.

Rettig: You see this in observing the shifting loyalties in the inmate social structure. Their individual loyalties are shifting ones, often temporary in nature, where they draw courage by association with the more powerful and privileged inmates.

Manny: Actually, both the old-time cons and the old-line guards are often conformists, wanting to hang onto the conventional prison morality. They want to keep the hickory shirts, the "red line" walkway from the yard to the cellblock, life like it's always been down along the mainline. There's a certain romantic notion about the convict code and "in the life" that permeates the maximum-security prison.

Rettig: You see this in guards and administrative personnel in their resistance to new types of treatment and rehabilitation programs such as work release and preparole home visits. Often the old-line officers can be very effective in keeping things as they were. But it is important for us to stress, as Manny has, that the "old con" mentality contributes as much or more to the static nature of prison than does the traditional guard resistance.

Manny: Sure. He doesn't want to give up his conniving, his bootlegging, his capering, and his pretty little boy-girl relationship. All that stuff thrives in the old-line joint.

Student: What can we do to change it? You paint a black picture.

Manny: Institutional changes are probably the only answer. You are not going to see the old-timers in prison lay down their biases and lifestyles merely in response to words that they refuse to listen to, that they misinterpret. That's why riots seldom work, even when adjustments are attempted afterward. Either it ends up in a lot of useless words or the cons use a few feeble concessions merely to reinforce their established values.

Rettig: The specific kinds of institutional change that can be implemented to modify these antiquated lifestyles are vague and experimental at this point. We may well need fundamental adjustments in our economic and political system. We must invent changes that will inhibit or eliminate the processes whereby these alienated and hostile identities are generated. The kinds of institutional change that will build personality rather than tear it down, that will channel hostility and despair into less degrading, harmful circumstances, are probably somewhere beyond our present social vision. Work-release centers, halfway-in rather than halfway-out houses are a couple of examples. But neither the penal administrators, the lawmakers, nor the public have a significant commitment to these alternatives as anything but token remedies presently.

Student: Manny, you made a very interesting observation when you said that inmates appeared to get involved in overt racism in the prison as a mode of adjustment. Can you go on with that?

Manny: There's a lot of group identification in prison. It's an overcontrolled environment with most of the territory in the hands of the establishment. The traditional superior-subordinate relationships that prevail in the joint almost insure that racist attitudes will develop. Contact is never on equal terms in prison. One is always measuring himself individually with another. One group measures itself up with another. Factionalism is reinforced by all the institutional patterns; there is no common goal, no higher unity that can serve to bring the prejudiced person in line with the object of his prejudice. Us Puerto Ricans used to say, when we had nothing else to do, "Let's go get us some niggers."

Student: I'm not sure I followed everything you said about prison homosexuality. My idea about it was that guys just ran around knocking down kids when they got the chance and raped them. But you talked as if rape wasn't that frequent in jails and prisons.

Rettig: A significant fact about the male prison community is that it is a world of men without women. Sexual starvation thus becomes a serious problem. You might say that homosexuality is institutionalized through the process of prisonization. Because there is nothing provided to help the inmate cope with his sexual needs, deviations from the conventional sex code are tolerated and regarded as inevitable. As in any other one-sex situation, homosexual behavior is to be expected.

Manny: Prison is an abnormal environment, men's normal impulses are often turned to perversions. Do you worry about the existence of homosexuality in prison? I'd worry if there wasn't any. If the sex drive is not satisfied in an abnormal manner, a stud's mental conflicts may be more disturbing than the screwing around itself. Sure, rape is a fairly frequent event in the joint, but it is not the only homosexual activity in prison. Do you guys read Irwin [1970] for this course? He's right on when he says that voluntary homosexuality often becomes a way to avoid the potential attacks of rapists. An alliance with some powerful jock can be a source of protection from other prisoners. Sometimes it is just a much-needed expression of love.

Student: Don't the guards and officials resist this behavior?

Manny: Oh, they don't stand around and let kids get raped; if they see it they break it up. Funny thing, though, the kid usually gets thrown in the hole same as the guy that attacked him. I never could understand that. Two guys get in a fight, they're both gone to the growler, makes no difference if one's fighting for his honor.

But homosexuals "sleeping" together by consent? In my experience, the prison staff is aware of the problem. But they feel that nothing can be done to stop it, so they tend to look the other way. Therefore, because of the lack of opportunity for normal sexual relationships, and the implicit encouragement on the part of prison guards and administrators, homosexuality thrives in most joints. And this implicit acceptance of homosexual "love" relationships tends to cool out the guard's attitudes toward the brutal rape incidents. "The kid over in D Block who was raped? He probably asked for it." Also, don't forget that once a kid gets raped, he is marked as a sexual victim for the duration of his stretch. And this mark follows him from institution to institution.

Rettig: It is damned obvious that not only does the joint fail to rehabilitate guys who are socialized into homosexuality, it is the prime breeding ground for the homosexual lifestyle. If you think the problem is bad in prison, take a look in the reform schools. All kinds of punks and queers are generated by our children's centers and training schools.

Manny: In the reform school kids are just learning what sex is all about. They are full of piss and vinegar. For this reason the incidence of homosexual play is even higher in juvenile institutions than in adult prisons.

Many boys in reform school have never before been confronted with abnormal sex behavior, yet they are naive to the point where they "drop their strides" for the first old-timer who thumps them in the chest.

Student: That's kind of what Irwin [1970] was talking about in his concept of the "state raised youth." Can you comment further on that in terms of your experience?

Manny: Although I didn't do much juvenile time, I met a lot of men in prison who'd been raised in the reformatories and boys' schools of America. By the time these guys get to prison they're gonners.

Rettig: The system of the "state raised youth" is rightly tagged by Irwin [1970, pp. 26-29] as the one "criminal" system represented in the prison world that is mostly indigenous to that milieu. Many youths come to an adult prison after repeated commitments to a juvenile institution where they have come in contact with and become a part of the preprison behavior system. These institutions actually create the prison experience; they get kids ready for the real thing. And it's not just the training school organization, it's the institutionalized process of how we relate to adolescence in our society. Those places that we reserve for the storage of our young problematic identities are truly "training schools," providing the initiating and processing rituals that will equip the young man for the future sequential process into criminality.

Manny: To be up front about it, the problems for the state raised youth begin when he or she is committed to a juvenile institution again and again for minor offenses like running away, incorrigibility, ungovernable behavior, and minor in need of supervision. Soon he gets the idea that because he is habitually in trouble with the law, and the school, and the home, for that matter, he comes to be identified by others as "trouble," a "delinquent," or a just plain shitty character, and he soon begins to view himself in the same way. He learns to identify himself as a deviant.

Student: Some of us are going to work in Preston, or at McLaren up in Oregon, or El Reno in Oklahoma. We are trained to do this kind of work. What you're telling us is hard to bear. How are we to survive and make a contribution?

Manny: By getting in and changing the whole system, that's how. Because if you don't you'll only be sucked in, regardless of your motives now. The correctional system sucks, and it'll co-opt anybody who becomes insensitive to the real issues.

Like, you'll join the Ramsey Clarks and the Jerry Browns, who are still fooled into pushing the same tired reformist ideology: more treatment, diagnosis, therapy. Hire more psychiatrists, beef up classification so that you separate the "bad ones" from the "good ones." And every one of these kind of reforms only makes possible that much more cloudiness and arbitrariness. The Number 1 public issue in regard to prisons should be their institutional failure; and the Number 1 question that the public should be asking is, why do we have these places?

Rettig: Yes, I agree. This system has failed wretchedly. As Irwin [1970] points out, once inside the juvenile institution, the youth realizes that the main themes of the organization are toughness and craftiness. He has to learn how to fight and to con others in order to survive. The top positions in the inmate social structure are maintained and preserved by physical force; and violence is accepted as the proper manner of settling any arguments. Craftiness and manipulation are the only alternative and coordinate methods of survival. The youth, then, necessarily becomes either extremely defensive or very offensive, learning to deal effectively with others by using aggressive methods of brute force and manipulation by insinuation. There is no place here for the cultivation of an existential awareness of self as person. No way to learn how to be understanding and outgoing to others.

Manny: The "state raised youth" that I knew in Chino and back in Sing Sing all ran in cliques, just like our gangs on the streets. These groups were not high on loyalty to each other. They were loose-knit and shifting—guys joining together for protection. Often riots in the joint are started by these hombres. Young guys up from reform school can exert a powerful force on the prison because they act weird and crazy just to impress each other. And there's seldom planning to their action.

Rettig: Manny, did you see more homosexuality among "state raised youth" in your opinion?

Manny: Yes. Although they argue with each other and shift around among their various cliques, in a way they are bound together as a reference group. These cliques establish territorial boundaries, attack and defend themselves from rival groups in the prison, and resolve internal conflicts by fighting. They are distrustful of guys outside their clique, thus they find it impossible almost to maintain normal social relationships inside or outside the prison.

Homosexuality is a dominant theme of the "state raised youth" because he is young and locked up. He has a strong sex drive and is in a place with no broads. Out of necessity he engages in sex with other dudes in the clique as a form of release. Probably he "punks" kids more than he masturbates because to play with himself would be a negation of his self-perceived toughness.

Rettig: I think that's a fair assumption. Unsure of his own manhood, he becomes extremely sensitive about his own perverse acts and constantly looks for ways to prove his manhood before his peers. "State raised youth" are often involved in prison "gang shags," where a group of inmates sequester a new young inmate and rape him repeatedly.

It is important for us to realize that we should not psychologize these kinds of problems. If the "state raised youth" has emotional problems—a troublesome identity—it is because he has had few options other than trouble from which to choose. It is in this abnormal world of the prison where he has acquired the meanings and definitions of sex, and that will make it very hard for him to maintain normal sexual relationships here or outside.

Manny: I agree! Man, that's just like I seen it happen, time and time again. It is easy for me to see how the world view of this kind of kid becomes distorted and irrational. The joint becomes his home, the only world to relate to—and his gang members become the family. A young kid raised in a world of sex perversion and brute force soon learns to function and prosper in that world. He learns all the angles, and this knowledge will serve him well when he matures in the adult prison. Really! A young kid's experience in jails and juvenile joints has prepared him for the world of the convict.

Student: You people talk a lot about the inmate subculture. Like the prison is run by them. What about staff, the administration, and their rules and regulations?

Rettig: A clear distinction should be made between the prison community and the prisoner community. To the casual visitor, the sole community at a prison location is the one maintained by the administration. However, a closer look at any prison reveals a covert organization composed entirely of inmates. Every inmate subsequently must recognize two opposite codes of behavior—that one written and legalized by the administration, and the code laid down and enforced by the inmates.

Manny: The inmate code may be unwritten but it is the more powerful of the two, and becomes the real rules that the convict learns to follow. Whenever the inmate code clashes with prison regulations, or the con's own personal code of ethics, for that matter, the inmate code will dominate his thought and action most of the time. That's who he's going to follow, the other cons, not the Man.

Rettig: It is this unwritten but powerful social code that keeps peace and relative quiet within the prison community. It keeps the inmate in line and forces loyalty to the other inmates, while at the same time forcing resistance to the administration, which is the enemy. When the code is broken, fights and killings are often the result.

Manny: You have to experience it to believe it. I know it seems strange when you hear that "cons run the prisons," or that "the inmate code predicts most of what happens in the daily life of prisoners." That's the reality, though, and I don't see how you're going to change it with the structure of prisons remaining the same. The unwritten code regulates the public and private life of the convict, telling him what he can and cannot do. Did you read Minton [1971] for this class? He points out that the inmate code colors the convict's own perception of self, and is like a giant chain that binds the inmates together.

Student: You have had us look at two fundamentally different perspectives on prisons and the inmate adjustment, which you identify as "situational" and "sequential": can you go over again the position of each rather clearly and then maybe Manny can relate to that in terms of his own experience?

Rettig: Sykes and Messinger [1960] see the inmate social organization as a social system made up of argot roles. These roles include: the "rat"—an inmate who betrays a fellow prisoner; the "tough"—a prisoner who quarrels and fights for no reason; the "gorilla"—a person who uses brute force for personal gain; the "merchant"—a crafty inmate who exploits his fellow prisoners; the "wolf" or "fag"—an inmate who epitomizes the ideal of the inmate code, the hero; and the "square John"—the inmate who gives the picture of conformity, "doing his time" and working.

Sykes and Messinger view this system of normatively interlocked roles as a functional system which arose out of the prisoner's effort to cope with what is called the "pains of imprisonment." As they see it, the prisoner comes to prison rejected by society, reduced to a level of living near bare subsistence, with an ego threatened by the lack of heterosexual relationships, and is then forced to live with possibly dangerous criminals. The inmate feels that the deprivations, the frustrations, and the fears of prison life somehow must be alleviated. It is as an answer to this need that the imprisoned criminal must find a device for rejecting his rejectors, if he is to survive physically and psychologically. He finds it in the subculture system of values or inmate code.

Besides maintaining order and providing protection, the code helps to bolster the prisoner's dignity and self-respect. Group cohesion, the dominant theme of the inmate code, provides the prisoner with a meaningful social group with which he can identify and which will support him in time of need.

Sykes and Messinger believe that the characteristics of this prison social system take shape within the situation itself, free of influence from external factors. They further suggest that the former identities, values, and norms of the prisoner are, for the most part, erased through various ceremonies upon entering prison.

Irwin [1970], however, takes the opposite stand in support of the sequential thesis. He views the criminal career as a total process influenced by the home, school, reformatory, criminal justice system, prisonization, and the streets again. It's a whole sequential process in identity formation.

Usually, the criminal's career begins with some contact with other criminals. Through this contact he acquires a criminal identity—a set of beliefs, values, and self-definitions relating to different criminal lifestyles. Irwin's typology of these various criminal identities and their major themes are: the "thief"—his major theme is the "big score" (money or goods from a burglary or armed robbery); the "hustler"—the major theme is sharpness in language and appearance, maintaining a good front; the "dope fiend"—the major themes are being hooked, scoring, fixing, and hustling; the "head"—the dominant theme is the lifestyle of seeking new, exotic experiences through the use of psychedelic drugs; the "disorganized criminal"—the major themes here are carelessness, self-defeatism, "screwing up"; the "state raised youth"—the major theme is toughness and a clique-forming propensity; the lowest and last, the "square John"—the major theme is conformity or convention.

Once the criminal forms an identity, from then on, any new phase in his career is influenced to some degree by these perspectives gathered earlier. In fact, many convicts bring with them a criminal identity which really prepares them for life in the prison, and they redefine and direct this behavior toward the larger criminal world of which prison is an important part. Therefore, Irwin concludes, the inmate system of norms is largely an extension of criminal norms and values. The roles found in prison are not innate to the prison, but rather, they originated within the criminal world.

Manny: You know, if you've listened to what I've said, I was a dope fiend on the streets, and I was a dope fiend in the joint. I hustled on the bricks, and I hustled inside. Your personality don't change that much from one time to another. Any changes the prison makes are for the worse, in the human personality, that is. When I was in prison I learned how to rip off more and better. You talk about reformation? Prison gives the cat an opportunity to get his shit together! I've actually been to safecracking school in the big yard. The teacher was an expert craftsman. That school was both entertaining and educational.

If you're a weak sister, you're going to die, morally, ethically, and maybe physically when you come to the joint. But, if your "Mammy" was the streets, you're gonna make it by hook or crook. I was a man when I got this number, and I'm gonna be a man when I get it off my back!

Student: You constantly refer to our institutions as prisons. I thought the new concept was "correctional institutions." Why isn't it working?

Manny: Prisons are in their own world, they don't relate to the world at large. Usually they sit way out in the sticks somewhere or across the bay in the marshes. They are built to be secure physically. Lots of concrete and stone, steel and barbed wire. "Correctional institutions" is what they are called, but what they provide is custody. The walls exist not only to keep convicts in but to keep the public out. Prisons are designed to control inmates, and cellblocks are built to segregate and separate them into controllable groups. I know that guards are now called "correctional officers," but their job is to manage the physical plant—to lock people in and let them out. They manage the internal security machine and that doesn't leave much time for correctional work. Actually, few officers that I ever knew had much training or skills in personal management or counseling. They are guards, plain and simple, coming oftentimes from the military. They like the work because it is civil service—for their own security—not because they are motivated to rehabilitate offenders.

Rettig: Correctional officers maintain their distance from the inmate body. There is little fraternization. Correctional officers don't take part in the social life of the prison: generally this is mandated by prison regulation. Most officers first come to know blacks, Chicanos, Puerto Ricans, poor whites, and other disenfranchised minorities as convicted criminals, not as social equals. Racist attitudes among the officers permeate most prisons and strongly affect their judgment. This gap between the correctional officers and inmates is one of the chief causes of tension in the prison and is responsible for the retention of the guard image in the collective mind of the inmate body.

Manny: Lots of convicts resist the change to newer, more innovative programs, and so do many of the guards. They don't want change. Cons and guards are often more comfortable with the lockup and the old style.

Student: Manny, you've talked about the different approaches of treatment and custody in prison, as if there are two sets of staff there. Can you clarify that and give your impressions about treatment practices in prison?

Rettig: Let's specify the theoretical differences between custody and treatment in the contemporary maximum-security prison first, and then

Manny can comment whenever he wants to get in here.

The principal objective of penal custody is protection of society from what is popularly considered to be the incorrigible and dangerous offender. In our history, prison has traditionally been delegated the responsibility of shielding society from the deviant behavior of criminal types. The justification for custody inheres in the legal obligations of the warden to maintain safekeeping and the community's concern for its own security.

Manny: What the professor means is that we, society, flush down the sewer anything that don't smell right to us. And prison is our cesspool! Dangerousness is lots of times a myth that clouds the real issue: are we going to personally deal with people that need help? Or are we going to ship them away? Maybe the myth of dangerousness is foisted on society to keep the prison rationale intact. I've seen thousands of prisoners come and go, and the vast majority are emotionally torn-up guys without a home or a job. That's all.

Rettig: Because of strong public support, and through rationalizations such as deterrence, incapacitation, and retribution, the concept of custody has historically overshadowed the penal organization's other prescribed functions: training for industry and treatment for personal problems.

Manny: Prison custody is more than just lockup and the prevention of escapes. Custody has to do with issuing standard prison clothes, restricting personal belongings, cutting the hair short, lack of privacy, numbers instead of names, regimentation, excessive rules and regulations, and excessive punishment for minor violations. These and other custodial practices are meant precisely to degrade the inmate and show him he is a second-rate person subject to punitive control because of his "evil outlook on life." Even the inmate subculture is a form of social control practiced by the inmates themselves and often supported and subordinated by the administration to keep individuals in line.

Rettig: Treatment, on the other hand, begins with entry evaluation leading to classification. As Manny has pointed out, this is generally a negative experience that strips the new inmate of all defenses, leaving him vulnerable to attack and self-rejection. His total "being" is neatly condensed and packaged in a folder from which determinations and conclusions will be drawn concerning his direction and future.

Manny: The new inmate has a tremendous problem at this point. He must somehow pull himself together and stand erect in front of his accusers—classification hearings, like parole hearings, always seem to be adversary proceedings— to save some remnant of his self-respect and his personal identity that they have tried to rip off of him through the intake and subsequent labeling process.

You know, the thirty-day admission and orientation process (the "fish tank") common to most joints used to be necessary for quarantine purposes, but the procedure now is perpetuated for the sole purpose of restructuring the new convict's identity so that the joint can impress its authority over him and convince him to "get his head right."

Student: You don't like custody and you don't like treatment, Manny. I thought the object of better prisons is to get better treatment.

Manny: "Treatment" supposedly includes all but lockup and the constant regimentation. This generally involves some unrewarding and noninstructive work programs, some education and recreation, and possibly a little counseling, which always involves more paperwork than communication. Generally, "treatment" is a front for control because rehabilitation under maximum-security circumstances is close to impossible.

As I've said before, one place where you can see the phony face of "treatment" is in the supposedly advanced notion of the indeterminate sentence, which is clearly a control mechanism to coerce convicts to conform and to regulate population intake and discharge as needed for smooth prison functioning rather than a "hold until cured" idea.

Rettig: Even in prisons where there is a genuine effort to effect good "treatment," custody and treatment are in constant conflict. But the more important issue, in my judgment, is what do we mean by "treatment"?

Many modern correctional institutions operate from a medical model where most inmates are defined as being mentally ill, emotionally disturbed, having character disorders or disorganized social attitudes. They are approached with treatment policies which are ever more similar to those previously reserved for the physically sick. What happens is that corrections defines itself as a quasi-medical specialty that diagnoses, treats, and controls criminal and delinquent behavior therapeutically.

In essence, much of what correctional casework is all about can be traced directly to a medical model of social psychiatry, even though its practitioners are not medical psychiatrists.

Manny: Most of the classification people I ever knew in prison were either ex-guards who went to night school or young guys out of college with psychology or sociology degrees.

Rettig: A central notion of the medical model of social psychiatry is that the concept of mental illness should help us to organize and understand the facts about an individual's behavior.

Manny: Diagnostic evaluation is a big thing in the California system. They depend on personality tests and psychiatric testimony to classify and evaluate convicts. A principal part of this process is to make judgments on an inmate's "escape potential" and "violence potential."

Rettig: Although the notion of mental defect or illness is alleged to be scientific, it is not at all value-free. In fact, classificatory policies in California and many other jurisdictions are tied to all the assumptions of an individualistic psychology that blindly accepts an ideology that internal and constraining variables on individual behavior predict the convict's state of "being" and faithfully delineate his possibilities. [Szasz, 1961a, 1961b, 1963, 1965.]

Manny: Calling a cat sick just adds another label to his jacket; we already got him labeled bad!

Rettig: Exactly! The psychiatric approach is directly opposed to legality. It ignores all our traditional libertarian principles and Anglo-Saxon legal traditions. When you are classified as being "sick," all individual right, due process, and protection of the individual against the group are destroyed. We really do move "beyond freedom and dignity" as the medical model of corrections adds a whole new dimension of coercion to the law.

Manny: If you get sent to Vacaville you are classified as having a serious personality or character disorder. And man, you'll wear that jacket for the rest of your life. The whole California system is blinded by the notion of mental illness in the criminal. What they don't see at all is the social circumstances leading to his getting busted. And more important, the social circumstances that might be used to help redeem him.

Rettig: The lines of our argument here should be clear. If the problem lies within the head of the criminal, then psychological techniques which treat the inmate to effect remission of his behavior are indicated. The available evidence regarding the success of psychiatry, psychiatric social work, and counseling psychology in the correctional field does not lead to optimism. Based on the California experience alone, the potential of clinical models to deal with criminality is not good. For example, "I"-level theory [Warren, 1971]: an attempt to make discrete judgments regarding offenders' personality characteristics, long heralded as the way, has been generally abandoned. Recidivism among low-income inmates is very high.

But if the problem of criminality lies in "the world out there," our emphasis should shift from psychological reductionism to address those structural features which exert powerful pressures to lock criminals into their deviant roles.

Student: Manny, you have a long record; you've been many kinds of criminal; you're an admitted long-term dope fiend. How did you change?

Manny: You mean, how am I changing? I haven't finished becoming somebody different than I was. Hopefully, we're all doing that. One reason that I'm changing is that the people up here in Humboldt County are something else! I've not experienced hardly any put-downs because of my past. I'm going to school and doing all right with it. I'm not setting the university on fire, but I'm making good grades and enjoying my work.

Student: Would you comment on what specific kinds of reforms are needed to make our prison system work?

Rettig: We should keep in mind that prisons are the terminal end of a much larger problem. Our prisons aren't working because the entire criminal justice system isn't working properly.

Manny: I don't believe in prison reform. Prisons are the cesspools of society, and I don't believe that our health specialists are trying to reform cesspools. They are trying to do away with them!

Rettig: The whole criminal justice system rests on highly inequitable discretionary processes. Problems for the inarticulate members of disenfranchised groups begin long before arrest, are specifically initiated on their arrest, are compounded at every subsequent step—the adversary trial, the sentencing process, the prison term, and the parole board decision.

Manny: Due process is a sham. You can have very legal due process every step of the way and still get screwed.

Rettig: That's because of the arbitrary nature of our legal system. All outcomes for a criminal depend on the discretion of the officials who process him. The single most significant step we could take toward turning the justice system around and giving it new direction would be to eliminate judicial and official arbitrariness. Discretion has always worked in favor of the articulate. As Justice Douglas has often said, the poor and the masses have never been articulate; the man of property is articulate and has always been heard in the courts.

Manny: And how about redemption for the man sent to prison? The prison environment discourages redemption. Any redemptive steps taken by the inmate are a struggle against the prison officials. Redemption happens in spite of the joint, not because of it.

Rettig: A major share of the blame for prison failure should be shouldered by society, you and I. We have never really made a commitment to the rehabilitative process. I assume that the money legislated for prisons, both federally and locally, is a pretty valid indication of citizen intent and desire. About 90 percent of the money spent in prison budgets is for security and about 10 percent for programs that might help prisoners. The costs of running our prisons are staggering, without any real success.

Manny: Warden John Case of Bucks County, Pennsylvania, said that if General Motors had the same failure rate that American prisons had, they'd be having a new board of directors every year.

Rettig: We have to look long and hard at the whole judicial process. There are a number of things drastically wrong.

Manny: You want to hear a good one? Parole boards are charged by law with the responsibility of determining when individuals are rehabilitated. That's illogical, because there is not one shred of evidence to show that any prison has a process that rehabilitates.

Rettig: All sentencing power should be returned to the judicial branch, in my opinion. Determinate sentences are the most practical and the most humane. The decision of when to release a prisoner should not be arbitrary. If you do the crime you should do the time. This should stand for everybody. Perhaps then we could talk about the general deterrent effect of the law.

Manny: I agree that society has a right to punish offenders. But they should punish all equally regardless of wealth or station. And reasonable punishment is one thing, excessive punishment is another. If you can't redeem a man in six or seven years, you might as well forget it.

Rettig: I'm for the establishment of local facilities in every community. There should be tight security for those who are demonstrably dangerous. The rest of the inmates, by far the larger number, should be reintegrated with their own community as soon as possible. Work furlough, work release, halfway houses, parole, and outright release should be options available to the judge in each case at any time during the sentence.

Manny: There's a very important point I want to make here. Under the present prison setup, the cons who conform best to prison life are least likely to make it in the demanding outside world. And yet, the institutionalized con-wise inmate is the one who makes parole usually. But the outspoken, politically aware, gutsy cons who could go a long way outside with the proper direction are kept in longer because of their "bad attitudes."

Rettig: There are several ways we can raise the money to change the system without increasing the tax burden severely. Prison populations could be cut in half by eliminating victimless crimes. Prison is a deadly way to "mother" people, which is what we do if we assume that a man can be a victim of his own act. First offenders should be diverted into alternate channels removed from penal justice. This should even include murders since it is proven statistically that most murderers will never commit another crime. A real functional arm of the diversionary process could be public service programs, where the man would pay his debt by working a stipulated time for society without significant remuneration. If these programs continue to be tokenistic we will not ever effect reform of the criminal justice system; if they become widespread, the system could be revolutionized.

However, the most enlightened prison program can only be a beginning. It is the postprison experience encountered by the ex-offender that will tell whether or not he will make it. Numerous long-time felons fall before public opinion, as personified by an eager prosecutor, for minor theft or the like. Prison is never a finishing school, in the good sense at least, and we must be accepting and patient as the ex-offender tries to work through his problems upon release.

Reformation and redemption are processes consisting of sequential steps. Ex-offenders must have the time and assistance needed to construct lifestyles in which they are socially anchored. They need every public and private assistance in restructuring a legitimate identity. To feel competent, they need jobs established; to feel useful, they need to feel that they are making a significant contribution; to feel that they belong, they need to be accepted by many and be allowed to have a wide range of social contacts; to have a sense of personal power or potency, they need to be encouraged to participate in every phase of the decision-making process that affects them.

Above and beyond all this theory, society needs to accept the fact that ex-offenders may continue to commit minor offenses for a time as they pass through the "latency stage" of their criminal careers. When our justice system "busts" them automatically for minor offenses, because of their ex-con status, they may often nip the bud of reformation that could have flowered into a successful citizen.

Selected References

Atchley, Robert C., & McCabe, M. Patrick
1968   Socialization in correctional communities: A replication. *American Sociological Review 33* (October), 774–785.

Becker, Howard (Ed.)
1964 *The other side: Perspective on deviance.* New York: The Free Press.

Clemmer, Donald
1958 *The prison community.* New York: Rinehart. (Originally published, 1940.)

Cohen, Albert K.
1955 *Delinquent boys: The culture of the gang.* Glencoe, Ill. The Free Press.

Cohen, Bernard
1969 The delinquency of gangs and spontaneous groups. In Thorsten Sellin & Marvin E. Wolfgang (Eds.), *Delinquency: Selected studies.* New York: Wiley.

Cressey, Donald R.
1959 Contradictory directives in complex organizations: The case of the prison. *Administrative Science Quarterly 4* (June), 1–14.
1960 Limitations on organization of treatment in the modern prison. In Richard A. Cloward, et al. (Eds.), *Theoretical studies in social organization of the prison.* New York: Social Science Research Council.
1965 Prison organizations. In James C. March (Ed.), *Handbook of organization.* Chicago: Rand McNally.

Durkheim, Emile
1958 *The rules of sociological method* (G. Catlen T., Trans.). New York: Macmillan.

Garbedian, Peter G.
1963 Social roles and the process of socialization in the prison community. *Social Problem II* (Fall), 139–152.

Gibbons, Don C. & Garrity, Donald L.
1962 Definitions and analysis of certain criminal types. *Journal of Criminal Law, Criminology, and Police Science* 53 (March).

1963 Some suggestions for the development of etiological and treatment theory in criminology. *Social Forces 38* (October), 51–58.

Glaser, Daniel
1964 *The effectiveness of a prison and parole system.* Indianapolis: Bobbs-Merrill.
1972 *Adult crime and social policy.* Englewood Cliffs, N.J.: Prentice-Hall.

Goffman, Erving
1961 On the characteristics of total institutions: The inmate world. In Donald R. Cressey (Ed.), *The prison: Studies in institutional organization and change.* New York: Holt, Rinehart & Winston. (Chap. 1.)

Irwin, John
1970 *The felon.* Englewood Cliffs, N.J.: Prentice-Hall.

McCorkle, Lloyd W., & Korn, Richard
1954 Resocialization within walls. *Annals of the American Academy of Political and Social Science 293* (May), 80-89.

Miller, Walter B.
1958 Lower-class culture as a generating milieu of gang delinquency. *Journal of Social Issues 14,* no. 3, 5-19.

Minton, Robert J. (Ed.)
1971 *Inside: Prison American style.* New York: Random House.

Ohlin, Lloyd E.
1960 Conflicting interests in correctional objectives. In Richard A. Cloward, et al. (Eds.), *Theoretical studies in social organization of the prison.* New York: Social Science Research Council. (Pp. 111-129.)

Schrag, Clarence
1969 The correctional system: Problems and prospects. *Annals of the American Academy of Political and Social Science 381* (January), 11-20. (This entire issue, edited by John P. Conrad, is devoted to "The Future of Corrections.")

Seeman, Melvin
1963 Alienation and social learning in a reformatory. *American Journal of Sociology 69* (November), 270-284.

Street, David
1965 The inmate group in custodial and treatment settings. *American Sociological Review 30* (February), 14-39.

Sykes, Gresham
1956 The corruption of authority and rehabilitation. *Social Forces 34* (December), 257-262.
1958 *The society of captives.* Princeton: Princeton University Press.

Sykes, Gresham, & Messinger, Sheldon
1960 The inmate social system. In Richard A. Cloward, et al. (Eds.),

Theoretical studies in social organization of the prison. New York: Social Science Research Council. Pamphlet no. 15, 5-19.

Szasz, Thomas S.
1956 Malingering: Diagnosis or social condemnation? *AMA Archives of Neurology and Psychiatry 76* (October), 432-443.
1957 On the theory of psychoanalytic treatment. *International Journal of psychoanalysis 38:* 166-182.
1961a *The myth of mental illness: Foundations of a theory of personal conduct.* New York: Hoeber-Harper.
1961b The uses of naming and the origin of the myth of mental illness. *American Psychologist 16* (February), 59-65.
1963 *Law, liberty and psychiatry.* New York: Macmillan.
1965 *Psychiatric justice.* New York: Macmillan.

Warren, Marguerite
1971 Classification of offenders as an aid to efficient management and effective treatment. *Journal of Criminal Law, Criminology, and Police Science 62* (May), 239-258.

Wheeler, Stanton
1969 Socialization in correctional institutions. In David A. Goslin (Ed.), *Handbook of socialization theory and research.* Chicago: Rand-McNally: 1105-1123.

Chapter 8

Perspectives on Manny's Life Story

In the introduction to this book, the purpose of the chapter Perspectives was discussed. To facilitate easy reference, these have been combined into a single chapter. Although the Perspectives will be useful in examining and analyzing theoretical issues that surface in Manny's life history, the student will want to make use of the bibliographies included at the end of each section of this chapter for more comprehensive coverage of theories and research studies.

Chapter 1:

Young Star Here!

Our purpose in the beginning of this Perspectives chapter is to present a brief outline of the structuralist position, which we will then use to interpret, sociologically, Manny's early experiences.

Durkheim (1958 pp. 65–75, 1960) was one of the first to reject theoretically notions of individual pathology with reference to deviant behavior. For him, the individual was not anomic, society is often anomic. He uses the concept of anomie to refer to a lack of solidarity in the division of labor. The breakdown in social cohesion results from numerous crises and conflicts in society. For example, Durkheim cites the up-and-down movement of the business cycle and the concomitant set of economic circumstances as acting to reduce cohesion in society. In times of crises and abrupt change, the ability of society to perform its regulatory function with respect to the collective implementation of traditional rules or norms tends to erode. The collective sentiments lose their authority as a general frame of reference and normlessness becomes relatively widespread. A social condition results to which individuals relate without reference to social norms.

Durkheim (1951) presents a general argument to the effect that when the goals that individuals seek have no relationship to the means that society prescribes for attaining goals, life, in effect, becomes unlivable. The guidelines for behavior set forth by society are ignored, as they are not pertinent to the goals sought. Anomic conditions are the result of this disjunction between means and ends.

One of the more useful formulations in this regard is that suggested by Robert Merton (1968), in which he lays the foundation for our consideration of differing deviant styles as responses to structural pressures or strains in the social structure.

Merton's work in anomie theory is intended to be clearly sociological in scope and purpose. He was reacting to biological biases so often intrinsic to theories of deviance. Merton presents anomie theory as a frame of reference for understanding the social and cultural sources of deviant behavior in individuals. In this form of functionalism, the theoretical focus is on structural strain, or the malintegration of roles and statuses within the social structure. Deviance is seen as the individual adaptation to stress that is generated by prominent disjunctures between the goals of success and the legitimate structural means for their achievement. The utilitarian calculus, more individualistic than collective, generates the willingness to deviate as a response to the lack of legitimate opportunity. Within the delinquent subculture, for example, the institutionalization of self-interest tends to legitimate amorality and foster alternative world views with respect to what is appropriate. Varieties in the official rates of deviance are seen, then, not as evidence of individual pathological states so much as "normal" responses by lower-class offenders to structural deprivation.

Cohen (1962) and Cloward and Ohlin (1960) present theories from the anomie tradition in which it is argued that almost all youth in American society are exposed to and internalize more or less standard success goals, e.g., occupational careers that are financially rewarding. However, they maintain that lower-class youth are systematically disenfranchised because of inequitable home, school, and neighborhood environments. This disenfranchisement and subsequent loss of "legitimate identity" leads to problems in the home, failure to achieve at school, and a resultant perception on their part of little stake in the legitimate, job-oriented economy.

Cohen (1962) elaborates important social-psychological considerations so as to move away from Merton's "atomistic and individualistic" focus. He shows how interaction with others gives meaning, valuing, and effect to one's behavioral pattern. For Cohen it would be the supportive nature of one's friends that determine opinions and actions. Substitute goals, diluted goals, and inverted values may be instigated in individual awareness by the sociocultural environment. The boy with delinquent friends is very likely to commit delinquent acts, especially when his ties to conventional society are weak from the outset.

Street gangs, for Cohen, become a meaningful "place" where the socially dislocated or drifting youth finds his identify confirmed in the pursuits of the gang and whatever social rewards it will bring. Short (1968) adds depth to this by pointing out that the most important status universe for youth in conflict gangs, that is, gangs principally oriented toward fighting, is other conflict-oriented gang youth. Life revolves around building up armor, enlisting troops, and going to war. Although leadership roles are not always formally defined, and gang solidarity may be somewhat ritualistic, there are specific ties of ceremonial deference within the group adding to a strong sense of individual identity and group cohesion. Interpersonal relationships within the gangs appear to vary in frequency and intensity. As Yablonski (1962) notes, conflict gangs are often characterized by "diffuse role definitions, limited cohesion, impermanence, minimal consensus on norms, shifting membership, disturbed leadership, and limited definitions of membership expectations." These behaviors vary from group to group, and there is evidence in the present case to indicate a fairly strong group identity and loyalty among its members. The focus in all conflict gangs is on its "turf," over which each group attempts to assert absolute territorial rights.

Cloward and Ohlin (1960) outline a theory of differential opportunity systems in which the lack of opportunity to succeed legitimately within the system is seen as probable for urban, working-class boys. As a consequence of this deprivation they often seek status and social reward in other ways. The social disorganization in slum areas fosters a breakdown of social control among youth. They are not only deprived entry into legitimate roles but also find the institutionalized channels to the criminal life closed in part because of their age. In their rebellion from the legitimate and acceptable forms of social life these boys take on a new set of illegitimate commitments and standards—their priorities focus on conflict subcultures as a means to gain status and success or as a means for striking back at a frustrating society. Fighting for territory becomes a dominant way of life under conditions of relative detachment from most local systems of opportunity and social control.

This barest outline of the structuralist position suggests a number of implications for viewing the linkages between Manny's early experiences in the gang and pervasive social conditions, in the first instance, and, second, his later criminality and drug life. First, from the structuralist perspective we can infer that the events revolving around his father's death and the subsequent family misfortunes represent one form of socially obstructed goal attainment; Manny's poor school performance and the societal response to it represent another. That is, the legal "rip-off" of his father's inheritance, the move to a lower-class neighborhood, and the ineffectual schooling experiences all appear to have influenced Manny's perception that success opportunities in the legitimate world were not really accessible. The supportive nature of his new friends soon influences him away from the "middle class" of his early homelife. Since the fighting gang was the most common institutionalized method of adjustment in Manny's new neighborhood, his commitment to the Young Stars can be viewed as a socially reinforced series of events. In addition, his ganging activities seem to have been preparatory activities for his future criminal adjustments.

Alternative approaches to the study of delinquency activities are provided in the cultural perspectives of Miller (1958) and of Karacki and Toby (1962), who reach agreement on the point that problematic youthful behavior occurs as a result of a fundamental lack of commitment to conventional middle-class standards and roles. Miller (1958) maintains that youthful gang misbehavior results largely because of discord between the values of the lower-class culture and those of a "middle-class"-dominated world rather than because of relative deprivation or obstructions in goal attainment. Miller argues that youth are thus acculturated into a lifestyle that emphasizes trouble, toughness, smartness, excitement, fate, and autonomy as "focal concerns." These expressions of endogenous values (physical strength and "masculinity," thrills, risks and dangers; being cunning; duping the authorities or enemies) are in significant contradiction to the more conventional world of the larger social surround.

For Miller, lower-class youth are on a collision course with conventional society in that their acceptance of lower-class focal concerns, which becomes necessary to earn status and prestige within their peer group, is almost certain to bring them into conflict with the law.

Karacki and Toby (1962), studying middle-class youth, found that some boys are "imperfectly socialized" so that they choose fun, trouble, freedom, and sometimes violence instead of becoming committed to a more middle-class style of adjustment to work, recreation, and school roles and statuses.

Yet another theoretical approach is offered in Reckless' (1973) "containment" theory, in which he attempts to merge psychological and sociocultural viewpoints of crime causation. Social pressures, such as economic conditions, minority-group status, and family conflicts act as "pull factors," drawing the individual away from accepted normative referents. One significant pull factor in this case would be the availability of a ganging subculture. When the structure of "external containment," e.g., the family and school, break down, "internal containment" is threatened because in the ghetto and slum areas the internalization of conventional norms has been a weak process anyway. Thus, the inner tensions, hostilities, and strong feelings of inadequacy and inferiority vis-à-vis the legitimate surroundings act as "push factors" diverting the individual toward deviant opportunities.

Miller's perspective may be the more useful one for viewing very disadvantaged ethnic and "bottomed-out" status groups in urban slum areas. However, Manny's experience suggests that many lower-class youth may have an early commitment to conventional norms and standards that tends to erode as they perceive that they have little apparent stake in community status patterns.

The relationship between these analyses of Manny's ganging delinquency and the aforementioned theories suggests that Manny's lack of commitment to legitimate society may have been engendered by his reactions to socially obstructed goal attainments.

Selected References

Becker, Howard S.
1960 Notes on the concept of commitment. *The American Journal of Sociology 66* (July), 32–40.

Bordua, David
1960 *Sociological theories and their implications for juvenile delinquency.* Washington D.C.: U.S. Government Printing Office.

Cloward, Richard A., & Ohlin, Lloyd E.
1960 *Delinquency and opportunity.* New York: The Free Press.

Cohen, Albert K.
1955 *Delinquent boys.* New York: The Free Press.

Durkheim, Emile
1951 *Suicide* (J. A. Spaulding & G. Simpson, Trans.). New York: The Free Press.
1958 *The rules of sociological method.* New York: Macmillan.
1960 *Division of labor in society* (G. Simpson, Trans.). New York: The Free Press.

Karacki, Larry, & Toby, Jackson
1962 The uncommitted adolescent: Candidate for gang socialization. *Sociological Inquiry 32* (Spring), 203–215.

Miller, Walter B
1958 Lower class culture as a generating milieu of gang delinquency. *Journal of Social Issues 3* (March), 5–19.

Merton, Robert K.
1968 *Social theory and social structure* (2nd ed.). New York: The Free
Press.

Park, Robert E., Burgess, Ernest W., & McKenzie, R. D.
1925 *The City.* Chicago: University of Chicago Press.

Reckless, Walter C.
1973 *The crime problem* (5th ed.). New York: Appleton-Century-Crofts.

Short, James F., Jr. (Ed.)
1968 *Gang delinquency and delinquent subcultures.* New York: Harper
& Row.

Sutherland, Edwin H., & Cressey, Donald R.
1974 *Criminology* (9th ed.). Philadelphia: Lippincott.

Thrasher, Frederic M.
1963 *The gang* (abridged ed.). Chicago: University of Chicago Press.

Yablonski, Lewis
1962 *The violent gang.* New York: Macmillan.

Whyte, William F.
1955 *Street corner society* (2nd ed.). Chicago: University of Chicago
Press.

Chapter 2:

A Piece of the Action

On a very fundamental level of analysis, Manny's introduction to criminal
activities can be viewed in the context of differential association (Sutherland and Cressey, 1974), which sees criminal behavior as learned like all
other behaviors. With respect to illegal gambling and bookmaking in particular, it is clear that Manny associated more with people who thought
these deviant acts were proper than with those in the majority who would
have defined those acts as wrong. Manny and his friends shared a cultural
tradition reinforced and redefined daily in face-to-face groups. Clearly,
Manny's self-report data support the central assumption of Sutherland and
Cressey's theory, which may be stated briefly: there exist crime cultures
and legal cultures and some groups will oppose the law while others will
uphold the law.

Again, his early deviance can be in part explained by the Merton (1968)
hypothesis with reference to the cultural goal referents available to and

valued by all members of society, and the definitively sharp restriction of institutionally legitimate means for his achieving these goals. Yet, while each of these theories contains some explanatory power with respect to the genesis of deviant behaviors and attitudes in Manny and his friends, none of these perspectives offers a unitary explanation of consistently deepening deviant behavior in Manny's life.

Howard Becker (1963a) borrowed the concept of "career" from the sociology of occupations, where it has been defined as the movement of a person through a series of positions within a given occupational system. The concept of career is central to our consideration of Manny's development at this point. We see how, much as in a career in the usual sense, Manny progressed so that he knew more about the job, knew how to behave properly within the Organization, how to get promoted, even knew when he couldn't maintain any longer. Things happened to him in a logical sequence up to the point of his addiction. The contrast between his career in the organized rackets and his venture into the life of drugs is striking.

Almost all theories of deviance assume the simultaneous action of simple variables. For example, they read so that the student might be led to believe that external constraints impinge on one instantly, i.e., absent father in the home, poverty, poor association, school failure, and law enforcement intervention happen at once, or nearly so, causing immediate criminality. From Becker we can see the consequence of events in Manny's experience as a career and view those factors that moved him from one step to another as "career contingencies."

The studies of Isador Chein and associates (1964, pp. 151–157) focus on the sequential steppingstone process leading to heroin use and addiction. Manny's case appears at first glance to be almost typical with respect to how older adolescents are introduced to heroin. The suggestion to use heroin was free from overt conflict; he was not constrained by undue pressure. Manny's first real chance to use the drug came at the initiative of a relative in a face-to-face situation. It is questionable whether or not one could reliably refer to the interaction with his uncle as "seduction."

Chein and associates report that late adolescence is a particularly vulnerable age with respect to drugs. The sixteen- or seventeen-year-old youth is more likely to continue heroin use after the initial try than either older or younger youths. We could speculate that in Manny's case there were some serious ambivalencies surrounding his transition from adolescence to adulthood. On the one hand, he built up a lot of self-confidence and self-esteem by making it in the Organization at such an early age. But his responsibilities were great, and he may well have been suffering something akin to the anomie of success in that presumably he had everything, but he had left his peers behind in the street. He had a lot of surplus money, and drugs became a way to pass it around in the neighborhood—still another way to add to his "big man" self-image.

We are not suggesting that the steppingstone theory of drug addiction is valid, or that one can scientifically identify a "drug addict personality pattern" in which basic character defects and weaknesses appear. In Manny's case, however, escalation from cannabis to opiates occurred, perhaps as an opportunity for something to do, a way to spend time and money.

One thing that can be seen in this chapter is Manny's rather swift retreat from his world and a realignment of his relevant social bases. Manny did fall into a lifestyle that has been conceptualized as a "retreatist role adaptation." Merton (1968, p. 153) advances the notion that in the drug user, "Defeatism, quietism and resignation are manifested in escape mechanisms which ultimately lead him to 'escape' from the requirements of society." In setting forth their theory of differential opportunity systems, Cloward and Ohlin (1960) propose that delinquent youths suffer alienation as a result of failure "or the anticipation of failure in achieving success-goals by socially approved means." They try to explain the ghetto drug phenomenon with a "double failure" hypothesis and advance a typology of delinquent subcultures to include the criminal, the conflict, and the retreatist subcultures. When conditions are such that youths cannot make it in the conventional social surround *or* the conflict or criminal subcultures, they suffer from "double failure." They retreat into a drug subculture as a means of resolving their status dilemmas. Clearly, however, the "double failure" hypothesis doesn't fit here. Manny experiences success both in the gang and in the criminal world. It would appear that rather than escaping into drugs from a world of failure, Manny deliberately propelled himself into the heroin world because he was attracted by the lifestyle of his uncle and the lure of the "high" experience.

As Sutter (1969) points out, the student should be aware of theoretical attempts to understand drug addiction by debunking or omitting the experience of the user. "Failure," "immaturity," and "defeatism" hypotheses are steeped in a middle-class bias.

Finestone (1957, pp. 3-13) talks about Chicago's "elite society of cats" who centered their entire existence around private, aesthetic kick experiences and who appeared to be in full retreat from relationships with the conventional world. We should remember which frame of reference is "ours" and which is "theirs," lest the analysis suffer from an overmoralistic tone and perhaps not enough of an emphasis on investigating the fun and enjoyment part of the using experience.

One thing is clear from Manny's present account: being hooked introduces the addict into an all-encompassing lifestyle that leaves little room for outside activities, except to the extent that these activities contribute directly to scoring and fixing heroin.

The totalitarian nature of heroin addiction as noted by Ashley (1972, p. 81) and in the work of Irwin (1970), for example, is fully supported in Manny's account. Although scoring the drug requires a significant portion of the committed user's time, because it is illegal and therefore very expensive and sometimes very scarce, one might consider that the drug effect itself also adds materially to the dominating aspect of the doper's world. Manny often reports being caught up in the experience of being high so that other aspects of his life get consistently overlooked and put off. "Everything gets filtered through the drug effect," he says. We suspect that not just the illegality of heroin procurement but the protracted use of it under any conditions would tend to collapse the addict's world view into one dominant dimension—being hooked.

Irwin (1970, pp. 16–18) sees scoring as one major theme of the dope fiend world, and Manny shows us how scoring can sometimes be a hard, painful process. While the illegal status of heroin sale certainly complicates the scoring function, we observe that fixing became the central theme of Manny's whole life. It didn't matter what he had to do to get heroin, the important thing was to *use.* When Manny talks about using, he almost caresses the word, and one gets the feeling that he remembers too well a time when the drug process totally encompassed his experience.

It is interesting that Manny coined (to our knowledge) the theme of "passing over" to indicate going from the straight life to the drug world. Manny saw his life in the Organization as being quite straight, regardless of the faint overtones of illegality. To "pass over" indicates in a sense that the dominance of the dope fiend identity is such that he lives, moves, and has his being in a subcultural world apart from the conventional society. In *passing,* Manny suffered a severe loss in status among his family members and old business associates. His financial losses were also severe. But he was compelled by his growing habituation to assume full membership in the drug culture so as to participate fully in the social advantages it has reserved for "members." At first Manny "shuttled" (Cox, 1948, p. 430) back and forth between the two cultures, leading a primary straight life and a secondary drug life. One of the dominant risks of shuttling is that you can't keep it together in two worlds at once. Manny couldn't live up to his obligations in the Organization while staying high all the time, nor could he find the necessary time to score, fix, and enjoy while committed to the system. Soon he began to subordinate his obligation to Leo in favor of spending more time "in the life." When the time for a complete break from his past came, Manny didn't care. After his surplus funds were used and he had sold everything of value, Manny was perfectly willing to pass over into a world he was now beginning to understand.

Many accounts have left the impression that heroin addicts are childish and immature. Desperate and insecure, they want all of life without effort (cf. Mills, 1966). The literature abounds with misconceptions that have been drawn about addict life and generalized to all its members. Prejudicial and ignorant opinions that tend to label the addict as lazy and stupid stem from an inability or unwillingness to understand alien lifestyles (Ashley, 1972, p. 71). The criminal schemes that Manny involved himself in were often sophisticated and ingenious. We note briefly the similarities that exist in comparing status and role, line and staff positions, planning and carrying out operations in the illegitimate check-passing and dock-boosting endeavors with those of a more conventional and legitimate business endeavor. The fronting behavior, the skilled, precise planning of sequential operational steps require energy, intelligence, and follow-through on the part of all group members.

Letkemann (1973, p. 28) suggests that the "amateur"/"experienced" distinction made by criminals bears some resemblance to the "amateur"/ "professional" distinction the layman makes. Status is distributed and roles deployed, as we saw in Manny's case, in the criminal world much as in regular business life. However, as many theorists have pointed out (cf. Sutherland, 1937; Maurer, 1940; and Letkemann, 1973), the true professional thief has little association with "rounders" and drug abusers. He is a highly skilled person who engages in crime for business purposes rather than a lifestyle. His attitude toward police will often be deferential or even friendly, whereas the "rounder" or "hustler" incorporates hostility toward law enforcers and other citizens into his world view (Letkemann, 1973, pp. 28–29; Irwin, 1970, pp. 16–20).

Manny does make it clear that professional, organized criminal activity, such as the check-passing ring or the dock-boosting gang, becomes a hardship for the dope fiend, not because of shortcomings in personality or intelligence but precisely because of demands on his time for scoring, fixing, and enjoying drugs. Time, for a drug addict, is organized around highs and lows, and Manny has indicated how difficult it is to be tied to a schedule. Events, things of importance, even people close to one are readily sacrificed if these threaten to intrude on getting from low to high.

Although the reader can draw many theoretical conclusions from this chapter, one point of special significance should be made. Manny shows us that one must *learn* to be a thief and a hustler. It is often the case, as it was in Manny's experience, that one is "apprenticed," or attaches oneself, to a journeyman in the business so that one becomes acquainted through a sequential learning process with the necessary abilities and tools of the trade. We note that the concept of career as developed by Becker (1963a, pp. 22–39) has a great deal of utility in helping to understand Manny's experience at this point of his life.

Selected References

Ashley, Richard
1972 *Heroin: The myths and the facts.* New York: St. Martin's Press.

Becker, Howard
1960 Notes on the concept of commitment. *The American Journal of Sociology 66* (July), 32–40.
1963a *The other side.* Glencoe, Ill.: The Free Press.
1963b *Outsiders: Studies in the sociology of deviance.* New York: The Free Press.

Berry, Brewton
1965 *Race and ethnic relations* (3rd ed.). Boston: Houghton Mifflin.

Burroughs, William
1953 *Junkie.* New York: Ace Books.

Chapel, T. L., & Taylor, D. W.
1971 Drugs for kicks. *Drug Abuse Law Review* 1 (June), 53–60.

Chein, Isador, Gerard, Donald L., Lee, Robert S., & Rosenfeld, Eva
1964 *The road to h.* New York: Basic Books.

Cloward, Richard A., & Ohlin, Lloyd
1960 *Delinquency and opportunity.* New York: The Free Press.

Cox, Oliver C.
1948 *Caste, class and race.* New York: Doubleday.

Edwards, Carl N.
1974 *Drug dependence.* New York: Aronson.

Eldridge, William Buller
1963 Myths and facts. In Dan Wakefield (Ed.), *The addict.* Greenwich: Fawcett Publications.

Engel, Madeline H.
1974 *The drug scene: A sociological perspective.* Rochelle Park, N. J.: Hayden Book Company.

Finestone, Harold
1957   Cats, kicks and color. *Social Problems 5* (July), 3–13.

Horman, Richard E., & Fox, Allan M., (Eds.)
1970   *Drug awareness.* New York: Avon Books.

Irwin, John
1970   *The felon.* Englewood Cliffs, N.J.: Prentice-Hall.

Lasagna, Lewis, von Felsinger, J. M., & Beecher, H. K.
1955   Drug induced mood changes in man. *Journal of the American Medical Association 157* (September), 1006–1113.

Letkemann, Peter
1973   *Crime as work.* Englewood Cliffs, N.J.: Prentice-Hall.

Lindensmith, Alfred R.
1947   *Opiate addiction.* Bloomington: Indiana University Press.

Maurer, David
1940   *The big con.* Indianapolis: Bobbs-Merrill.

Merton, Robert K.
1968   *Social theory and social structure.* (2nd ed.) Glencoe, Ill.: The Free Press.

Mills, James
1966   *The panic in Needle Park.* Toronto: Ambassador Books.

Mulcary, John F., Jr. (Ed.)
1963   *The Chatham conference: Perspectives on narcotic addiction* Chatham, Mass. (September), 9–11.

O'Donnel, John A., & Ball, John C. (Eds.)
1966   *Narcotic addiction.* New York: Harper & Row.

Sutherland, Edwin
1937   *The professional thief.* Chicago: University of Chicago Press.

Sutherland, Edwin H., & Cressey, Donald R.
1974   *Criminology* (9th ed.). Philadelphia: Lippincott.

Sutter, Alan
1969   Worlds of drug use on the street scene. In Donald R. Cressey & David A. Ward (Eds.), *Delinquency, crime, and social process.* New York: Harper & Row.

Thomas, Piri
1968   *Down these mean streets.* New York: Signet.

Winick, Charles
1963 The addict psychology. In Dan Wakefield (Ed.), *The addict.* Greenwich: Fawcett Publications.

Chapter 3:

Sing Sing Prison

Sociologists have for some time understood the institutional arrangements within prison organizations to be complex in nature and "total" in scope (Goffman, 1961, Chapter 2). Traditionally, prisons function as isolated social systems with autonomous sets of clearly defined roles, expectations, and rigidly established patterns of interrelationships among the people within them. Our special task in this chapter should be to underscore clearly the autonomy of the inmate subculture in relation to the larger society in general and the correctional system specifically.

Two basic theoretical perspectives can be identified in the literature dealing with inmate subculture. The first paradigm can be classified as a situational view that uses the structural-functional method of analysis for ordering its central concepts, themes, and modes of action with respect to the prison experience. The advocates of this position include, among others, Sykes (1958), Sykes and Messinger (1970, pp. 401–408), McCorkle and Korn (1954), and Clemmer (1958).

In the tradition of the social-system model, this perspective examines the structure of prison, emphasizing adaption and coping mechanisms of the individual in response to imprisonment. The need to cope with the exigencies of prison life, according to most situational theorists, forces the new inmate to develop one of the available identities in the inmate subculture. For example, in order to face the "pains of imprisonment" (Sykes, 1958), the convict social organization evolved a social system composed principally of argot roles (Sykes and Messinger, 1970, p. 19). A group of normatively interlocked role identities ("rats," "center men," "merchants," "wolves," "punks," "fags," "hipsters," etc.) emerged as a functional network of coping mechanisms. Sykes and Messinger suggest that in direct response to the deprivation of prison life the inmates maintain their own social code, a code that is initiated primarily to reassert their autonomy and manliness. Through the code they can organize and control their reactions as a group; they can systematically cultivate opposition to the established order, the staff, and the values upheld by the institution. Thus, Clemmer (1958, pp. 293–304) equates prisonization with an assimilation process in which an individual takes on "in greater or lesser degree—the folkways, mores, customs, and general culture of the penitentiary." It is not suggested by the situational school of thought that the inmate code commands complete loyalty. As we discovered in Manny's account, inmate roles often emerge that tend to contradict particular code tenets. For example, one way a weaker member can combat specific deprivations is to accept exploitation by certain "punks," "jockers," or "merchants" in return for specific favors or definitions of normatively acceptable status. However, the situational perspective presents an indigenous origin theory in which a principal assertion is that the characteristics of the inmate subsystem emerge and take shape within the situation itself, largely devoid of influence from external factors.

A second theoretical perspective emphasizes the sequential development of criminal identities. Wheeler (1961, pp. 706-711), comparing penal institutions in Scandinavia and the United States, challenges the notion that the form a prison culture takes is the same everywhere, and that it can be best understood simply in terms of an indigenous response to the pains of imprisonment. He contends that the kind of society from which the inmates originate will also contribute to the degree of cohesion, solidarity, and the values of the inmate society.

Irwin (1970) presents an argument emphasizing the importance of primary and semiprimary groups that often stand in opposition to other members of the prison population. This argument opposes the construct of social systems as important theorizing for capturing the reality of prison subcultural experience. The sequential perspective intends to show, for example, that the "world views" of the thief subculture, which are established outside prison, become an important element in establishing the prison values and norms. For example, the thief's major themes call for "honesty, rightness, responsibility and loyalty" (Irwin, 1970, p. 8). Thieves believe that one of their major responsibilities is "never divulge information to anyone which may lead to the arrest of another person" (Irwin, 1970, p. 8). Significantly, this is the same set of characteristics attributed to the "right guy" in the inmate code that Sykes and Messinger explain as being indigenous to the prison and generated within the prison structure.

Manny's experiences appear to support the sequential view. For example, Irwin argues that the thief and hustler subculture, as well as the reform school or convict subculture, have the greatest influences on norms and role emergence in the adult prison. Manny shows us how the toughness theme, learned on the streets and in reform schools, explains much of the violence that is reposited in prison. Time after time, Manny makes the point that hustling and doping and conning and conniving within the prison are merely extensions of similar street behaviors.

Even though we can identify various aspects of the inmate subculture that display street-origin themes, the importance of the situational elements, including rejection, de-masculinity, mortification, and isolation, cannot be rejected as explanations of life within the penal compound. However, any theory one constructs to account for inmate life should range beyond the prison experience itself, taking cognizance of preprison variables.

There can be little doubt that the life chances of the prison inmate are profoundly affected by the wide range of sanctions imposed on him by guards and administrative personnel. The systematic patterning of punishments directed against Manny when he was unable to cope with the initiation rituals resembles a process of "identity spoilage" that accompanies stigmatization. Manny was seen as "not quite human" (Goffman, 1963, p. 9), and it is clear that an ideology explaining his inferiority and accounting for his dangerousness was well institutionalized as standard policy at Sing Sing.

One might wonder if it is an appropriate expectation that our Mannys always be passive receptors of stigma. The environment of inmate-staff relationships creates a considerable amount of psychological and physical pain for many unadaptive youths. In fact, it is precisely the uninitiated, the unsophisticated, the tender first-timer, who is most seriously damaged by these "ceremonies of degradation." One way the stigmatized individual has of contending with these situations is to develop a set of techniques that allows him to neutralize the values permeating the "legitimate" social surround. This technique was noted among delinquent youths by Sykes and Matza (1957, pp. 664–670), whereby these youths "condemn the condemners," and, as McCorkle and Korn (1954, pp. 88–89) determined in their study of prison inmates there occurs a "rejection of the rejectors." This reaction, perhaps already partially internalized from encounters with law enforcers on the street, can be most important to the self-protection and autonomy of the individual by "deflecting" the sanctions that were meant to produce future conformity.

One fundamentally important aspect of this stigma-neutralization process is that it feeds directly into out-group supports of hostility and aggression against the prison system. There are few isolated, alienated individuals violently contending with failure and rejection on their own. Whatever evidence we can glean from Manny's account suggests the existence of numerous primary and semiprimary groups—call it a subculture as long as you understand that its origin is not totally indigenous to the prison setting—of alienated individuals who work somewhat in concert both to provide effective neutralization and to generate trouble for the system and success for themselves.

Manny's account sheds some light on prison homosexuality. According to his estimate, about 30 percent of the inmates are actively involved in homosexuality. About 90 percent of these are situationally homosexual. An important point in Manny's account is that in his observation the deprivation of heterosexual relationships does not even *usually* lead to homosexual intercourse. We have developed a crude diagram intended to represent the types of homosexual relationships in the male prison.

Coercive and economic relationships ←――――――→		Reciprocated and romantic relationships ←――――――→	"Degenerate" and coercive relationships ――――――→
Kid Boy Commissary punk	One not known as a "Jocker" but has relations	"She" Queen Girl	Pervert Queer Fag
	The "Jocker" or "Daddy": primarily hustlers, long-timers, state raised youth	Broad Bitch	

Figure 1
Sexual Relationships in the Male Prison

Manny informs us that the status and trustworthiness of prison homosexuals are ordered hierarchically. The jocker is considered to be the most trustworthy and holds the most status among the prisoner population. Status and trustworthiness decline in order beginning with the queen, who often has high status, and descending to the kid, the boy, the punk, the pervert, and the queer, who has the least status. All but the jocker play the role of the woman. The pervert and queer are often "finks," cooperating with the officials. The queen, according to Manny, is a "legitimate woman," in reality often acting and looking like a "beautiful broad." Sometimes a jocker will have a kid for his sexual outlets, while also playing the role of a kid for the sexual gratification of another jocker.

Homosexuality in male prisons functions to permit convicts to cope with life in a unisexual society. Sykes (1958) and Sykes and Messinger (1970) characterize the social system of homosexuality as a way to deal with the problem of heterosexual deprivation and the accompanying problem of living side by side with other deviants who are possibly repugnant and dangerous to each other. These physiological and psychological deprivations may influence prisoners in different ways. Jim Terra, in "25,000 Eunuchs" in *Inside* by Robert Minton (1971, p. 122), clearly states the alternatives he sees to the lack of heterosexual relations: "I can masturbate; I can revert back to my adolescence and let nature take its course; I can go to bed with a homosexual; or I can force a weaker inmate into anal intercourse or fellatio." Manny shows that when these are the inmate's only alternatives and he begins to question his masculinity after an extended period of deprivation, the chances of an inmate engaging in a homosexual relationship increase. This type of logic is consistent with the situational analysis of prison, which uses the structural-functional approach for explaining homosexuality in prison.

This orientation typifies the interlocking homosexual role structure that emerges in the prisons. In discussing "argot roles," Sykes (1958) explains the types of homosexual roles that the situational approach identifies. The wolf, or jocker as other sources label this type, is the least stigmatized of the homosexual roles. He is identified by his aggressive sexual role. He uses different techniques in many circumstances to "bait" the younger or newer members of the prison community into participating in homosexual relations. For example, he gives candy bars or cigarettes to young kids in the prison and expects in return sexual favors. If he doesn't get these sexual favors he may resort to violence or force and if the individual he has "baited" doesn't attempt to fight back violently, he will be forced into the role of the "punk," or commissary punk, who can be manipulated by bribery or forced into participating in homosexual acts.

The commissary punk is the second role type in the homosexual typologies of the prison. This typology is usually characterized, as already mentioned, by the younger or newer inmates, who will engage in homosexual acts for bribes or because of the threats of the jocker. Typically, these individuals are more passive than other prison inmates, who are willing to fight the jocker when they are threatened or bribed by him.

The commissary punk, who is usually young and immature when he first is forced into his role, often develops into one of two homosexual roles in prison. Behavioristic learning theory, which is based on the idea of learning because of rewards or from models, predicts the development of these two roles. One role the punk often develops into is the queer or queen homosexual. In this case the behavioristic learning theory would argue that the homosexual role was rewarding to the commissary punk and so he continued to seek rewards by becoming a queer or queen. The second option is that the commissary punk will later become one of the prison jockers when he develops and gains power in the prison. In this case the behavioristic school would argue that the punk has been rewarded by the jocker through bribes and has been associated with a model who uses aggressive techniques which, according to their theory, would work to teach the punk to use the same techniques to gain the sexual outlet provided by homosexual acts. The idea is quite similar to the child who has very aggressive parents. This child is more likely to follow the parental model he is provided with and act aggressively with other children to get what he wants.

The next two role types already mentioned are classified as the "fags" by Sykes but can be divided into the queers and queens. The queen role is what one would call a pseudo-transvestite, someone who dresses and tries to take on a woman's appearance by shaving his legs, by designing or wearing his clothes differently, by putting on make-up, or by attempting to mimic women's gestures. It is possible that the queen may establish some type of relationship with the jocker for a short period of time or even, in extreme cases, for extended periods of time. The queer in the prison would also be considered a fag by Sykes' definition but can be distinguished from the queen because the queer either no longer has the sexual attractiveness that is part of the queen role or never attempted to play the female role. Instead, the queer is the complete sexual deviant who engages in the complete realm of homosexual activities with other inmates.

An important point is that the queer, queen, and jocker can also be part of a sequential process that begins outside of prison, continues in prison, and will continue after prison. In many cases the jocker may be the sex offender who has been committed for rape and just continues his aggressive role in prison with the weaker male inmates. The queens or queers could also be queens or queers before entering prison. What may be occurring in prison is that the individuals who were participating in homosexual roles outside prison add to the "pains of imprisonment" by creating more situational homosexual encounters with members who haven't established themselves in heterosexual relationships outside of prison, and these encounters plus the psychological and physiological deprivations of heterosexuality in prison help to create more homosexual role development of individuals in prison.

Homosexual activity in the reform school setting takes similar forms, with many of the same types of roles appearing. One important point is that the age of the individuals who are sentenced to terms in reform schools coincides with the age at which the onset of puberty begins. This age is typified by sexual curiosity as well as greater sexual arousal. A second important factor is that many studies have pointed out that peer group pressure may be much more effective during adolescence, when young boys are trying to establish their manhood or male identity.

What often takes place in both the juvenile and penal settings, but much more often is a juvenile phenomenon, is that the stronger individuals take what they want sexually from the weaker members of the inmate body. A duke or jocker, who is a leader because of his strength, makes the weaker boys prove their masculinity by either being a jocker like he is or by forcing them into homosexual activity. The options presented to individuals are to become the dominant member of a homosexual relationship or to become the weaker member of the relationship. We see that the jocker, by forcing as many as possible to participate in some form of homosexuality, validates his masculinity.

In summary, the sequential and situational aspects affecting prison inmates blend to create an atmosphere that perpetuates and encourages defeatism, homosexuality, and criminality. The danger that prisons will be dominated by the most "disreputable" and criminal elements among their population gives valid cause for concern. They have the longest experience in the system, know the ropes best, have the greatest investment in the prison community, and by anybody's theory of socialization will tend to be the most committed to criminal values.

If all the above is not to be misleading, these data must be hedged with caveats and qualifications. Even then the theories discussed and our present findings can lead to oversimplifications and unwarranted generalizations that can prematurely affect public opinion and political decisions. Research into prisons is still in its infancy, findings are still most tentative, the information on which they are based is often questionable and inadequate, and the methods of handling it often crude. We would suggest, however, that studies such as Wheeler (1961) and Irwin (1970), which are supported by Manny's present account, hold forth hope in that they bring out the fact that particular categories of offenders, taken separately, tend to manifest behaviors and attitudes of different types. Also, these behaviors and attitudes have historical reference to *our* communities, perhaps even over and above contemporary reference to *their* penal situation. What this suggests is an argument for smaller, community-based institutions, for dealing with such groups as first offenders, short-term prisoners, and the well behaved so as to fit *our* societal response to *their* need.

Selected References

Atkins, Burton, & Glick, Henry G., (Eds.)
1972 *Prisons, protest & politics.* Englewood Cliffs, N.J.: Prentice-Hall.

Chaneles, Sol
1972 *Losing in place.* New York: Avon Books.

Chessman, Caryl
1958 *Cell 2455, Death Row.* New York: Avon. Books.

Clemmer, Donald
1958 *The Prison community.* New York: Rinehart. (Reissue).

Davidson, Theodore
1974 *Chicano prisoners: The key to San Quentin.* New York: Holt, Rinehart & Winston.

Goffman, Erving
1961 *Asylums.* Garden City, N.Y.: Doubleday.
1963 *Stigma: Notes on the management of spoiled identity.* Englewood Cliffs, N.J.: Prentice-Hall.

Irwin, John
1970 *The felon.* Englewood Cliffs, N.J.: Prentice-Hall.

McCorkle, Lloyd W., & Korn, Richard
1954 Resocialization within walls. *The Annals of the American Academy of Political and Social Science 293* (May), 89–98.

Minton, Robert (Ed.)
1971 *Inside: Prison American style.* New York: Random House.

Radzinowicz, Leon, & Wolfgang, Marvin
1971 *The criminal in the arms of the law.* New York: Basic Books.

Sutherland, Edwin H., & Cressey, Donald R.
1974 *Criminology* (9th ed.). Philadelphia: Lippincott.

Sykes, Gresham
1958 *Society of captives.* Princeton: Princeton University Press.

Sykes, Gresham M., & Matza, David
1957 Techniques of neutralization: A theory of delinquency. *American Sociological Review 22* (December), 664–670.

Sykes, Gresham M., & Messinger, Sheldon L.
1970 The inmate social code. In Norman Johnston, et al. (Eds.), *The sociology of punishment and corrections.* New York: Wiley.

Wheeler, Stanton M.
1961 Socialization in correctional communities. *American Sociological Review 26* (October), 706–711.

Chapter 4:

Synanon

It is interesting to note the processual development whereby Synanon norms and goals were integrated into Manny's personality structure over time. Charles Dederich's Synanon appears to have as its chief philosophical architect one George Herbert Mead. Mead (cf. Morris, 1934) suggests that the development of self involves a continuing conversation between the "me" and the "I," which he calls "minding." The "I" represents the spontaneous, unique, and natural characteristics of each individual;

the "me" represents the specifically social component of the self. The "I" develops first; the "me" takes much longer. New ex-addict members are seen as having an "I"-"me" lag, so to speak. They are perceived as being babies, having no rights, unable to assume any responsibilities or make any significant contribution. In reading Manny's account, one can anticipate each step in the process wherein his "me" began to act as a social control mechanism for his "I."

Mead also points out that there is a difference between the social demands and expectations made by those with whom you have a close contact and personal relationship with and whose judgments are important to you ("significant others") and the impersonal demands made by society ("generalized others"). Synanon views the world outside its boundaries as a breeding ground for stupidity (Kanter, 1972, p. 203). People become addicts because they are stupid people in a stupid world, according to the Synanon philosophy. In Synanon, group pressure is a primary form of social control, responsible not only for the solidarity of its community but for the dramatic changes wrought in its individual members. Manny relates his tribulations in identifying with the group and its significant members when he failed to live up to standards of the community.

One of the principal criticisms of the Synanon philosophy, that of coercive control, receives some support from Manny's report. When one is made totally vulnerable to such a group ethic, the pressures may require one to violate one's individual inner nature in order to conform. In one of his novels, Kosinski (1965) describes a similar form of socialization, desocialization, and resocialization in relating "how I learned to love Josef Stalin."

According to Mead (cf. Morris, 1934), the self develops in three distinct stages. First is the "imitative" stage, when the child copies what he sees his parents doing. In the second or "play" stage, the child plays more creatively at adopting social roles. The third or "game" stage comes when the child is able to take a role in a social situation with a real awareness of his importance to the group and the group's importance to him. The philosophy of the Synanon approach appears to insure that the new recruit is always assumed to be in the "imitative" stage and must be walked step by step through the "play" and "game" stages.

With respect to Synanon, Manny reports that "hardened addicts," crippled by the socioeconomic ethic, are fed a combination of mental health rhetoric and the mirage of constant community. Synanon can be seen as a form of supersocialization, an "acceptable" corollary of enemy brainwashing techniques (Friedenberg, 1965, pp. 256–261). As Manny learned, so long as one remains a willing captive of the organization and an obedient subject of its leadership, one can navigate safely within protected waters.

But, it may be that Synanon works for the same reason that the children's program "Sesame Street" works: the adults are in control of the program and the "children" do as they are told. Both programs operate out of a massive source of direct instruction and mental oppression that may be antagonistic to the development of thoughtful habits that involve choosing, seeing, and freely doing.

The Synanon experience, for many, is nontransferable. You never pass Go, and if you do, you can't take it with you. In fact, it is not Synanon's purpose to effect transfer of its membership back into the real world. Rather, its purpose is to create a utopian society similar to *Walden Two,* where the principles of behavioralist psychology are consistently implemented to bring in "the perfect society" (Kanter, 1972, pp. 36-37).

The difficulties in judging the method of social control in Synanon are those inherent in definitional problems. If control is defined as making the drug abuser abandon his behavior and return to social conformity and usefulness in the broad sense, then most would argue that Synanon's means of control are highly unsuccessful. If, however, control is defined as the identification and permanent isolation of deviants from the general population (because in some cases their behavior may have proven harmful to others), then Synanon's system of control would be considered successful.

It is our assumption, however, that to be effective, social control programs and philosophy must address themselves to the problem of reintegrating the ex-addict into the larger social surround. Any long-term programs must have as a principal thrust some means of reducing such potential causes of drug abuse as poverty, discrimination, slum subcultures, and poor housing.

Selected References

Abramson, E., et al.
1958 Social power and commitment: A theoretical statement. *American Sociological Review 23* (October), 15-22.

Becker, Howard S.
1960 Notes on the concept of commitment. *American Journal of Sociology 66* (July), 32-40.

Berne, Eric
1966 *The structure and dynamics of organizations and groups.* New York: Grove Press.

Bittner, Egon
1963 Radicalism and the organization of radical movements. *American Sociological Review 28* (December), 928–940.

Buber, Martin
1958 [*Paths in Utopia*] (R. F. C. Hull, Trans.). Boston: Beacon Press.

Clark, Burton R.
1956 Organizational adaptation and precarious values. *American Sociological Review 21* (June), 327–336.

Dornbusch, Sanford
1954 The military academy as an assimilating institution. *Social Forces 33* (May), 316–321.

Eaton, Joseph W.
1952 Controlled acculturation: A survival technique of the Hutterites. *American Sociological Review 17* (June), 331–340.

Endore, Guy
1968 *Synanon.* Garden City, N.Y.: Doubleday.

Fairfield, Dick
1971 *Communes U.S.A.* San Francisco: Alternatives Foundation.

Friedenberg, Edgar Z.
1965 The Synanon solution. *Nation 200* (March 8), 256–261.

Goffman, Erving
1961 *Asylums.* Garden City, N.Y.: Doubleday.

Goodman, Paul
1964 *Utopian essays and practical proposals.* New York: Vintage.

Gouldner, Alvin W.
1960 The norm of reciprocity: A preliminary statement. *American Sociological Review 25* (April), 161–179.

Hoffer, Eric
1963 *The true believer.* New York: Avon Books.

Kanter, Rosabeth M.
1972 *Commitment and community.* Cambridge, Mass.: Harvard University Press.

Kosinski, Jerzy
1965 *The painted bird.* Boston: Houghton Mifflin.

Morris, Charles W. (Ed.)
1934 *Mind, self, and society*. Chicago: Chicago University Press.

Yablonski, Lewis
1967 *Synanon: The tunnel back*. Baltimore: Penguin Books.

Zablocki, Benjamin
1971 *The joyful community*. Baltimore: Penguin Books.

Chapter 5:

After "Sesame Street"

In an effort to see Manny's criminal behavior within the context of the sane and the rational rather than the pathological and the bizarre, we can view his activities within the rubric of the sociology of work and occupations. For instance, we see that Manny rather systematically developed certain skills necessary for the successful completion of work tasks. He learned new skills rapidly and moved from occupation to occupation with a great deal of facility. Probably his addict status discouraged specialization in that he frequently shifted living quarters as a response to "heat" or drug shortage. As we have noted, Manny refrained from continuing in the more sophisticated and drawn-out criminal specialties "because it was too much like work" and he couldn't be hassled.

Conklin (1972, p. 64) defines professionals "as those who manifest a long-term commitment to crime as a source of livelihood, who plan and organize their crimes prior to committing them, and who seek money to support a particular life style that may be called hedonistic." Accordingly, Manny and his friends were professionally involved in this line of work because it was fast, direct in rewards, and usually quite profitable.

Manny's lack of sophisticated planning was compensated for by his sheer bravado and ability to cower his victims. It appears that the constant need for junk-money contributed to the momentary nature of his criminal activities. Manny's cash was constantly being exhausted, and he seldom had savings or reserve. Consequently, plans for the day's business developed rapidly, often on the spot.

Although the status of "criminal" is never descriptive of the person in totality, because "criminal" is only one of the statuses a person may occupy, it appears at this time in his life as if all of Manny's roles and statuses were related to his identity as a criminal. His principal status as a dope fiend was always affected by the success or failure of his role as a robber or a thief. In some ways, Manny was as locked into his lifestyle and work circumstances as the most oppressed and burdened assembly-line worker.

Although he never punched a clock or lined up at a window for his pay, Manny's habit, together with the expectations of his friends and connections, predicted his status continuity as a professional criminal.

Manny's "job"-related activities varied in duration, intensity, and complexity. Although he experienced a long and varied criminal career, at times he was engaged in very complex and intense jobs. On other occasions the vocational climate was much more simple and relaxed. If we take Manny's perspective seriously, his experiences for what they were to him, we will avoid imposing an "outside" order upon the data. The student should look to Manny for answers to questions having to do with the meanings and motivations of his actions (Irwin, 1970). We know, for instance, that the economic imperative fails to explain totally varieties of worker behavior and satisfaction in the legitimate world. The data presented by Manny indicates that this is also true for those involved in "underworld" occupations. It is evident that he was motivated in part by the rewards inherent in craftsmanship, expertise, and social standing.

We see that Manny learned technical skills basically by experiment and experience. He wasn't usually involved in on-the-job training by an expert teacher so much as just venturing out to master a technique with someone of more or less equal status. The prerequisites for Manny's success in crime include numerous social and perceptual skills gleaned only by participation in a lengthy career process. The student should read Letkemann (1973) for insight into "crime as work." Most important, a certain foolhardiness that extends beyond sheer bravado appears to be a substantial element of Manny's successful career. The "need for drug effect" may be part of this personality matrix, but a journeyman's approach to the work at hand is also evident in Manny's criminal behavior.

We note that Manny's sensitivity to various symbols of his occupation (casing a job, not overwriting bum checks) tended to erode as he got further and further into drugs each time. The conventions and requirements of doing a good job as a thief always gave way to the drug imperative. This tends to substantiate Irwin's (1970, pp. 16–18) assertion that the need to score and fix becomes the dominating aspect of the dope fiend's life.

Selected References

Becker, Howard
1963 *The outsiders.* New York: The Free Press.

Cloward, Richard, & Ohlin, Lloyd
1960 *Delinquency and opportunity.* New York: The Free Press.

Conklin, John E.
1972 *Robbery and the criminal justice system.* Philadelphia: Lippincott.

Einstadter, W. T.
1969 The social organization of armed robbery. *Social Problems 17*
(Summer), 64–83.

Irwin, John
1970 *The felon.* Englewood Cliffs, N.J.: Prentice-Hall.

Jackson, Bruce
1969 *A thief's primer.* New York: Macmillan.

Letkemann, Peter
1973 *Crime as work.* Englewood Cliffs, N.J.: Prentice-Hall.

Maurer, David
1964 *Whiz mob.* New Haven: College and University Press.

Shaw, C.
1930 *The jack roller.* Chicago: University of Chicago Press.

Sutherland, Edwin
1937 *The professional thief.* Chicago: University of Chicago Press.

Chapter 6:
_____

The Turnaround

Manny makes us aware of the castelike characteristics of the prison social
system. The rigid, authoritarian model of prison noted by Ohlin (1956,
pp. 14–30) receives support in Manny's account of the well-defined status
demarcations, lack of communication between subgroups, and well-articu-
lated though rather inane regulations. Although corrections administrators
tend to categorize penal institutions as to their custody and purpose,
Manny draws attention to the eternal conflict that exists between staff
and inmates in every type of institutional milieu.

The authoritarian structure of prison relationships institutionalized theft,
dishonesty, and craftiness in Manny and his friends because "everything
settled around one idea: take good care of yourself by learning how best
to con and connive." Manny reports that he picked his shots and hung out
with only those few convicts who could do him some good. He was on the
hustle constantly in the Chino experience. Again, we see that his total life
there was identified with the inmate social system and its codes of behavior.

We note that not only did he stay out of trouble with the officials, he
was for the most part isolated from staff personnel. There were only a few

officers with whom he had to communicate. This isolation indicates that most learning that takes place in prison is through a process of communication among inmates themselves. It appears that when staff-inmate communication is limited, as in Chino during Manny's stay, the formal authority of the staff is maintained and the possibility of staff being corrupted by inmates is reduced. However, tthe probability that inmates will corrupt other inmates is increased (cf. Glaser, 1969, p. 83).

In California, when a convicted felon goes to regular prison he is assigned an "A" or a "B" number. When a criminal goes to a hospital-treatment center he is assigned an "N" (for narcotics) number. In Manny's case even though he had pleaded guilty to armed robbery, the judge sent him to the California Rehabilitation Center for drug addicts. This was because his criminal career was considered to be drug related, and Manny was assumed to have a nonviolent character—the two prerequisites for entry into CRC.

The basic intent of California's program is to provide recovery from drug addiction. The theory hinges on the assumption that addicts become criminals because they must acquire drugs. A recovered addict will no longer be criminal if he is off drugs and rehabilitated into the mainstream of society. Manny points out several inconsistencies existing between the assumptions and the operation of the system. Before arriving at CRC he was led to believe that it was a hospital. He not only expected an easier route than the joint, he wanted a cure. But he was shocked and irate to find that CRC was just another prison complex complete with cells, gun towers, and barbed-wire barriers. He soon determined that CRC was basically a maximum-security warehouse to clean up dope fiends—a place where one kicked for a while. It is considered by some to be an easier way out, but most solid cons in the joint see CRC as just another jail for weaklings and rats. Manny points out that the failure rate is high and recidivism is frequent. Addicts come and go, processed in and out by what the public assumes are professional social work techniques.

The general feeling, according to Manny, is "once a dope fiend, always a dope fiend," so CRC and the "N" number system in reality do little to help a drug addict kick his habit.

According to Irwin (1970), specialized programs are often central to the addict's return to deviance. Rehabilitation becomes a programmed source of pressure encouraging drug use because each time the parolee is confronted with the "dope fiend" reference world the other addicts serve as judges who may be evaluating his progress. "The prison standards of doing good are impossible to forget when the dope fiend is forced to appear each week for judgment."

Irwin (1970) perceives the nalline clinic as a source of enticement back into drug addiction. Drug connections are at the clinic or available through others attending the clinic. Some who have returned to drugs report they are able to "beat" the nalline test. Many begin to use drugs immediately after being tested, as they have time to "clean up" before the next test. The nalline clinic, while it has helped to induce and entice him into drug use, serve as a control on his habit. It is likely, though, that an addict will slip from this routine. The dope fiend may use too close to his testing date, so decide not to appear for testing. He may even jump parole.

Continued use will usually lead to an addict's arrest on a new charge or for a technical violation of parole. He will subsequently probably be returned to prison. There is little hope for an offender sentenced under the "N" number, as the purpose of CRC and the nalline program is rarely met.

Manny has noted a striking similarity in the way CRC inmates and juvenile offenders are treated. Both are handled as civil cases under the guise of rehabilitation as opposed to punishment. Manny recalled that almost every spring CRC is cleared of inmates so as to make room for a new crop of junkies fresh off the streets of Los Angeles. One summer the Green Hornet Patrol picked up one thousand junkies on the streets of Venice, California. They were arrested if they showed track marks on their body. The charge is "internal possession," and appears to be unconstitutional because it infringes on one's right to remain silent and the evidence discovered under duress is self-incriminating. These kinds of quasi-legal procedures demonstrate the differential vulnerability of street addicts. The well-to-do addict seldom if ever gets rousted in this manner.

Although Manny's assertions with respect to the psychiatrist's naive role in prison settings are not without support in the literature (cf. Mathison, 1965, pp. 166–178; Sloan, 1971, pp. 136–138; Irwin, 1970; Robitscher, 1968, pp. 38–42), some further evidence on psychiatric practices in corrections-related contexts is needed to lend special significance to his point. The National Institute of Mental Health (1969) reports that 18,750 psychiatrists were identified as practicing psychiatry according to the criteria of the association. Of the 16,449 who responded to a survey on their location, training, work status, work area of specialization, and other pertinent personal and occupational characteristics, only 1.3 percent—211—listed their area of specialization as forensic and correctional. There is a highly disproportionate distribution of forensic and corrections psychiatrists by state. The states of Kansas, Kentucky, Vermont, Oregon, Hawaii, Florida, and Missouri account for 24.5 percent of all psychiatrists involved in the field of law and corrections. Interestingly enough, only 7.4 percent of all United States psychiatrists live in these seven states, yet they do 24.5 percent of all the work in the corrections field. In addition, the data indicate that 10 percent spent no time in direct services; 46 percent spent no time in consultation. However, 65.9 percent spent from 1 to 35 hours per week in administration, while only 40.8 percent spent 35 hours or more in direct services or consultation.

These figures tend to show that, with the exception of spotty areas of involvement, psychiatry's role in corrections is almost nil. However, there are additional revealing figures from another source that we should consider.

According to "The National Profile on Corrections," there were 121 psychiatrists employed in adult correctional institutions in this country. The task force placed the need for psychiatrists in this area at 335. Thus, as a conservative estimate, adult corrections could use 214 additional psychiatrists merely to help administer diagnostic and treatment programs that are in some sense ongoing presently.

It is evident from a brief glance at these statistics that there is a major shortage of trained personnel, at the psychiatric level, in the correctional field. Is the solution purely an economic one? Are adequate numbers of psychiatrists waiting in the wings ready to put on their correctional hat if funds to compensate them become available?

It is difficult to find substantial and accurate survey data from informed subjects as to the need for psychiatric services in a correctional facility. One such study (O'Brian, 1970) yielded the following information. Two institutions were studied: the Correctional Complex (young offenders, adult) and the Youth Center (juvenile offenders).

Correctional Complex staff identified 46 disturbed inmates (3.6 percent of the institutional population). Youth Center staff identified 48 disturbed inmates (12.7 percent of the institutional population). These two measures of incidence were quite close to the 4.4 and 12.8 percent, respectively, derived in the Dellinger study (1968), which was based on a case-folder analysis.

Symptoms of the disturbed cases at the Correctional Complex fell most frequently into the categories of Anti-Social Behavior, Aggressiveness, and Disturbed Thought Patterns.

Symptoms of the disturbed cases at the Youth Center emphasized Poor Thought Patterns, Poor Attitudes, and Anti-Social Behavior.

Conspicuous staff differences were evident in the nominations. Teachers frequently indicated that no inmates were in need of psychiatric care. Security personnel at the Youth Center, more than any other class of personnel, described the disturbed inmate in terms of Anti-Social Behavior and Poor Attitude. Classification and Parole Officers at the Complex described the disturbed inmate in terms of Aggressive Behavior, Immaturity, and Disturbed Thought Patterns, more than any other staff members.

A close reading of this study indicates that a number of findings may be in order. It is clearly evident that those personnel who have learned to cope with "disturbed behavior" as part of their own school experience (teachers, counselors) were far less willing to impute behavioral problems to the inmates. However, the principal findings indicate that there is a definite need for expanding and strengthening guidance services at this major corrections facility. Particularly is this true in the Youth Center, where guidance and consultation is needed both on the inmate and staff levels.

In addition, to make these services effective, it would be necessary to involve many more trained personnel than are currently available, both in the research phase, wherein more systematic and accurate methods of identifying disturbed individuals should be developed, and in the direct services phase, where individuals can be counseled, treated, and materially aided toward understanding the social self. Far too often inmates with spoiled identities are identified as "abnormal personalities" when their biggest problem has been systematic disenfranchisement—being without friends, advocates, and work opportunities.

There is a growing body of literature arguing that the M.D. degree as it is conventionally offered may not be the proper preparation for the practicing psychiatrist. The difficulty stems from the fact that the ideal foundations of a psychiatric education differ substantially from those in all other fields of medicine. As Lidz and Edelson (1970, pp. 2-3) comment:

> The time has come for us to start specifically training students for psychiatry while they are still in medical school by offering them a program far different from what they are currently receiving. . . .
> Psychiatry, more than any other field of medicine, has its foundations both in the biological and the behavioral sciences. It requires an understanding of the biological basis of human behavior, a grasp of neurobehavioral mechanisms, and an understanding of psychopharmacology; and it needs a behavioral science background to understand the essentially human aspects of human adaptation and maladaptation and to comprehend psychodynamic theory.

Jay Ziskin (1970, p. 184) has this to say regarding educational qualifications of psychiatrists:

> The psychiatrist holds an M.D. degree with Specialization in Psychiatry. One of the most obvious and serious defects of psychiatric formal education lies in the fact that a large portion of time is devoted to the study of general medicine, most of which is irrelevant to the subject matter of the work he will perform. More serious is the lack of training in psychology, the basic science with which the psychiatrist works.

Members of our society attribute exceptionally high status to all doctors. In any field of medicine the average layman is not prone to question the education, training, and even the "good advice" of the physician. The question arises, then, if all psychiatrists are competent to make decisions and render "good advice" in every respect in the correctional institution. Mariner (1967) is relevant to this discussion:

From a theoretical point of view, to an observer unhampered by institutional concerns, it would seem apparent that a knowledge of human behavior, thought and emotion, would be the logical and necessary foundation on which a professional practice dealing with disturbance of behavior, thought and emotion would have to rest. Thus psychology—or more generally "behavioral science"—would seem unquestionably to be the basic academic discipline of choice. (That this should be considered a heretical statement when made by a psychiatrist is evidence of the almost incredible irrationality of the medical profession in this area; a psychological background for dealing with psychological problems would seem as obvious a choice as a biological background for dealing with biological problems.)

Dr. Mariner's remarks are especially pointed when you consider that the dynamic new emphasis in corrections is toward the diffusion of treatment and custodial responsibilities into less rigidly ritualized roles. Today's correctional model assumes that custodial and treatment roles are compatible and should not be seen as inversely correlated (Pennsylvania Department of Justice, 1969). Therefore, administration must promote both custody and rehabilitation priorities equally, and all administrative staff should be sufficiently competent and versed in both areas to function appropriately.

In order to examine the role of psychiatry in corrections it would be fruitful to look into psychoanalytic theory as it pertains to the motives of criminal behavior. It is held by students of Freud and Jung that the invisible motivations that exert a major influence on the causation of human conduct are sustained from the unconscious level of the human personality and interact with that phenomena known as the collective unconscious.

According to Jung, there are innate psychic dynamisms closely connected with the basic structures of the human psyche, whose language is expressed in symbols and whose validity is collective. The directions of normal and pathological human behavior can ultimately be reduced to a particular reciprocity between the ego and some archetypal constellations. Thus, man's life is conditioned not only by external situations but primarily by interior psychic factors, represented by archetypes present in a particular moment in a given individual (DiTullio, 1969).

According to psychoanalytic theory, the "pleasure principle" is the first step in an individual's emotional development. Any delay in those gratifications the person deems as indispensable generates an attitude of distrust. Thus, the external world often becomes a source of insecurity, threat, and even aggression.

Freud held that only when the child experiences an atmosphere of familial trust do acceptance, good affective relationships between parents, and the "pleasure principle" become subliminated gradually by the "reality principle." If this occurs, the individual learns to behave in harmony with what those in his immediate circles want of him, thus acquiring a sense of "social reality." When he matures in these kinds of affective surroundings he learns "oblavity," or how to give freely to others without the need for profit. Accordingly, he will be less motivated by the "pleasure principle."

A principal point we might make here is that, generalizing from this theoretical prespective, it is not hard for an analyst to find a *dormant capacity for delinquency in any normal individual.* All of us at one time or another are extremely selfish; all of us dream crime at one time or another; most of us have known Porter's feeling when he wrote, "I have a panther in my breast." It is not easy for the analyst to determine on what layer or level of the ego structure these thoughts exist or how far in the past our "pleasure principle" is buried.

Indeed, the whole theory has been questioned by many competent writers. For example, Woodmansey (1967, p. 113) states:

There can be no more urgent or conspicious problem in psychiatry as a scientific discipline than that it lacks a generally agreed theoretical framework on which to base practice and teaching. . . . This state of affairs has led to an emphasis in psychiatric education and training on psychoanalysis theory and concepts, an emphasis which is based upon a premature and uncritical acceptance of that theory.

According to Polk [1969, p. 78], it would be sheer folly to continue the present practice of nonaccountable education where virtually no systematic attempt is made to assess the extent to which an educational program reaches an explicit set of learning goals. Learning goals for the young medical student are very explicit and very elitist.

Universities have long accustomed themselves to their role of training elites. . . . The university assumes that the universe can be divided into the "able" and "unable." Its mission, of course, is to train the able. Simultaneously, the university must protect itself from the unstable, and the lowering of "standards" that would occur if the unable were admitted. The danger here to correctional training programs is that most of both clients and staff lie in the unsafe range.

Relevant to our thesis here is the logical assumption that the young doctor, who has spent four years in medical school and several years of additional specialty training in one or another school of psychiatry, has never come into contact with corrections as a possible field of endeavor, and, as Lidz and Edelson (1970) have pointed out, probably does not have the tools to repair, much less blueprints to comprehend, the trouble he might find in that milieu.

Kadushin (1961, pp. 517–531) studied the effect of social distance between client and professional on the stability of their interactions as self-reported by ministers, physicians, and psychologists. On the four dimensions of social distance—normative, interactive, cultural, and personal—ministers were found to be closest, general physicians were more distant, and psychotherapists were the most distant from their clients. Since the theory holds that stable interaction between client and professional is more probable when internalized norms, mutual expectations, and optimum cathexis exists among role partners, it is surprising that these conditions appear, from this study, to be less met in the psychoanalyst-client relationship.

Kadushin points out that one of the social mechanisms psychoanalysts use to minimize the "social distance gap" yet keep their professional distance is the community of "friends and supporters of psychotherapy," but the majority of patients are left out of this community, certainly all of them in the institutional setting, and have difficulty obtaining adequate treatment. Kadushin intimates, however, that the mental hospital and custody facility create an "artificial community," which is recognized as a potential aid or "bridging device" between analyst and patient.

We should note that plans are now being carried out in major universities not only to update the curricula but to bring the various psychiatries together. Let us glance briefly at the plan for Yale Medical School currently being put into operation: On the completion of this program, the student will have a reasonable familiarity with (1) psychodynamic and psychoanalytic theory and personality development, (2) the neurobehavioral sciences and psychopharmacology, both at the theoretic and practical level, (3) various psychologies of potential pertinence to the field, such as the work of Piaget, operant conditioning, learning theory, dissonance theory, and psycholinguistics, (4) the foundations of sociology, social psychology, and ethnology, (5) techniques and attitudes needed for interviewing patients, (6) the various psychiatric syndromes, (7) various types of therapy that will enable him or her to function as a resident from the start of his or her residency training (Lidz and Edelson, 1970, p. 10).

It seems to me that this kind of training will better enable the psychiatrist to go into prison with the attitude Alfred Loos (1955, p. 137), former Commissioner of the New York Board of Parole, called for in an article somewhat dated but still cogent:

Elementary as it may sound, it appears that among the basic qualifications of the psychiatrist and the psychologist who plan to enter the correctional field, and essential to effective therapy, are a sincere personal interest in the inmate and an attitude of hopeful assurance in the inmate's ability to cure his maladjustment by adhering faithfully to a treatment program. They also should recognize that the average inmate regards his confinement as punishment and that he is not there because he is an emotionally ill person. What this means to the development of a mutually satisfactory relationship is self-evident.

The treatment of prisoners should emphasize not their exclusion from the community but rather their continuing part in it. All community agencies should be enlisted to assist staff in the task of social rehabilitation. Rehabilitation takes place best in "open institutions," where social life is most like any community.

We have found that there are not many psychiatrists active in prison or reformatory work. Those that are usually take the role of an administrator or institutional staff member. The psychoanalytically oriented model of noncoercive therapy is not offered to prison inmates. A necessary restructure of the concept of therapy in penal institutions would involve the implementation of new rules designed to engender equality between patient-prisoner and doctor-therapist so that the program created between them would enable free relationships to develop. Neither equality nor equity relationships currently exist in prisons.

Further, we find that "headshrinkers" and "pill pushers" receive little formal education in those social disciplines that would enhance their understanding of what prisons are all about and what inmates of those facilities must endure and surmount. As Stoll (1968, pp. 199–227) points out, the ideology of social control agents, including psychiatrists in corrections work, shapes the mode of treatment recommended and used. The psychological models of criminal causation tend to be atomistic in that external variables are minimized or ignored—and control-oriented in that the deviant is managed within a system that predicts its own problems.

Selected References

Allchin, W. H.
1969 The psychiatrist, the offender and the community. *Medical & Biological Illustration 13* (March), 157–160.

Brennen, William T.
1963 Law and society must join in defending mentally ill criminals. *Journal of the American Psychiatric Association 49.*

Cormier, B. M.
1969 Psychiatric services in penal institutions. *Laval Medical 40* (September), 939–943.

Dellinger, J. B.
1968 Alcoholic, narcotic, and emotional problems among correctional inmates. District of Columbia Research Report.

DiTullio, Benigno
1969 *Horizons in clinical criminology.* New York: Rothman.

Glaser, Daniel
1969 *The effectiveness of a prison and parole system.* Indianapolis: Bobbs-Merrill.

Hollingshead, E. R., & Hollingshead, Redlich
1958 *Social class and mental illness.* New York: Basic Books.

Irwin, John
1970 *The felon.* Englewood Cliffs, N.J.: Prentice-Hall.

Kadushin, Charles
1961 Social distance between client and professional. *American Journal of Sociology 67* (July), 517–531.

Lidz, Theodore, & Edelson, Marshall
1970 *Training tomorrow's psychiatrist: The crisis in curriculum.* New Haven: Yale University Press.

Loos, Alfred
1955 Psychiatry in the correctional process. In Paul Hoch & Joseph Zubin (Eds.), *Proceedings of the forty-fifth annual meeting of the American Psychopathological Association.* New York: Grune & Stratton.

Mariner, E. S.
1967 A critical look at professional education in the mental health field. *American Psychologist 22* (April), 271–281.

Mathison, Thomas
1965 *Defenses of the weak.* London: Tavistock.

National Institutes of Mental Health
1969 *The national psychiatrists.* Chevy Chase, Md.: Public Health Service Publication Number 1885.

O'Brian, Kathleen
1970 Inmates with psychiatric problems: A survey of staff perceptions of incidents and symptoms. District of Columbia Research Report 27 (June).

Ohlin, Lloyd
1956 *Sociology and the field of corrections.* New York: Russell Sage Foundation.

Pennsylvania Department of Justice
1969 Planning report. Bureau of Corrections (April).

Polk, Kenneth
1969 *The university and corrections: Potential for collaborative relation-*

ships. Washington D.C. Joint Commission on Correctional Manpower and Training.

President's Commission on Law Enforcement and Administration of Justice
1964   *Task force report: Corrections.* U.S. Government Printing Office.

Robitscher, J. B.
1968   Non-coercive therapy in a prison setting. *Prison Journal 48* (February), 38–42.

Rozowski, A. S.
1969   Community psychiatry and the education of psychiatrists. *Community Mental Health Journal 5* (February), 129–139.

Rubin, Jesse
1968   Who is involved in the treatment process? In Alan Ferster & Jesse Rubin (Eds.), *Readings in law and psychiatry.* Baltimore: Johns Hopkins University Press.

Scott, G. D., & Gendrear, P.
1969   Psychiatric implications of sensory deprivation in a maximum security prison. *Canadian Psychiatric Association Journal 14* (April), 337–341.

Sloan, Nellie
1971   The psychiatric unit. In Robert Minton (Ed.), *Inside: Prison American style.* New York: Vintage Books.

Stoll, C. S.
1968   Images of man and social control. *Social Forces 47* (February), 119–127.

Walters, R. F., & Jackson, G. W.
1969   The mentally ill offender in Arkansas. *Journal of Arkansas Medical Society 65* (December), 474–476.

Woodmansey, A. C.
1967   Science and the training of psychiatrists. *British Journal of Psychiatry.*

Ziskin, Jay
1970   *Coping with psychiatric and psychological testimony.* Beverly Hills: Law and Psychology Press.

Chapter 9

An Integrated Theoretical Perspective

The purpose of writing this chapter is to set forth some of the major theoretical concepts pertinent to adolescent development within those social circumstances where the Mannys of our society must live and survive. It is not our intention to account precisely for Manny's experience with explicit reference to our theory at each point. This would not be conceptually sound. So we will advance the notion that the broad, general, run of street-criminal careers similar to his can best be understood by referring to theories of social strain, differential opportunity, and institutional labeling processes rather than by casting them within a pathological frame of reference. Our focus is intended to be primarily sociological. We intend to provide an overall interpretative skeleton in terms of types of sociological theory, the substantive foci of the theories, and the logical interrelationships among the theories. In Chapter 8 the student has been provided with in-depth material that should serve to flesh out the material provided below.

One of the more useful formulations is that suggested by Merton (1968), in which he lays the foundation for the consideration of differing deviant styles as responses to structural pressures. In Merton's theory of anomie (1968, Chapters 6 and 7), deviant behavior is elaborated as a socially constructed phenomenon, the extent and distribution of which depends on the frequency and location of value-access disjunctions and anomie in society. Merton's guiding assumption is that especially in our differentiated society, dominant emphasis gets placed upon success values or achievement of goals.

These goals are ordered primarily along occupational, monetary, and material concerns, but also include the rather pervasive intrapersonal concerns of leadership and independence. Merton asserts that the socially approved or institutionalized lines of access to the legitimate means for achieving emphasized cultural goals are disproportionately distributed throughout the social structure. That is to say, the lower social classes, including racial and ethnic minorities, represent significantly disadvantaged social locations. Thus, the lack of integration between the dominant cultural values and socially structured access to these values engenders strain and a propensity toward the breakdown of normative consensus. This kind of anomic social condition leading toward the dissemination of alternative, illegitimate means is greatest where educational and occupational channels to legitimate means are limited, and this is why one should expect to find higher rates of criminal activity in the lower socioeconomic classes and among marginal social groups, such as those located in the New York ghetto.

Theoretically Merton's statement presents a plausible explanation for certain types of theft or robbery, but as an explanation of all delinquent behavior it has several limitations. As Cohen (1955, p. 36) has indicated, this perspective does not explain the nonutilitarian and destructive nature of much youthful deviance nor the fact that delinquency is found in the middle as well as the upper classes.

In general terms, Cohen's (1955) theory of delinquent subculture is a somewhat similar explanation to that of Merton but considerably more specific. Cohen's theory is of the "middle range" in that it does not stand as a theory of delinquency in general but is limited to acts of delinquency committed by subcultural gangs. Cohen suggests that delinquent gangs spring up as a consequence of class stratification in American society. Assuming a distinctive working-class culture and a distinctive delinquent subculture integrally related to it, Cohen suggests delinquent-gang behavior as a product of group solutions to status problems and to the unfulfilled needs and consequent frustrations of the American working-class culture in a system of predominantly middle-class values.

Cohen's perspective appears to center on the supposition that since middle-class goals are unattainable and therefore become meaningless to the working-class male youth, he reacts to initiate a reversal process "whereby the delinquent subculture by means of this process becomes an inversion, so to speak, of middle-class values" (Bloch and Geis, 1970, p. 372). In distinguishing between the youthful gang member and the adult criminal, Cohen alludes to the following differences (1955, pp. 24-30):

1. Stealing is usually nonutilitarian for the gang member. This differs from other theft, which is often for profit.
2. Delinquent gang behavior is usually malevolent and negativistic. Hostility is directed toward "good children" as well as adults. Their "escapades" often flout ordinary community standards.
3. Gang stealing goes hand in hand with malicious mischief, vandalism, trespassing, assault, etc. It is unsystematic when compared to adult criminal behavior.

4. Gang capers reflect a "generalized protean orneriness" and "short tun hedonism." They are spur-of-the-moment affairs with the youths usually taking no care for consequences.

Cohen describes gang boys as individuals who find a way of survival within their own delinquent subculture. This subculture is characterized as having values that are antithetical to those of the dominant culture. He conceptualizes the problem of the gang boy as one in which there has been a "reaction formation" to the community's codes of behavior. In repressing these codes the gang boys have internalized a new set of values based on rules of conduct in direct opposition to those of the general community.

The problems of Cohen's working-class boys are largely problems of status and self-respect, and these tend to arise because the socialization of working-class children fails to prepare them to meet the standards of the larger culture. In competition with middle-class peers, the working-class boy is more likely to find himself shut out of the higher status "locations." One might assume that working-class youth would avoid status competition with middle-class rivals. However, our system of compulsory education suggests a prime setting, the school, where this competition is institutionalized. Cohen (1955, pp. 112–115) demonstrates that status in the school, to the extent that the school is a controlled environment, is allocated according to middle-class standards. He shows precisely how the "structural imperatives" of the school tend to militate for order and discipline. The teacher is by origin or orientation a middle-class authority figure. Most important, the middle-class board of education, middle-class parents, and many of the working-class parents expect teachers to work on the middle-class manners and skills of their students.

Cohen claims that the working-class boy is neither fully prepared nor properly motivated to dance to the middle-class tune. He argues (1955, p. 119) that "to the degree to which he values middle class status . . . he faces a problem of adjustment and is in the market for a solution." The delinquent subculture provides one solution that justifies "the free expression of aggression against the sources of his frustration" (1955, p. 132). Cohen's theoretical explanation of the "solution" takes the form of an alternative status system that provides the kinds of status criteria working-class boys are able to meet: "The hallmark of the delinquent subculture is the explicit and wholesale repudiation of middle class standards and the adoption of their very antithesis" (1955, p. 129). Cohen assumes that delinquent boys are ambivalent about middle-class norms, and this mediates against the stability of their delinquent adaptation. He therefore introduces the psychological concept of "reaction formation" to explain what he sees as their exaggerated response in the form of malicious and negativistic delinquent actions.

Clearly, Cohen is positing the existence of a rebellious type of "reaction formation" here that takes the form of nonpurposive, expressive behavior as opposed to a more rational, instrumental kind of act. A significant part of Cohen's theoretical concern was to understand the rebellious responses of high school boys as they related to various status forces in the community.

The most extensive documentation in the sociological literature of delinquent behavior patterns in lower-class culture (cf. Miller, 1958) describes a tradition that integrates youthful delinquency with adult criminality. In the central value orientation of youths participating in this tradition, delinquent and criminal behavior is accepted as a means of achieving success goals. The dominant criteria of in-group evaluation stress achievement, the use of skill and knowledge to get results. In this culture, prestige is allocated to those who achieve material gain and power through avenues defined as illegitimate by the larger society. From the very young to the very old, the successful "haul"—which quickly transforms the penniless into a man of means—is an ever-present vision of the possible and desirable. Although one may also achieve material success through the routine practice of theft or fraud, the "big score" remains the symbolic image of quick success (cf. Irwin, 1970, Chapters 1 and 2).

The means by which a member of a criminal subculture achieves success are clearly defined for the aspirant. At a young age, he learns to admire and respect older criminals and to adopt the "right guy" as his role model. Delinquent episodes help him to acquire mastery of the techniques and orientation of the criminal world and to learn how to cooperate successfully with others in criminal enterprises. He exhibits hostility and distrust toward representatives of the larger society. He regards members of the conventional world as "suckers," his natural victims, to be exploited when possible. He sees successful people in the conventional world as having a "racket"—e.g., big businessmen have huge expense accounts, politicians get graft, etc. This attitude successfully neutralizes the controlling effect of conventional norms. Toward the in-group the "right guy" maintains relationships of loyalty, honesty, and trustworthiness. He must prove himself reliable and dependable in his contacts with his criminal associates, although he has no such obligations toward the out-group of noncriminals.

One of the best ways of assuring success in the criminal world is to cultivate appropriate "connections." As a youngster, this means running with a clique composed of other "right guys" and promoting an apprenticeship or some other favored relationship with older and successful offenders. Close and dependable ties with income-producing outlets for stolen goods, such as the peddler, the junkman, and the fence, are especially useful. Furthermore, these intermediaries encourage and protect the young delinquent in a criminal way of life by giving him a jaundiced perspective on the private morality of many functionaries in conventional society. As he matures, the young delinquent becomes acquainted with a new world made up of predatory bondsmen, shady lawyers, crooked policemen, grafting politicians, dishonest businessmen, and corrupt jailers. Through "connections" with occupants of these half-legitimate, half-illegitimate roles and with "big shots" in the underworld, the aspiring criminal validates and assures his freedom of movement in a world made safe for crime.

One role model in the conflict pattern of lower-class culture is the "bopper," who swaggers with his gang, fights with weapons to win a wary respect from other gangs, and compels a fearful deference from the conventional adult world by his unpredictable and destructive assaults on persons and property. To other gang members, however, the key qualities of the bopper are those of the successful warrior. His performance must reveal a winningness to defend his personal integrity and the honor of the gang. He must do this with great courage and displays of fearlessness in the face of personal danger.

The immediate aim in the world of fighting gangs is to acquire a reputation for toughness and destructive violence. A "rep" assures not only respectful behavior from peers and threatened adults but also admiration for the physical strength and masculinity it symbolizes. It represents a way of securing access to the scarce resources for adolescent pleasure and opportunity in underprivileged areas.

Above all things, the bopper is valued for his "heart." He does not "chicken out," even when confronted by superior force. He never defaults in the face of a personal insult or a challenge to the integrity of his gang. The code of the bopper is that of the warrior who places great stress on courage, the defense of his group, and the maintenance of honor.

Relationships between bopping gang members and the adult world are severely attenuated. The term that the bopper uses most frequently to characterize his relationships with adults is "weak." He is unable to find appropriate role models that can designate for him a structure of opportunities leading to adult success. He views himself as isolated and the adult world as indifferent. The commitments of adults are to their own interests and not to his. Their explanations of why he should behave differently are "weak," as are their efforts to help him.

Confronted by the apparent indifference and insincerity of the adult world, the bopper seeks to win by coercion the attention and opportunities he lacks and cannot otherwise attract. In recent years the street-gang worker who deals with the fighting gang on its own "turf" has come to symbolize not only a recognition by conventional adult society of the gang's toughness but also a concession of opportunities formerly denied. Through the alchemy of competition between gangs, this gesture of attention by the adult world to the "worst" gangs is transformed into a mark of prestige. Thus does the manipulation of violence convert indifference into accommodation and attention into status (cf. Miller, 1958).

Retreatism may include a variety of expressive, sensual, or consummatory experiences, alone or in a group. In this analysis, we are interested only in those experiences that involve the use of drugs and that are supported by a subculture. We have adopted these limitations in order to maintain our focus on subcultural formations that are clearly recognized as delinquent, as drug use by adolescents is. The retreatist preoccupation with expressive experiences creates many varieties of the "hipster" cult among lower-class adolescents that foster patterns of defiant but not necessarily delinquent conduct.

Subcultural drug users in lower-class areas perceive themselves as culturally and socially detached from the life style and everyday preoccupations of members of the conventional world. The following characterization of the "cat" culture, observed by Finestone in a lower-class Negro area in Chicago, describes drug use in the more general context of "hipsterism." It should not be assumed that this description in every respect fits drug cultures found elsewhere. We have drawn heavily on Finestone's observations, however, because they provide the descriptions available of the social world in which lower-class adolescent drug cultures typically arise.

The dominant feature of the retreatist subculture of the "cat" lies in the continuous pursuit of the "kick." Every cat has a kick—alcohol, marijuana, addicting drugs, unusual sexual experiences, hot jazz, cool jazz, or any combination of these. Whatever its content, the kick is a search for ecstatic experiences. The retreatist strives for an intense awareness of living and a sense of pleasure that is "out of this world." In extreme form, he seeks an almost spiritual and mystical knowledge that is experienced when one come to know "it" at the height of one's kick. The past and the future recede in the time perspective of the cat, since complete awareness in present experience is the essence of the kick.

The successful cat has a lucrative "hustle" that contrasts sharply with the routine and discipline required in the ordinary occupational tasks of conventional society. The many varieties of the hustle are characterized by a rejection of violence or force and preference for manipulating, persuading, outwitting, or "conning" others to obtain resources for experiencing the kick. The cat begs, borrows, steals, or engages in some petty con game. He caters to the illegitimate cravings of others by peddling drugs or working as a pimp. A highly exploitative attitude toward women permits the cat to view pimping as a prestigious source of income. Through the labor of "chicks" engaged in prostitution or shoplifting, he can live in idleness and concentrate his entire attention on organizing, scheduling, and experiencing the aesthetic pleasure of the kick. The hustle of the cat is secondary to his interest in the kick. In this respect the cat differs from his fellow delinquents in the criminal subculture, for whom income-producing activity is a primary concern.

The ideal cat's appearance, demeanor, and taste can best be characterized as "cool." The cat seeks to exhibit a highly developed and sophisticated taste for clothes. In his demeanor, he struggles to reveal a self-assured and unruffled manner, thereby emphasizing his aloofness and "superiority" to the "squares." He develops a colorful, discriminating vocabulary and ritualized gestures that express his sense of difference from the conventional world and his solidarity with the retreatist subculture (cf. Miller, 1958).

The word "cool" also best describes the sense of apartness and detachment the retreatist experiences in his relationships with the conventional world. His reference group is the "society of cats," an "elite" group in which he becomes isolated from conventional society. Within this group, a new order of goals and criteria of achievement are created. The cat does not seek to impose this sytem of values on the world of the squares. Instead, he strives for status and deference within the society of cats by cultivating the kick and the hustle. Thus, the retreatist subculture provides avenues to success goals, to the social admiration and the sense of well-being or oneness with the world that the members feel are otherwise beyond their reach.

Friedenberg (1965) relates the myriad problems of coming of age in America. In dealing directly with the notion of school rebellion, Nordstrom, Friedenberg, and Gold (1967) also extend the work of Max Scheler (1961) and his predecessor Nietzsche (1956) by integrating their classic concept of *ressentiment* into a theory of adolescence. Scheler (1961, pp. 45–56) sees *ressentiment* as being a kind of free-floating rancor, "a lasting mental attitude, caused by the systematic repression of certain emotions and affects which, as such, are normal components of human nature." Scheler (1961, p. 48) has said that *ressentiment* is "chiefly confined to those who *serve* and are *dominated* at the moment, who fruitlessly resent the sting of authority." This systematic repression, according to Scheler, "leads to the constant tendency to indulge in certain kinds of value decisions and corresponding value judgments." In his words, the "emotions and affects primarily concerned are revenge, hatred, malice, envy, the impulse to detract and spite" (1961, pp. 45–56).

Scheler points out, for example, that criminals seeking to collect scarce valuables are not motivated by *ressentiment,* but that certain subtypes, such as arsonists, are. He thereby suggests a point of differentiation between "deviant behavior that is oriented toward specific goals and deviant behavior that is purposelsss in terms of utilitarian values" (Coser, 1967,

p. 27). As Coser notes, this brings us to bear on a logical distinction between two types of "juvenile delinquency": "One of which is oriented
against symbolic targets such as schools or other symbols of middle class
values, and the other, which aims at providing instrumental benefits."

Rebellion, in this context, becomes a problem when the natural development of a young person's independence meets with consistent opposition.
It is clear from Friedenberg (1959) that it is natural and proper for youth
to rebel. This rebellion becomes a serious problem when it has to fight its
way against parental and school domination and oversolicitude. Rebellion,
for Friedenberg (1959, p. 127), "means a revolt against an authority
whose legitimacy the rebel concedes, though he may object to it as unjust
or arbitrary." The impersonal and remote character of those in authority
is fatal to any proprietary interest in society on the part of the ordinary
adolescent.

Rebellion seems to be a more frequent expression of life in the last few
decades, climaxing in a contemporary existential position that rebellion
can be an exercise of the individual's fundamental freedom. This isn't to
say that in our conforming society rebellion is generally regarded as an
acceptable pattern of behavior. In fact, it is most often feared. Lindner,
(1952, pp. 218-219), who, significantly, was the first to focus on the delinquent as a "rebel without a cause," describes the reaction to rebellion as
follows:

> Rebellion is a word, and a concept that has been mauled, maltreated, and corrupted.
> . . . Dictionaries give it as a sense of opposition, chiefly adding fuel to the notion that
> as an act of pattern of thought and behavior, it is immoral, blameworthy and scan-
> dalous. . . . An immediate value-association of good and worth applies to that which
> is rebelled against, while the deed of rebellion and its actors acquire the stigma of
> wrong and reprehensible.

Polk and Halferty (1966) demonstrate that there are no hard and fast
rules for determining what comes first in patterns of deviant behavior—
rebellion or delinquency. They offer six possible temporal sequences using
the variables of commitment, delinquency, and rebellion, and conclude that
although commitment variables tend to increase probabilities for a "drift
into delinquency," other combinations are possible. Delinquency or rebellion could precede commitment and rebellion, and *one* legally defined act
of delinquency could lead to rebelliousness and further entrenchment
in delinquent patterns.

Our argument at this point is to say that in our somewhat authoritarian
and totalitarian society, rebels and delinquents are often treated alike.
That is to say, that in certain organizations such as the school little pro-
nounced deviation from the norm is permitted, and severe sanctions are

used against those who persist in any style of patterned nonconformity. The larger society may at times treat the adult criminal differently from the heretic, but it is seldom that the adolescent is given the freedom to innovate, create, or criticize.

Erik Erikson (1968), who views development in the individual as a maturational cycle, says that in each stage of development there is a "central problem that has to be solved." In adolescence this problem is the establishment of what Erikson calls "the sense of identity" (cf. Witmer and Kotinsky, 1952, p. 6). The adolescent seeks to carify who he is and what his role in society is to be. Thus, adolescence is a time of crisis when rebellion may play its most important formative role. If society doesn't clarify the adolescent's role for him and doesn't reward him with status, or in fact is hostile, the adolescent is likely to define himself through his rebellion. He may turn to youth groups and gang peers for the sense of identity denied him from other more "legitimate" sources.

Clearly, Manny was disappointed in the secondary school experience. Middle-class standards are imposed on all students regardless of ethnic or cultural background; conformity is encouraged and creativity is stifled. Far too many youngsters are being made aware that they cannot be themselves in school or that they are not wanted, and "a group response of pessimism and hostility results" (Stinchcombe, 1964, p. 7).

Stinchcombe (1964) seriously examined the phenomenon of rebellion in the high school within a closely related theoretical framework to that of Cohen's (1955). He used the concept of "expressive alienation" to explain some of the sources of boredom and rebellion in the high school classroom. Characteristics of expressive alienation include (1) short-term hedonism, (2) negativism with respect to conformity and those who conform, (3) perceptions of persons that the status system is unfair in its expectation of inputs and distribution of outcomes, particularly as administered by school authorities, and (4) demands for autonomy and freedom from adults.

Stinchcombe notes that the "attitudinal characteristics of high school rebels are similar to characteristics attributed to juvenile delinquents" (1964, p. 51). That is to say, that defiance of legal norms and organizational regulations can be observed in either case, rebelliousness or delinquency. But Stinchcombe does note significant attitudinal differences in those who confront the law of school or the society head on and those who "merely evade the law." This is the basis of our subtle distinction between the categories rebellion and delinquency. As Stinchcombe points out (1964, pp. 51–52), when rebellion involves defiance of the law and its official representatives, it becomes for legal purposes delinquent behavior. But what of that rebellious behavior directed primarily at home, neighborhood, and school authority? Stinchcombe noted the tendency of rebellious boys to behave in patterned ways—that is to say, that their behavior was normatively (for them) hedonistic, irresponsible, and expressive. In spite of the wide variety of dissimilar forms of expressed behavior it seemed useful and reasonable to Stinchcombe to designate this behavior as "rebellious" (rather than deviant, delinquent, or alienated—although he was aware that it may become these) because it is in a large part the *autonomous* response of subcultures of the recalcitrant young. Thus, for Stinchcombe, rebellious responses of a nonutilitarian, negativistic, hedonistic, and autonomous variety are adaptive responses by *some* adolescents to problems presented to them by the parent society and culture (for example, norm contradictions and imbalances, structure of opportunity, ambiguities in age-grading, the prospect of meaningless work roles, etc.), and particular forms that they take in specific groups reflect a choice of alternatives from options available to them.

According to Stinchcombe, this psychological state of rebellion may be instigated from an inability to meet school demands; the attitudinal set may arise from a loss of cognitive articulation between school activity and future status. For those students whose class or ethnic background or demonstrated intelligence allows their expectation that they will not achieve the desired level of occupational status in any case, achievement in school makes no sense. For them, one can assume that grades and the usual indicators of successful progress have little meaning. Perhaps, says Stinchcombe, in the search for predictors of maturity, these youth prematurely demand adult status and reject the cultural assumptions that authority and the right to rebel belong exclusively to adults. To the extent that the deprived youth has externalized success goals, he will evidence rebellious attitudes and behaviors. Stinchcombe (1964, p. 179) concludes:

The major practical conclusion of the analysis above is that rebellious behavior is largely a reaction to the school itself and to its promises, not a failure of the family or community. High school students can be motivated to conform by paying them in the realistic coin of future adult advantages. Except perhaps for pathological cases, any student can be made to conform if the school can realistically promise something valuable to him as a reward for working hard. But for a large part of the population, especially the adolescents who will enter the male working class or the female candidates for early marriage, the school has nothing to promise.

Polk and Schafer (1972, p. 114) argue convincingly that "Stinchcombe gives too much weight to the future social class and economic ramifications of school experience." They advance this thesis:

An alternative explanation is that the rebellion of failing youngsters is a response to the *immediate* effects of failure rather than to its implications for future low status in the essentially external economic world. Placement in non-college tracks of the contemporary high school means consignment to an educational oblivion without apparent purpose or meaning; but the effect of this placement in producing rebellion may stem from the stigma, humiliation, and hostility generated within the school itself, rather than from a reaction to anticipated consignment to a work-class role.

The implications for theoretical development, and for understanding the practical situation our Mannys find themselves in, are important if we are to comprehend the concepts of rebellion and delinquency as they affect the experience of adolescent males in society.

Traditionally, rebellion and delinquency have been treated as more or less identical symptoms of adolescent dissidence and conflict, expecially by parents, school authorities, and police. Social scientists have tended to follow along in this regard. To be sure, these concepts appear to have a strong interdependent relationship, but we argue that adolescent rebellion, and a more enterprising delinquency, may stem from different attitudinal matrices insofar as the individual is concerned. Further, we contend that these "deviant" attitudes and behaviors, while not unrelated to socio-economic class position, can be better understood if considered within the broader perspective of their respective organizational and institutional situations, e.g., lack of success in school and lack of legitimate work opportunities.

We set forth the possibility that official delinquents sometimes are junior criminals, while rebellious youth usually are not—at first. Cohen (1965) argues that all human behavior consists of individual and group efforts to solve problems. Successful actions tend to reduce tension and discomfort, while unsuccessful actions create new problems and compound previously unsolved problems. Perhaps we can best understand the adolescent rebel's behavior in terms of problem solving if we take a close look at the problems he faces. Again, youthful patterns of breaking and entering or auto theft are problems of a criminal nature, youthful impiety in the presence of school authorities or the local cop is a problem of maintaining orderly social intercourse. Breaking and entering, car theft, and the like are usually covert, arbitrary actions and have little to do with exchange relationships. While there are often extenuating circumstances, responsibility for the action can be attached to the "offender," at least in the first analysis. On the contrary, rebellious impiety, for example, is usually an action by one party involved in interaction with another. It may often be the case that the teacher's or cop's behavior is equally as "impious" toward the adolescent. According to the doctrine of adolescent inferiority, however, the significant other is both actor and judge in this situation; he has the status and therefore the power to judge both his and the young person's behavioral and attitudinal input into the situation in question.

Stinchcombe (1964) touched on this aspect briefly in developing his sophisticated concept of "expressive alienation." Generalizing from Stinchcombe, one can see how rebellious attitudes come about when the student perceives that the school status system appears to him to be unfair in its expectation for his inputs—work, effort, attendance, attention, etc.—relative to their inputs—grades, relevance, providing interest, playing fair etc.

According to Stinchcombe, the psychological state of "expressive aliena-tion" may be instigated in the cognitive processes of the student when he perceives that he is unable to meet school demands—or, as in the case of many lower-class youth, when he perceives that the school has no relevance for where he is at now or where he wants to be in the future.

Clearly, the indication from Cohen (1955), Friedenberg (1959, 1965), and Stinchcombe (1964) lends assistance to our case for conceptualizing rebellion as one form of deviant response to the insitutionalized pressures of the educational process. But it is not yet clear from the theory to what extent we can define youthful misconduct as "delinquent" when the term is used synonymously with "criminal."

The work of Cloward (1959) and Cloward and Ohlin (1960) provides us with categorical descriptions of deviant responses that have some utility for the present discussion. Their work was entirely accomplished within the urban setting and focused generally on male gang delinquency, so their concepts of "expressive" and "instrumental" deviant behavior are useful in our notion of "rebellious" and "delinquent" responses.

As we have seen above, the primary emphasis of Merton's formulation is upon the instigation to use illegitimate means as a way of adapting to value-access disjunction. In addition to instigation to deviance, value-access disjunction, when widespread, results in the weakening of regulatory norms or in the withering of legitimacy relative to normative controls and sanctions—a state of anomie. To some extent, Merton's theory describes both the sociocultural pressures toward deviance and the sociocultural sources of deviance control. The anomie formulation, however, is only in a very general sense applicable to all forms of deviance and fails to specify the conditions under which instrumental theft will occur, for instance, rather than expressive rebellion. Cloward and Ohlin (1960, pp. 166–168) point to the importance of assessing the relative dominance of expressive or instrumental components in deviant behavior. They point out that access to illegitimate means is also differentially distributed in the social structure and that the appropriation of specific alternatives to legitimate means is dependent not just on value-access strains and weakened norma-tive referents but also upon differential access to specific kinds and styles of illegitimate means.

Cloward and Ohlin submit that young people in the ghetto buy into the egalitarian ideology of American society, in which they are promised their share of the "good life," but they recognize that ethnic and class barriers will seriously restrict them from cashing in on the promise. This anticipation of failure, then, takes a form of "alienation," which is defined as "a process of withdrawal of attributions of legitimacy from established social norms" (1960, p. 110). After being "freed from commitment to and belief in the legitimacy of certain of the existing organizations of means" (1960, p. 110), these "alienated" youth must then seek support from others to develop a collective rather than an individual solution to their adjustment problems. They also learn differential rationalizations, "appropriate means for handling the problems of guilt and fear" (1960, p. 110), which may result from engaging in different deviant acts. Cloward and Ohlin (1960, p. 132) suggest that this may be accomplished by "a supporting structure of beliefs and values that provide *advance justification for deviant conduct*" (italics supplied).

It is important to note that Cloward and Ohlin (1960, p. 86) do not propose that deprivation must result in the evolution of delinquent subcultures but that it can have this result. Deprived youth may find their way into "criminal," "conflict," or "retreatist" gangs. Cloward and Ohlin developed a typology of gangs in an effort to explain norm violations sanctioned by delinquent subcultures, and nowhere do they propose a general theory of delinquency. Important to our purpose here is the observation that Cloward and Ohlin (1960, pp. 161–171) identify the "criminal" subculture precisely to account for instrumental acts they saw as existing in fact. Not only does the individual have to learn role performances in the process of becoming a criminal, the social structural milieu must support the actual performance of the criminal role.

Thus, Cloward and Ohlin's theory provides us with a theoretical step beyond Merton's structural argument. They specify a number of deviant modes of "integration of values" around both "expressive" and "instrumental" reactions. What they are saying essentially is this: when a community limits its ability to provide opportunities for all to achieve in accordance with standard middle-class values, it closes out legitimate opportunities for success and achievement, thus insuring that somewhat differential forms of illegitimate or deviant behavior will occur systematically. In other words, the societal reaction (this is not their term) makes it somewhat certain that particular forms of deviant behavior will occur in areas where there is social support for those particular forms of criminal or rebellious behavior (1960, p. 164).

Kitsuse and Detrick (1959), in their critique of Cohen (1955), add substance to Cloward and Ohlin's (1960) criminal typology. They see many delinquents as organized into groups that are busy tending to serious activities. "There is no absence of rational, calculated, utilitarian behavior among delinquent gangs as they exist today" (1959, p. 212). Contrasting delinquent and rebellious subcultures, they infer that the enterprising delinquent who operates subterraneanly, covertly, and rationally, ripping off what he needs for survival, is fairly certain about his commodity goals and instrumental means scheme; whereas the rebellious subculture persists because, once established, it creates for those who participate in it the very problems of uncertainty and ambivalence that were the basis for its emergence (1959, p. 215).

We see that the theoretical literature on deviance and delinquency supports the notion that young boys sometimes behave criminally and sometimes behave rebelliously in response to structural and environmental pressures. But this is only half the picture. A more contemporary sociological perspective would have us examine those institutional pressures that generate the societal reaction to these various forms of inappropriate behavior. This, in a sense, is a central issue in Cohen's (1965, pp. 5–15) later work. This paper, published about the same time as Stinchcombe's book (1964), appeared some ten years after *Delinquent Boys* and elaborates and integrates concepts in that volume with Merton's theory. Cohen (1965, p. 7) suggests that Merton's contribution suffers from "the assumption of discontinuity." That is to say, there appears to be an abrupt shift from a "state of strain of anomie to a state of deviance." Cohen observes that human behavior, whether deviant or not, "typically develops and grows in a tentative, groping, advancing, backtracking, sounding-out process." By integrating anomie and self-role theory, Cohen (1965) shifts his focus to the process whereby one becomes tentatively involved in and progressively committed to social roles. He suggests, therefore, that deviant behavior is often expressive of one's role(s) and that one's deviant behaviors may serve to affirm that "one is a certain kind of person." The implication here is that not all deviance involves just structural strain; deviant acts may express and confirm a particular identity. Clearly, the later Cohen (1966, p. 65) leads us toward institutional labeling theory:

... young people's self feelings depend very large upon how they are judged by others. In this country the stages on which they perform and the situations in which they are judged—most notably, the school situation—are dominated by middle-class people, and the standards or measuring rods by which they are judged are those current among middle-class people.

We look to the labeling or interactionalist perspective of deviant behavior as discussed by Lemert (1967), Becker (1963), Kai Erikson (1964), and others for the root thinking behind institutional labeling theory. Their view is based on the notion that deviancy is not something inherent in the act but is created out of the definitions of those who define and enforce social standards of behavior. For example, Becker (1964) states:

Social groups create deviance by making the rules whose infraction constitutes deviance, and by applying those rules to particular people and labeling them outsiders. From this point of view, deviance is not a quality of the act the person commits but rather a consequence of the application by others of rules and sanctions to an "offender." The deviant is one to whom that label has successfully been applied; deviant behavior is behavior that people so label.

Becker should be read for an understanding that casual, offhand deviance differs significantly in form and sometimes in content from secondary (Lemert, 1964) or "habitual" deviance. Becker's model is developmental, with every step requiring explanations perhaps independent of the others. The sequence of events in the experience of a deviant is a career, and factors that move the deviant from one step to the next are "career contingencies." Thus, the societal reaction that arbitrarily identifies the neighborbood gang member, who at this point may only be acting out his frustrations at lack of success in the classroom, as a *young criminal* may operate as a career contingency: "If I have the name, I may as well play the game."

Becker advances the notion of commitment as that pressure that leads one to remain in a social identity or follow expected lines of behavior. People engage in consistent lines of behavior because they are threatened (or perceive threat) by certain penalties for not doing so. In this sense of commitment, the actor rejects certain alternatives, and behavior associated with the identity or expectation to which one is committed persists over time.

Although Becker identifies commitment as that cognitive state that restrains people from sequential deviance, his main concern is with those actors who build their life around a deviant career. Becker shows how the individual advances step by step through a deviant career by learning the moves he should make. One first begins a career when a decision to act is made; then the techniques of action are learned, step by step. At each step there is a contingency awareness.

Becker deals to some extent with the relationship of power to the deviant label. His concept of "moral entrepreneur" is another way of organizing a view of deviant career. Becker finds the sequential model applicable to an explanation of rule enforcement. When the deviant comes into contact with agents and agencies of control his status gets progressively focused, redefined, and finally institutionally fixed.

Kai Erickson (1964) furnishes some helpful insight here in his consideration of the "community screen" concept. For Erickson, deviance is not a property *inherent in* certain forms of behavior; it is a property *conferred upon* these forms by the audiences that directly or indirectly witness them. The critical variable in the study of deviance, then, is the social audience rather than the individual actor, since it is the audience that eventually determines whether or not any episode of behavior or any class of episodes is labeled deviant (Kai Erickson, 1964, p. 10). While this definition will not cause us to turn away from an examination of the differential attitudes and behaviors manifested by our subjects it does serve to bring the concept of "societal reaction" into focus: when a community acts to control the behavior of one of its members, it is engaged in a very intricate process of selection. After all, even the worst miscreant in society conforms most of the time, if only in the sense that he uses the correct spoon at mealtime, takes good care of his mother, or in a thousand other ways respects the ordinary conventions of his group; and if the community elects to bring sanctions against him for the occasions when he does misbehave, it is responding to a few deviant details set within a vast array of entirely acceptable conduct. Thus it happens that a moment of deviation may become the measure of a person's position in society. He may be jailed or hospitalized, certified as a full-time deviant, despite the fact that only a fraction of his behavior was in any way unusual or dangerous. The community has defined their own limits by the use of "boundary maintaining mechanisms" such as courts, probation officers and psychiatric appraisal. These boundary maintaining mechanisms are constantly subject to change so that it becomes incumbant on the deviant to define those characteristics of the community which make it "special." These transactions between deviants and agencies of control are referred to as "deployment patterns" whereby the "deviant"—automatically an inferior—is deployed or relegated to a caste or class. For all practical purposes they reflect what kind of person he "really" is. An important observation for the present purposes is that it may well be that the "worst miscreant" in the society, according to the selection processes of the social "screen," is the rebellious boy who almost by definition fails to conform most of the time. His "moments" of deviation become the measure of his position in that society. He may be stigmatized, jailed, certified as a full-time delinquent, despite the fact that only part of his behavior was unusual or dangerous in the criminal sense. The screening device that sifts these telling details out of the person's overall performance, then, is a very important instrument of social control. We know very little about the properties of this screen, but we do know that it takes many factors into account that are not directly related to the deviant act itself: it is sensitive to the suspect's social class, his past record as an offender, the amount of remorse he manages to convey, and many similar concerns that take hold in the shifting moods of the community.

This may not be so obvious when the screen is dealing with extreme forms of deviance like serious crimes, but in the day-by-day filtering processes that take place throughout the community this feature is easily observable. Some men who drink too much are called alcoholics whereas others are not, some men who act oddly are committed to hospitals whereas others are not, some men who have no visible means of support are hauled into court whereas others are not—and the difference between those who earn a deviant label and those who go their own way in peace depends almost entirely on the way in which the community sifts out and codes the many details of behavior to which it is witness.

Participation in the general culture is both rewarding and punishing. One who is consistently punished often comes to deny that there are acceptable solutions or alternatives for him in the general cultural role he is in. Usually, he is recognized as a "failure" by others, but he may feel discomfort rather than failure. However, "failures" usually come to employ one or more psychological "mechanisms of adjustment." They may attempt to rationalize, they may attempt to project, or they may try to compensate in terms of their personal status problems. These mechanisms of adjustment often take the form of rebellious responses to perceived status discontinuities. Others, in a similar situation, may use illicit means—lying, cheating, drugs, or stealing—in an attempt to escape an unrewarding social situation. Of course, it goes without saying that many people learn to live with status discontinuities and frustration and then there is little visible evidence of any attempts at adjustment.

The institutional focus outlined above does not deny the occurrence of individual pathology, or that states of "mental illness" are occasionally implicated in delinquency and criminality. However, we maintain that theories of individual pathology have failed to address the problems of basic societal design, and they are the dominant operating assumptions of our principal social institutions.

Examining the problem of delinquency and criminality within the institutional perspective, we are led to suggest—as numerous others have—that a wide variety of our social organizations are programmed so as to inhibit significant segments of our adolescent population from learning socially acceptable, responsible, and personally gratifying roles. Rather than being responsive to these appropriate needs, our social institutions and organizations may even foster negative role development.

A viable institutional focus must identify those features of the social environment that interact with the human personality to produce malignant behavioral effects, and then proceed to effect dialogue with the deviant by deliberate alteration and correction of institutional processes.

Dopers and criminals, often broken in health, substance, and spirit, marked with tracks on the arms and in the mind—both restless and impotent, timid and revolutionary—are human identities whom we have institutionally fashioned. Since the self-fulfilling prophecy of institutionalized negative labeling is apparent, it follows that institutionalized positive labeling could lead to self-fulfillment. That is, granting our youth trust through responsibility might encourage them to live up to that trust and demonstrate constructive responsibility.

We maintain that the process of institutional logic is clear in the case of Manny and his friends. Their individual pathological states appear to be traceable directly to the damaging experiences encountered as a member of the school, the prison, and various peer groups.

Looking at Manny Torres' career in terms of the theory presented above we can see that the early years in the Young Stars should properly be viewed as socially induced rebellion instead of delinquency. Manny reports that members of his group rarely stole, hardly ever engaged in drinking or drug use; their activities were oriented around the defense of territory and a growing sexual awareness. When Manny was forced to relocate in a "disadvantaged social location," he came into contact with a peer group whose well-defined mores supported an "expressive" as opposed to an "instrumental" (theft) type response to the strains of adolescence.

Circumstances later forced him out of a ganging pattern that he was about to abandon anyway because he had begun to form some significant contacts with the organized criminal element in his neighborhood. It is clear that legitimate models of "getting by" were never as available to Manny as were the illegitimate models, i.e., Leo and his boys. His drift from ganging to organized criminal endeavor was not accidental, it was opportunistic. Society had effectively withheld legitimate opportunities. Illegitimate ones became, for him, legitimate. Through his contacts with the Organization Manny acquired a criminal identity and perspective. This world view was well institutionalized in his environment and had permeated, or affected, every organizational form and activity of which he was a part (cf. Irwin, 1970, Chapter 1).

The drug culture, at first illegitimate in Manny's mind, gradually drew him because of its immediacy in the social surround. His uncle became the significant other from which Manny began to acquire a set of beliefs, values, understandings, and self-definitions relative to the world view of the dope fiend.

Manny's criminal career was not simply a single stream of thought and action, a unilateral commitment to one criminal behavior system. On the contrary, we see how his early attachments were often tentative and weak, especially with respect to his commitment to drugs. We see how these commitments were systematically bolstered and reinforced because of the consistent presence of significant others who argued for criminality and nonconformity, and the nearly total absence of referents arguing for a meaningful and remunerative conformity.

Throughout Manny's ciminal career he butted up against official agents of social control who contributed to his criminality both by omission and commission; by committing acts of atrocity upon his person from their protected penal advantage, for example, and, by omitting to use procedures calculated to contribute to his redemption—such as find, and support him in, work placements after release. Most of the "change agents" he encountered, particularly in prison, actually guided him along the pathway of further deviance because they misinterpreted his motives and actions time and time again, e.g., the incident with the doctor in Sing Sing Prison. Manny's personal trouble clearly elucidates a cardinal public issue: the correctional philosophy often supports deviant acts and responses because of its completely misguided policies.

Manny discovered a sense of enlightenment in spite of penal procedure. Prison life is calculated to extinguish higher ethical normative values in its clients, not to foster them as some naive publics would believe. Institutional correctional pratices work against the emergence of love and concern in their clients. For example, the prison co-opts its chaplains and requires that they function as administrative personnel who owe allegiance to the superintendent, not to their constituency.

Manny had to wait until he was thirty-three years old before any official bothered to "discover" what must always have been a possibility in him. One man at CRC was able to look beyond the conventional viewpoint, the official image of the criminal-convict, to visualize for Manny the opportunities of a successful career in higher education. Where diagnosis, therapy, and treatment in the medical-corrections tradition have failed, it is possible that one caring individual, acting to maximize social opportunities for success and legitimate identity for Manny Torres, may have succeeded.

Selected References

Allport, Gordon W.
1948 *ABC's of scapegoating.* Chicago: Roosevelt Press.

Becker, Ernest
1967 *Beyond alienation.* New York: Braziller.

Becker, Howard S.
1963 *Outsiders.* New York: The Free Press.

1964   *The other side.* Glencoe, Ill.: The Free Press.

Bernard, Jessie
1961   Teen-age culture. *The Annals of the American Academy of Political and Social Science 338* (November), 1–12.

Bloch, Herbert A., & Geis, Gilbert
1970   *Man, crime and society.* New York: Random House.

Camus, Albert
1957   *The rebel.* New York: Knopf.

Cicourel, Aaron, & Kitsuse, John I.
1963   *The educational decision makers.* Indianapolis: Bobbs-Merrill.
1968   *The social organization of juvenile justice.* New York: Wiley & Sons.

Clark, John P. & Wenninger, Eugene P.
1962   Socio-economic class and area as correlates of illegal behavior among juveniles. *American Sociological Review 27* (December), 826–853.

Clinard, Marshall B.
1944   The process of urbanization and criminal behavior. *American Journal of Sociology 50* (July), 202–213.
1973   *Sociology of deviant behavior.* New York: Holt, Rinehard, Winston.

Cloward, Richard
1959   Illegitimate means, anomie, and deviant behavior. *American Sociological Review 24* (April), 164–176.

Cloward, Richard, & Ohlin, Lloyd
1960   *Delinquency and opportunity.* Glencoe, Ill.: The Free Press.

Cohen, Albert K.
1955   *Delinquent boys: The culture of the gang.* Glencoe, Ill.: The Free Press.
1965   The sociology of the deviant act: Anomie theory and beyond. *The American Sociological Review 50* (February), 5–14.
1966   *Deviance and control.* Englewood Cliffs, N.J.: Prentice-Hall.

Cohen, Albert K., & Hodges, H.
1963   Characteristics of the lower-blue-collar clan. *Social Problems X* (Spring), 303–334.

Coleman, James S.
1965   *Adolescents and the schools.* New York: Basic Books.

Coser, Lewis
1967   *The functions of social conflict.* New York: The Free Press.

Davis, A.
1948 *Social class influences upon learning.* Cambridge, Mass.: Harvard University Press.

Dentler, Robert A., & Monroe, L.
1961 Social correlates of early adolescent theft. *American Sociological Review 26* (October), 475-483.

Dubin, Robert
1959 Deviant behavior and social structure: Continuities in social theory. *American Sociological Review 24* (April), 147-164.

Durkheim, Emile
1947 [*The division of labor in society*] (George Simpson, Trans.). Glencoe, Ill.: The Free Press

Eaton, Joseph W., & Polk, Kenneth
1961 *Measuring delinquency.* Pittsburgh: University of Pittsburgh Press.

Eisner, Victor
1969 *The delinquency label: The epidemiology of juvenile delinquency.* New York: Random House.

Empey, LaMar T.
1967 *Studies in delinquency: Alternatives to delinquency.* Washington, D.C.: U.S. Government Printing Office (HEW).

Empey, LaMar T., & Erickson, M.
1966 Hidden delinquency and social status. *Social Forces 44* (June), 546-554.

Erickson, Maynard, & Empey, L.
1965 Class position, peers, and delinquency. *Journal of Sociology and Social Research 49* (April), 268-282.

Erikson, Erik
1968 *Identity, youth, and crises.* New York: Norton.

Erikson, Kai T.
1964 Deviance and definition. In Howard Becker (Ed.). *The other side.* Glencoe, Ill.: The Free Press.

Finestone, Harold
1957 Cats, kids, and color. *Social Problems 5* (July), 3-13.

Flacks, Richard
1971 *Youth and social change.* Chicago: Markham Publishing.

Friedenberg, Edgar Z.
1959   *The vanishing adolescent.* Boston: Beacon Press.
1965   *Coming of age in America.* New York: Random House.
1970   Toward a more human secondary education. In Alvin Eurich (Ed.),
       *High school 1980: The shape of the future in American secondary
       education.* New York: Pitman Publishing.

Friedson, Eliot
1965   Disability as social deviance. In Marvin G. Sussman (Ed.), *Socio-
       logy and rehabilitation.* Chicago: American Sociological Association.

Havighurst, Robert J.
1961   How do we postpone youth's coming of age? In R. M. MacIver
       (Ed.), *Dilemmas of youth in America today.* New York: Harper
       & Row.

Havighurst, R. J., Bowman, P., Liddle, G., Matthews, C., & Pierce, J.
1962   *Growing up in River City.* New York: Wiley & Sons.

Havighurst, R. J., & Newgarten, B.
1967   *Society and education.* Boston: Allyn & Bacon.

Havighurst, R. J., & Taba, H.
1949   *Adolescent character and personality.* New York: Wiley & Sons.

Hollingshead, A. B.
1949   *Elmtown's youth.* New York: Wiley & Sons.

Inkeles, Alex
1960   The industrial man: The relation of status to experience, percep-
       tion and value. *American Journal of Sociology 66* (July), 1–31.
1968   Society, social structure, and child socialization. In J. A. Clausen
       (Ed.), *Socialization and society.* Boston: Little, Brown.

Irwin, John
1970   *The felon.* Englewood Coiffs, N.J.: Prentice-Hall.

Jackson, Brian
1963   *Streaming: An educational system in miniature.* London: Routledge
       & Kegan Paul.

Jencks, Christopher, et al.
1972   *Inequality: A reassessment of the effect of family and schooling in
       America.* New York: Basic Books.

Kahl, Joseph A.
1957   *The American class structure.* New York: Rinehart.

Karacki, L., & Toby, J.
1962   The uncommitted adolescent: Candidate for gang socialization. *Sociological Inquiry 32,* (Spring) 203–215.

Kelly, Delos H.
1970   *Social class, school status, and self-evaluation as related to adolescent value, success, and deviance.* Unpublished doctoral dissertation, University of Oregon, Eugene.
1971   School failure, academic self-evaluation, and school avoidance and deviant behavior. *Youth and Society 2* (June).

Kelly, Delos H., & Balch, R. W.
1971   Social origins and school failure: A re-examination of Cohen's theory of working-class delinquency. *Pacific Sociological Review 14* (October).

Kelly, Delos H., & Pink, W.
1971   School commitment and student career flows. *Youth and Society 2* (December), 225–236.
1972   Academic failure, social involvement, and high school dropouts. *Youth and Society 3* (September), 47–59.
1973   Social origins, school status, and the learning experience. *Pacific Sociological Review 16* (January), 121–134.

Kenniston, Kenneth
1965   *The uncommitted: Alienated youth in American society.* New York: Dell.

Kitsuse, John L., & Detrick, D.
1959   Delinquent boys: A critique. *American Sociological Review 2* (April), 208–214.

Koval, John
1967   *The drifters and the directed: an anatomy of educational involvement.* Unpublished doctoral dissertation, University of Oregon, Eugene.

Lemert, Edwin M.
1964   Primary and secondary deviation. In H. Becker (Ed.), *The other side.* Glencoe, Ill.: The Free Press.
1967   *Human deviance, social problems, and social control.* Englewood Cliffs, N.J.: Prentice-Hall.
1971   *Instead of court: Diversion in juvenile justice.* (Public Health Service Publication No. 2127.) Washington, D.C.: U.S. Government Printing Office.

Lindner, Robert M.
1944 *Rebel without a cause.* New York: Grune & Stratton.
1952 *Prescription for rebellion.* New York: Rinehart.

Matza, David
1964 *Delinquency and drift.* New York: Wiley.
1973 Subterranean traditions of youth. In Harry Silverstein (Ed.),
       The sociology of youth: Evolution and revolution. New York:
       Macmillan.

Mechanic, David
1962 *Students under stress.* Glencoe, Ill.: The Free Press.

Merton, Robert
1955 The social-cultural environment and anomie. In H. L. Witmer &
       R. Kotinsky (Eds.), *New perspectives for research on juvenile de-
       linquency.* Washington, D.C.: U.S. Government Printing Office
       (HEW).
1959 Social conformity, deviation, and opportunity structures: A com-
       ment on the contributions of Dubin and Cloward. *American Socio-
       logical Review 24* (April), 177–189.
1968 *Social theory and social structure.* Glencoe, Ill.: The Free Press.

Miller, Walter
1958 Lower class culture as a generating milieu of gang delinquency.
       Journal of Social Issues 14 (May), 15–19.

Miller, Walter, & Kauraceus, William
1955 *Delinquent behavior.* New York: The Free Press.

Nash, Paul
1966 *Authority and freedom in education.* New York: Wiley.

Nietzsche, Friedrich
1956 [*The birth of tragedy and the genealogy of morals*] (Francis Golf-
       fing, Trans.). Garden City, N.Y.: Anchor Books.

Nordstrom, Carl, Friedenberg, Edgar Z., & Gold, Hilary A.
1967 Society's children: A study of resentment in the secondary school.
       New York: Random House.

Parsons, Talcott
1951 *The social system.* New York: The Free Press.
1962 Youth: Change and challenge. *Daedalus* (Winter), 97–128.
1967 *Sociological theory and modern society.* New York: The Free Press.
1968 *The structure of social action.* New York: The Free Press.

Pearl, Arthur
1972 *The atrocity of education.* St. Louis: New Critics' Press.

Pearl, Arthur, & Riessman, F.
1965 *New careers for the poor.* New York: The Free Press.

Piliavin, Irving, & Briar, Scott
1964 Police encounters with juveniles. *American Journal of Sociology 70* (September), 206–214.

Polk, Kenneth
1969 Class, strain and rebellion among adolescents. *Social Problems 17* (Fall), 214–224.
1973 Social class and the bureaucratic response to deviance. *Humboldt Journal of Social Relations 1* (Spring), 2–7.

Polk, Kenneth, & Halferty, David S.
1966 Adolescence, commitment and delinquency. *Journal of Research on Crime and Delinquency 4* (July), 82–96.

Polk, Kenneth, & Kobrin, Solomon
1971 *Effective programming for youth development and delinquency prevention: Proposed principles.* Los Angeles: Public Systems Research Institute, University of Southern California.

Polk, Kenneth, & Schafer, W. E. (Eds.)
1972 *Schools and delinquency.* Englewood Cliffs, N.J.: Prentice-Hall.

Riessman, Leonard
1959 *Class in American society.* Glencoe: The Free Press.

Rettig, Richard R.
1974 A study in student development: rebellion and delinquency as alternative responses to schooling. Unpublished doctoral dissertation. University of Oregon, Eugene.

Robison, Sophia
1960 *Juvenile delinquency.* New York: Holt.

Schafer, Stephen, & Knudten, Richard D.
1970 *Juvenile delinquency: An introduction.* New York: Random House.

Schafer, Walter E.
1968 Deviance in the public schools: An interactional view. In Edwin Thomas (Ed.), *Behavioral science for social workers.* New York: The Free Press.

Schafer, Walter E., & Olexa, Carol
1971 *Tracking and opportunity: The locking out process and beyond.*
Scranton, Pa.: Chandler.

Schafer, Walter E., & Polk, Kenneth
1967 Delinquency and the schools. Task Force Report: Juvenile Delinquency and Youth Crime. Washington, D.C.: U.S. Government Printing Office. (Pp. 222–277.)

Scheler, Max
1961 [*Ressentiment*] (William W. Holdbeim, Trans.). Introduction by Lewis A. Coser. Glencoe, Ill.: The Free Press.

Stinchcombe, Arthur L.
1964 *Rebellion in a high school.* Chicago: Quadrangle Books.
1968 *Constructing social theories.* New York: Harcourt, Brace, & World

Sutherland, Edwin, & Cressey, Donald R.
1955 *Principles of criminology* (5th ed.). Chicago: Lippincott.

Witmer, Helen L., & Kotinsky, Ruth
1952 *Personality in the making: The fact-finding report of the mid-century White House conference on children and youth.* New York: Harper & Bros.

CDEFGHIJ—SM—7987